Shooting the Muzzleloaders

Shooting the Muzzle loaders

Edited by
R. A. Steindler

JOLEX INC.
Paramus N. J.

Distributed by
The John Olson Company
299 Forest Avenue Box 767
Paramus, New Jersey 07652

Copyright © 1975 by Jolex, Inc.
Published by Jolex, Inc.
in cooperation with the John Olson Company

Photographs: R. A. Steindler, Gerd E. Haida,
Hans Kubach, Richard Horlacher, Röpke.

LC Number: 74–29423
ISBN: 0–87955–490–8

Published simultaneously in Canada
by Plainsman publications Ltd, Vancouver B. C.

First Printing: May, 1975

TABLE OF CONTENTS

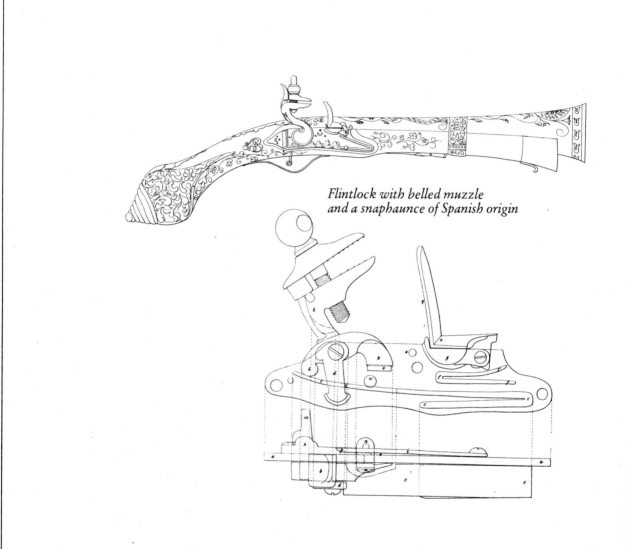

Flintlock with belled muzzle and a snaphaunce of Spanish origin

FOREWORD

Back in the 1920's, grandpappy's old musket, and perhaps even his ancient cap and ball revolver, peacefully rusted somewhere in the attic or the barn. Then came gun collectors who were willing to pay good money for those sorry-looking relics of yesteryear, and thus the interest in those old guns was revived – at least somewhat.

In the early 1930's, a few shooters unearthed a couple of armloads of black powder guns in their homes, and idly wondering just how accurate those old guns were, they began shooting informal matches with them. Of course, since none of them had much experience with black powder or the guns using this propellant, there were some mishaps, and a number of the guns were damaged beyond repair.

Those hardy Ohioans found out several things about their guns. With some care in cleaning and loading, they functioned surprisingly well. And with a good load, in the hands of a good shot, those guns also delivered groups which were in keeping with the accuracy reported by many of the early westerners – pioneers, mountain men, adventurers and bad men. Thus, in 1933, the National Muzzle Loading Rifle Association was formed and to this day, the NMLRA is the official watchdog at all competitive black powder events in the United States. For almost 30 years, the shooter who wanted to punch holes into paper, or bark a squirrel with a black powder gun, had to find an original and then restore it to its original appearance and make sure that it functioned properly. During this time, collectors began to complain about those who fired the sometimes priceless guns and wrecked them in the process. Shooters, some of them misguided by self-styled experts, ruined perfectly good guns by following bad advice. It was only in the mid-50's that the first of the replicas appeared. These early replicas, some of which have almost achieved collector's status today, were spitting images of their original counterparts, but were made from modern steels. Since all of them were imported from countries where each gun must undergo proof testing, they were quite safe when fired with black powder. Of course, there were those who believed that modern steel should withstand modern pistol powders, but fortunately, they tried such a foolish stunt only once.

NEVER LOAD ANYTHING BUT BLACK POWDER INTO ANY BLACK POWDER GUN, BE IT AN ORIGINAL OR A REPLICA.

Today's replicas, and some of them are a far cry from the originals, are every bit as good as modern cartridge guns, and like their forerunners, with the right load in the hands of a cool shot, they will shoot incredibly small groups and kill the biggest game in the world.

R. A. Steindler

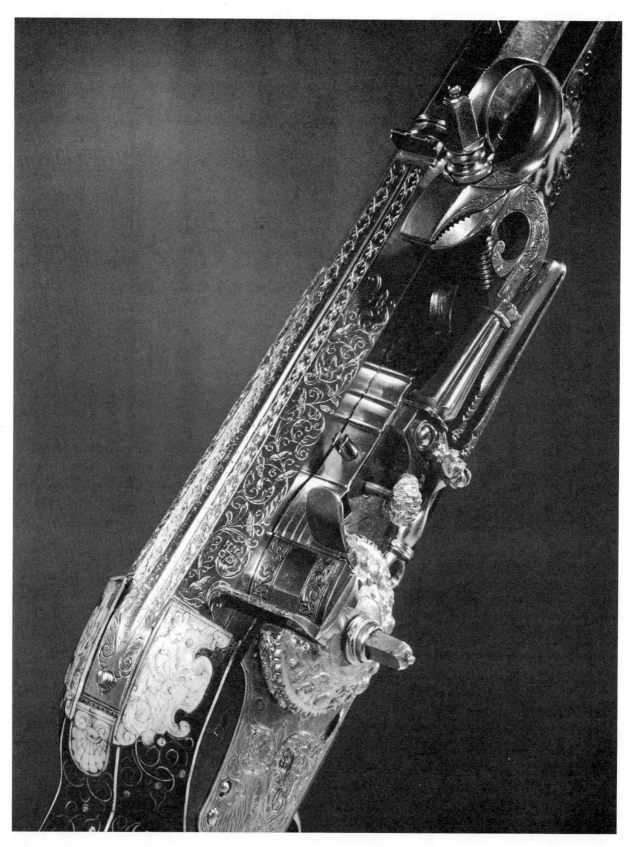

Wheellock rifle signed GNM and HK with Bavarian proofmarks of 1612

Chapter 1 AT THE BEGINNING

When radio station WLW in Cincinnati announced that there would be a full-dress reenactment of a pioneer rifle match, on a wintry day in 1933 at the NMLRA range in Friendship, Indiana – the same range where matches are still held today – droves of curious onlookers arrived! The curiosity about yesteryear's guns was as great then as it is now, and not only among shooters. Many non-shooters have found, after watching a match or even an informal plinking session, that there is a great deal of fascination in shooting the muzzleloaders.

Those who have tried to learn the reason for this revived and constantly growing interest in black powder guns believe that many black powder shooters are seeking an escape from the humdrum world of today. Others feel that the entire sport is a challenge. Still others reason that the black powder shooter is essentially a tinkerer and do-it-yourselfer, thus gets a great deal of satisfaction not only from the actual loading of the gun, but also from casting his own projectiles, and lately even from building his own black powder guns from kits. Whatever the reason, there is still spiraling interest in black powder guns and shooting, and despite the antiquity of black powder shooting much new work has been done in this field in the past few years.

In the following pages, you will find some of these new developments discussed, and you can even see how easy it is to build your own black powder rifle or handgun.

Even non-shooters often use phrases or terms which derived directly from the black powder days. Keep your powder dry and flash in the pan are but two. A guy either ramrods a job or is straight as a ramrod, but has a hair trigger temper, especially when an idea misfires. A double-barreled program is one that includes everything – lock, stock and barrel. There is always the chance that some trigger-man goes off half-cocked, is not a straight shooter or overshoots the mark. Of course, the whole thing can blow up in your face if you don't hold your fire, and then you sit on a short-fused powder keg. If there's a hangfire, you won't hit the bullseye, even if you are loaded for bear.

Today's black powder guns can be grouped two ways – by the ignition system or by the type of gun – that is, handgun, either single-shot or revolver, rifle or shotgun. By far the best and most widely used ignition system is the percussion or caplock system. There are handguns with more than one barrel, there are double rifles where the two barrels rotate around a central axis for a fast second shot for the hunter who missed with the first barrel, and there are single and double-barrel shotguns, the latter with the twin barrels arranged side-by-side.

The early history of the gun cannot be readily separated from its propellant, that mixture now commonly referred to as black powder, sometimes also simply called gunpowder. While the use of even the simplest of guns is well documented in Europe, the earliest gun records come from the east. The Arabs learned about guns from their eastern neighbors, and most of the historians believe that the Chinese used guns and gunpowder long before the rest of the world knew about this newfangled invention.

There seems to be little doubt that gonnes or cannons were the first guns used. These were relatively crude and cumbersome affairs and were probably every bit as dangerous to the cannoneer as to the recipients of the gun's charge.

9

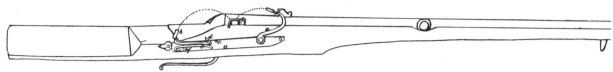

Matchlock rifle

The earliest handguns, made either from brass or cast from iron, were simple tubes with one end closed, and this closed end was connected to the outside of the tube by means of a small hole which was the place where the shooter eventually applied the glowing match or cord to the charge in the gun. The effective range of such guns was quite limited, and it re-quired nerve as well as luck to ride close to the opponent and fire in the hope of unseating him. Even the early matchlock rifles were clumsy to shoot, awkward to load, and in bad weather there was always the chance that the glowing match might drown in a sudden deluge.

The use of gunpowder in early guns goes back to the 14th century in Europe. The famed Swiss firearms designer and writer, Col. Rudolf Schmidt, traced the history of the use of powder in the various European countries. He found that the earliest use of black powder guns in Belgium was in 1313, in Germany 1324, in Italy 1326, in England 1327, in Spain 1331, in France 1338, in Switzerland 1371, in Russia 1389, and in Sweden 1400.

While black powder or gunpowder was first used in warfare, its widespread use in Europe in sporting arms is well-known and authenticated. Soon regular shooting stands or ranges sprang up, and matches using highly ornate targets became popular, not only with participants, but also with spectators. Of course, hunting supplied food for the table, and hunter's matches soon came into vogue, with some of them strongly resembling today's Running Deer and Running Boar matches.

Arquebusier firing a matchlock rifle

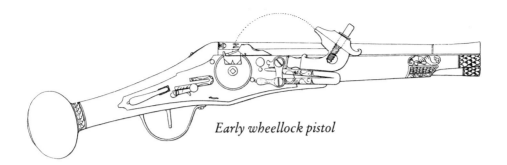

Early wheellock pistol

Of the numerous ignition systems once in use, only the percussion and the flintlock have survived. Once in a while some ambitious and skilled shooter will make his own wheellock, and such scale drawings with complete instructions will become available in the near future.

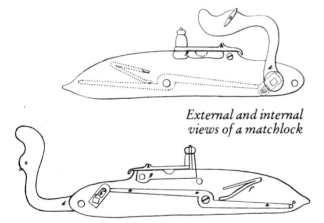

External and internal views of a matchlock

In the sequence of evolution, here are some of the basic ignition systems:

1. Hand cannon: Once loaded from the muzzle, the powder charge was ignited with a torch or burning wick, often simply called a match. Ignition took place at the touch hole at the rear of the barrel.

2. Matchlock: Again the barrel was loaded from the muzzle. A small charge of powder was placed into the flash pan. A length of match cord was clamped into a metal holder, the serpentine. The cord was then lit at both ends, and as the trigger was pulled, the glowing match cord made contact with the priming charge in the pan, which then started the primer charge burning. This, in turn, ignited the main charge through a vent hole in the rear of the barrel.

3. Wheellock: A coil spring operated wheel is the mechanical system used to ignite the charge. The charge is loaded from the muzzle, and iron pyrites, clamped into small jaws of the cock, are brought into contact with the rough edges of the wheel. As the trigger is pulled, the wheel rotates, thus produces sparks which ignite the charge in the priming pan. This, in turn, ignites the main charge by means of a touch hole at the edge of the priming pan.

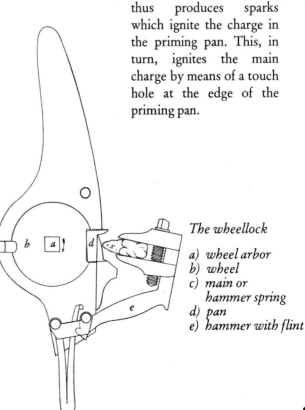

The wheellock

a) *wheel arbor*
b) *wheel*
c) *main or hammer spring*
d) *pan*
e) *hammer with flint*

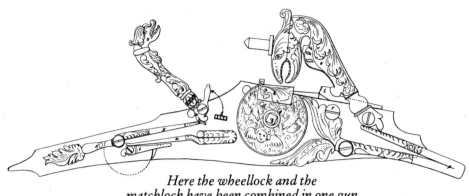

Here the wheellock and the
matchlock have been combined in one gun

4. Snaphaunce, dog lock, Snaplock, Miquelet lock, and several other systems are basically alike. The main charge is muzzle-loaded, a priming charge is placed into the pan and the pan cover is closed. When the trigger is pulled, the flint, fastened to the hammer, hits the edge of the priming pan. Depending on the system, the cover of the priming pan may open when the hammer is cocked or the lid is lifted by hand. The spark from the flint hitting the frizzen ignites the priming charge, and the flash from this passes through the vent hole and ignites the main charge.

Most of these ignition systems were not only exposed to the weather and hence not very reliable, but some, such as the wheellock, were costly to make and troublesome to maintain. There are a great many overlapping ignition designs. As the percussion system began to take hold, the dual ignition system found favor with some shooters. This system incorporates a flintlock system as well as a percussion cap. The Reverend Alexander John Forsyth, a Scottish minister, patented his fulminate ignition system on April 11, 1807, and though he did not live to see his invention widely used, most historians agree that Forsyth was the father of the modern percussion system.

Chemically, the fulminates are salts which are formed by the chemical reaction between an acid and a metal. They are highly explosive, especially when struck a blow. The late fulminate system called for

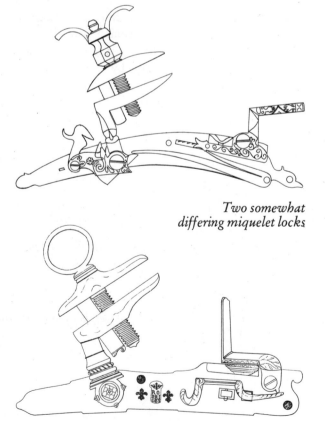

Two somewhat
differing miquelet locks

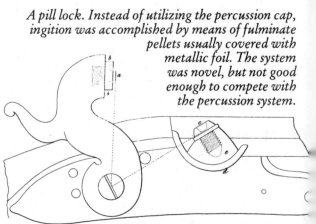

A pill lock. Instead of utilizing the percussion cap, ingition was accomplished by means of fulminate pellets usually covered with metallic foil. The system was novel, but not good enough to compete with the percussion system.

Shooting the Muzzleloaders

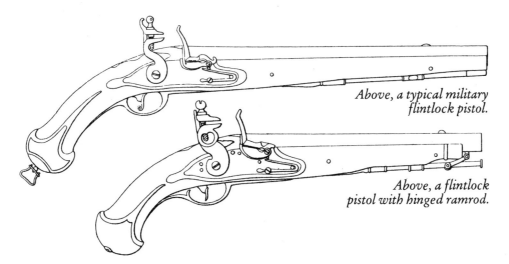

Above, a typical military flintlock pistol.

Above, a flintlock pistol with hinged ramrod.

the salt to be made into small pellets, with a pellet being placed on a nipple which had an internal passage to the main charge. When the hammer fell on the fulminate pellet, it detonated, and the resulting flame passed through the nipple into the main charge, igniting it.

The fulminate was tricky stuff to handle, and from it evolved the percussion system. Again, as with the earlier systems, there were a variety of designs, some good, others leaving much to be desired.

The percussion cap, originally made from a thin piece of copper, contained a charge of fulminate. Placed over the nipple which contained a passage directly into the main chamber of the barrel, the percussion cap, often simply called cap, detonated when struck by the hammer. The resulting flame passed

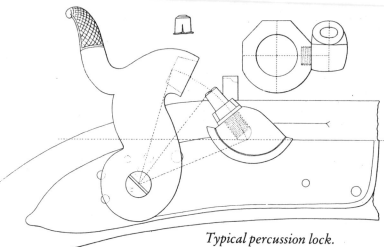

Typical percussion lock.

through the nipple, thereby igniting the charge in the chamber. Guns were, of course, loaded from the muzzle, hence you will often hear the term front-loader.

A refinement of the percussion cap was the tape primer of a Washington, D.C. dentist, Dr. Edward Maynard. Here the charge contained in the cap was located in a paper strip, each charge sealed, and this tape primer is very similar to the tapes used in cap

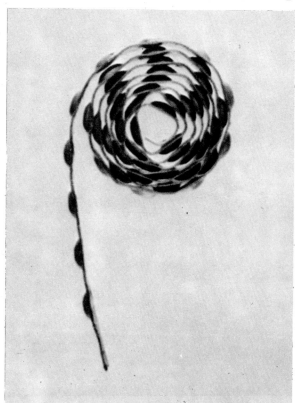

A tape primer, similar to the Maynard design. Note how it resembles the cap pistol tape of today.

pistols. At the present, no replicas of the guns using the Maynard tape have become available, and there seems little likelihood of them reaching the market since even ignition tapes for cap pistols are prohibited in some localities.

In some instances, the ignition system of a gun is linked to its historic past. Kentucky pistols, and here we are talking only about replicas, are usually flintlock guns. The Brown Bess Musket copies, sometimes simply called the Model 1776, are also flintlocks. But there are, for instance, two different models of Harper's Ferry handguns, the Model 1806 which is a flintlock, and the Model 1855 which is a percussion single-shot handgun.

Especially fine copies of the famed Enfield rifles are imported from England, and these are of course percussion guns.

While modern flintlock guns are excellent, they require a bit more care and attention during loading and shooting than percussion guns, and flints must be shaped properly for maximum effectiveness. Thus, most of the beginning black powder shooters prefer the percussion or caplock guns, as they are easier to handle.

As ignition systems changed, many of the guns with the older firing systems were converted to the newer mode of ignition. Thus, flintlocks were changed to percussion, and some of these conversions clearly show that the gunsmiths of those days knew their business – in most cases.

Early percussion caps contained potassium chlorate or fulminate of mercury. Seated on the nipple, the cap detonated when struck by the hammer, and again, the ensuing flame passed through the nipple into the main charge. The obvious advantage of the percussion system lies in the fact that rain and snow does not affect the ignition system and the gun would fire, providing of course that the charge at the rear of the barrel did not get wet. Since the firing mechanism is relatively simple, the easiest way to keep the powder dry was to carry the gun unloaded, and to load or charge the gun before the target presented itself.

Some refinements were made in the caps, but the major changes were in the locks which were greatly improved as time went on. Not only did locks become simpler to make and hence less costly, but they were also refined. Double triggers were introduced, two locks – each with its own barrel – were joined to make a double gun, and the armies of the world greeted the percussion lock with glee. Now warfare was no longer restricted to good weather when soldiers could keep their powder and ignition systems dry and working.

Prussia switched to the percussion system in 1839, with France following a year later although the first of the new guns were issued to some troops the same year the Prussian army adopted the caplock system. Sweden and the United States began the change in 1833, and England and Switzerland changed arms in 1842.

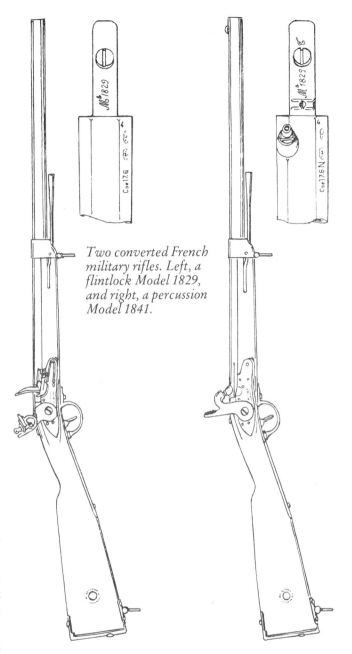

Two converted French military rifles. Left, a flintlock Model 1829, and right, a percussion Model 1841.

Converted Kuchenreuter duelling pistol

Colt Paterson Belt Pistol

This gun was offered in .31 and .34 caliber with a five-shot cylinder. Between 1836 and 1840, 2600 revolvers of this type were made in Colt's Paterson, New Jersey plant.

As guns were modified, designs improved and multi-shot guns were made, there was one more great era for the percussion guns of the future – the revolving cylinder made famous by Col. Samuel Colt. It seems uncertain just what led Samuel Colt to the idea of using the cylinder for more than one shot from a gun – yes, there are also revolving cylinder rifles, and while the originals are true collector's items, the replicas are fun to shoot. The idea that he saw a ship's wheel lashed down during an Indian Ocean voyage has often been proposed in conjunction with the cylinder idea.

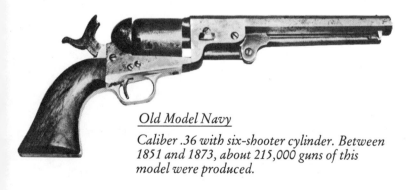

Whitneyville Walker Dragoon

Offered in .44 Caliber with six-shot cylinder. The Walker Model was made for Colt in Eli Whitney's factory in Whitneyville, Connecticut between 1847 and 1848. The finished product was the result of Col. Colt's meeting with Captain Walker of the Texas Rangers.

Old Model Navy

Caliber .36 with six-shooter cylinder. Between 1851 and 1873, about 215,000 guns of this model were produced.

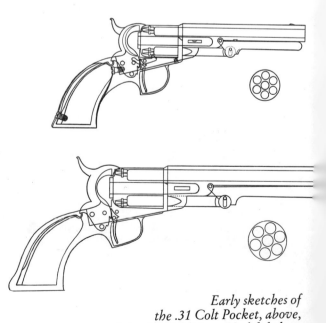

Early sketches of the .31 Colt Pocket, above, and the .36 Colt Navy Model, below.

Replicas of Colt's Whitneyville Walker Dragoon and his other early designs can now be bought by the black powder shooter. Especially the bigger and heavier models have proved to be very accurate and quite satisfactory for hunting.

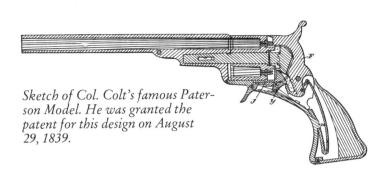

Sketch of Col. Colt's famous Paterson Model. He was granted the patent for this design on August 29, 1839.

The first Colt patent was granted in 1836. Cocking the hammer rotated the cylinder, aligning another chamber of the cylinder with the rear of the barrel. While the finish and some details have changed, this is essentially the same system used in revolvers made today. Colt's Model Paterson was the first of the Colt guns.

The design of the Colt revolver cylinder ultimately led to newer and better ignition systems, such as the pinfire, and finally to the self-contained brass cartridge of today. Call them replicas, frontloaders, muzzleloaders, or charcoal burners – the latter thanks to the major ingredient of black powder – and you are talking about shooting fun that costs but pennies per shot. More black powder is burned up annually just in plinking than any other propellant powder. But if you want to see just how accurate some of these replica guns are, take that new smokepole of yours out to the range and shoot a couple of groups from a rest.

While perhaps not on a par with the modern benchrest rifles, you will find that the special match or target replicas, both long guns and handguns, are capable of delivering a high degree of accuracy. Thanks to special sights – and some black powder buffs even put a scope on their rifle to improve the sight picture – the black powder target guns, with suitable loads, will open up a new world of target shooting for those who are so inclined. Many states have set aside special black powder gun hunting seasons, sometimes called Primitive Weapon Season, and many states have also set aside special tracts of land where only black powder guns are allowed.

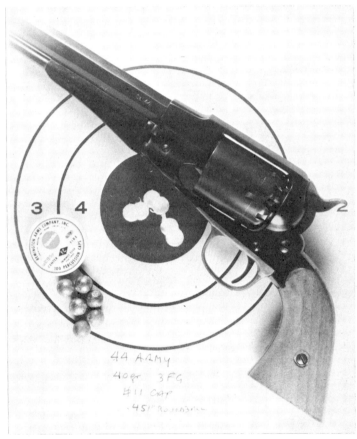

This is the sort of accuracy you can expect and can get from a replica cap and ball revolver. Firing distance was 25 yards, and gun was fired from a sandbag rest.

17

Shooting the Muzzleloaders

Chapter 2
REPLICAS VERSUS THE ORIGINALS

Why buy a replica if original guns are still available to some extent? Basically, there are three reasons for the existence of the replicas.

Many of the originals are valued collector's items, and any accident or even the slightest damage caused by use or perhaps abuse of the gun can seriously affect the value of the gun. Some 20 or 30 years ago, a Colt in good condition – and we are not talking about the ultra-scarce models – traded often for less than $ 100.00. The same gun today sells for three, four or even five times as much.

Secondly, there is the matter of gun failure and safety. Many of the originals have seen hard use, were often doctored up by some backwoods gun tinkerer. As steel ages, it also gets brittle, nipples are damaged, springs break. Original replacement parts are either non-existent, or they are prohibitively expensive. Although black powder is a forgiving propellant, and only extreme carelessness in loading will destroy a replica gun, some of the stiffer charges which a replica gun can handle easily can damage or possibly even wreck an original.

With the fantastic growth of black powder shooting, replicas have become a necessity, since not enough original guns in good shooting condition are on the market, even if price were not a consideration.

Most of the replicas come from Italy, with Spain, Belgium and, to some extent, England, also manufacturing replicas. A few black powder guns are made in the United States, but some of the black powder guns sold today are really not copies or even kissin'-cousins of the original designs.

Before attempting to fire this old relic, be sure that there is no charge left in the barrel, and have a competent gunsmith check the gun to be certain that it is in safe condition to fire. Remember, never use any propellant other than black powder.

One of the first of the .44 caliber replicas. Except for new finish, the gun is mechanically identical to the original gun.
↓

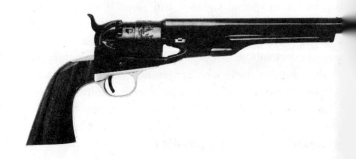

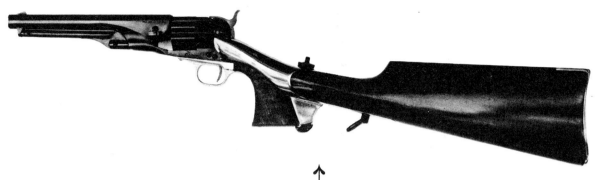

↑
Only the bright finish and untarnished brass indicate that this caplock revolver with shoulder stock just came from the factory. This early replica carries serial number 2.

The early replicas were very exact copies of well-known guns, and thanks to the efforts of a number of gun collectors, the replica makers and importers soon made a few minor changes – a healthy trade in artificially antiqued replica guns was threatening the collector's market. Some of the early replicas were so precisely copied from the original that even the length and pitch of the screw threads had been copied. Thus, spurious "antique" replicas soon began to command the same price as the originals, and only X-ray examination and metallurgic tests could differentiate between the real and the phony Colt revolver, for example.

Therefore, the currently manufactured replicas differ somewhat from the originals, and the differences can be found in the location of the screws, the engraving, and of course in the maker's name which is stamped on the barrel or the frame. To prevent the use of replica parts as original parts when an original gun is restored or repaired, most makers also mark the internal parts of guns, such as locks and springs, in some fashion.

True is that you will occasionally find a replica sixgun that is not timed properly, and once in a great while you may encounter a gun where the finishing touches leave something to be desired. On the whole, however, the modern replicas, no matter what the country of origin, are as good or perhaps even better than the originals.

The fact that most of the replicas come from Europe has another advantage. All of the European countries have proof laws, and these laws also cover black powder guns.

19

German Proofmarks

Cologne

Proofmarks prior to 1939

Marks of German Proofhouses

 Provisional or First Proof

Ulm   Berlin   Kiel   Hanover   Munich

 Final or Second Proof

Belgian Proofmarks

Proofmark for Imported Guns which passed Proof Test

Shotguns

 Optional Provisional Proof

Proofmarks 1939–1945

 Final Proof for Muzzleloading Guns with Standard Black Powder Charge

 Provisional or First Proof

 Mark Applied to Black Powder Guns

 Final Proof with Black Powder

 Proofed Two or Three Times Provisional Black Powder Proof for Breech and Muzzleloading Shotguns

 Optional, Provisional Double Proof

Proofmarks since 1945

 Optional, Provisional Triple Proof

 Provisional Proof

  Definitive Black Powder Proof

Final Proof with Black Powder

  Definitive Black Powder Proof for Rifled Long Gun Barrels

British Proofmarks

London   Birmingham

       Provisional Proof

       Definitive Proof with Black Powder

NOT NITRO   **BLACK POWDER**   Additional Marks on Barrels

       Special Definitive Proof

French Proofmarks

St. Etienne   Paris

       Provisional Proof

     Definitive Proof for Finished Barrels

       Special Double Proof for Barrels in Finished and Assembled Condition

French Proofmarks

       Definitive Black Powder Proof with Standard Load

       Special Double Proof of Finished Firearm

Italian Proofmarks

PN   Definitive Black Powder Proof

FINITO   Mark Shows that Gun was Proofed in Finished Condition

Italian Proofhouses

     Brescia

     Gardone

Austrian Proofmarks

 Provisional Proof, Vienna

 Provisional Proof, Ferlach

 Definitive Black Powder Proof, Vienna

 Definitive Black Powder Proof, Ferlach

*This is what happens
when a gun is not carefully tested.*

Spanish Proofmarks

 Mark of Admission to Eibar Proofhouse

 Definitive Black Powder Shotgun Proof

 Definitive Black Powder Proof of Breechloading Shotgun

 Definitive Proof for Long Rifled Barreled Guns

 Definitive Proof for Rifled Non-Automatic Pistols

Revolver Proof Mark

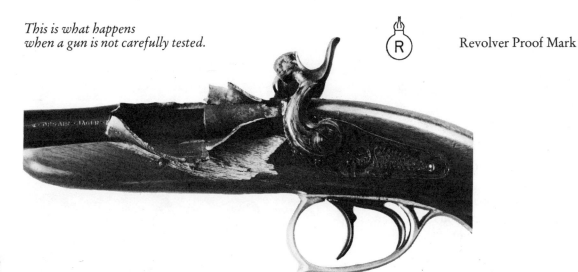

Thanks to the increased interest in black powder guns and black powder shooting, a number of custom shops have survived. Most of the men who build these guns learned their trade from their fathers, and some of the old-timers in the business still make all of their lock parts by hand, cast their own furniture, and some of them even rifle their own barrels on old-fashioned rifling machines or home-made copies of the many surviving rifling machines.

Of course, these guns cost considerably more than their mass produced replica counterparts, but they are also much truer copies of the originals. Most of these guns can be classified as Kentucky rifles, although here and there some Pennsylvania rifles and even copies of Hawken rifles are painstakingly made by hand. These handcrafted guns are invariably exceptionally well-made, beautifully finished and superbly accurate. Some of these guns are sold complete with all the needed accoutrements, others come without the accessories which you can either buy or make yourself. If accoutrements and accessories come with the gun, chances are that these too are hand-made. As a matter of fact, in the past 10 years or so, a number of accessories shops have sprung up. Here you can get not only all of the needed paraphernalia for shooting, such as ball starters, cappers and the like, but also copies of some of the clothing, hats, pouches and other sundries used and worn by early settlers, traders and mountain men.

While using an original Colt Walker or some other valuable gun is generally not recommended, there are some shooters who feel that shooting an original Kentucky, in perfect mechanical condition, adds to the challenge. As a matter of fact, some of the NMLRA matches are still fired with original guns. If

Dressing the part of the early settler or frontiersman is part and parcel of the fun you can find in black powder shooting.

Above left: Frame of replica percussion revolver is hand-finished, the assembled gun is then inspected, later is proof fired by official state proof master.

you acquire such a shooter, before loading for the first time, have a competent black powder gunsmith examine the gun.

Springs may be weak or broken, nipples damaged or rusted into place. Many of the old guns discovered in attics and barns still contain a charge, often complete with ball. If there is a ramrod with the gun, remove the rod from the thimbles, and lay it alongside the exterior of the barrel, with the tip of the rod held flush with the chamber end of the barrel. Make a

Note how rifleman in foreground has the muzzle of his rifle leaning away from him, and also how each shooter tends to his gun with care.

pencil mark on the rod where the muzzle of the barrel is, and you now have the inside length of the barrel marked off. Gently insert the ramrod into the barrel, but do not permit the rod to slam down in the chamber end of the barrel. If the muzzle and the mark on your rod coincide, there is no charge in the gun, but if the pencil mark on the rod is an inch or so above the gun muzzle, there is still a charge in the barrel.

When working with such a gun, never stand in front of the muzzle, do not permit the hammer to rest either on the half-cock or the full cock notch, and do not place a percussion cap on the nipple. Charges that have been stored in guns for many years sometimes go boom suddenly, and of course the same safety rules apply as with any other firearm.

If there is a charge in the barrel, do not attempt to shoot it out by firing the gun. First of all, the nipple

may either be broken, plugged or damaged, or the vent may be blocked. It is best to inactivate the charge before attempting removal. Pour some light penetrating oil down into the barrel and let it stand for at least a day. Then, with the help of a worm on a cleaning rod or ramrod, remove the ball. On old guns, the nipple may be rusted into place and may be so badly damaged that a percussion cap won't fit. Some of the older nipples differ in size from our modern nipple wrenches and you may have to alter a wrench until it can be used to turn out the nipple. A rust-removing spray, such as Bust Rust, will often make it easier to remove the stubborn nipple.

Once the ball has been removed, the worm can be used to remove the rest of the charge that is by now well-caked thanks to the penetrating oil. Remove the nipple and clean out the vent. Should the ball be seated so tightly that the oil does not appear to penetrate into the powder, run some penetrating oil into the charge, either through the nipple or through the vent. If you cannot budge the charge, have a gunsmith do the job, but be sure to emphasize that there may be a charge in the barrel.

If the old nipple is badly worn or damaged, it should be replaced with a new one. Stainless steel nipples by Michaels of Oregon and AMPCO nipples sold by Dixie Gun Works are good choices for replacement nipples. The AMPCO nipples look like brass, but are made from Beryllium which is quite hard. Most of the nipples found on old sporting guns of domestic manufacture have nipples which have 28 threads per inch and have a .250-inch diameter, taking a No. 11 percussion cap.

Before trying to shoot this old caliber .32 Remington percussion rifle, replace the nipple and have the gun checked for safe functioning.

The .245 x 28 nipple fits the Colt Dragoon, as well as many of the Civil War guns, including Remington, Manhattan, and Savage revolvers. It is possible to force a somewhat oversize nipple into the old threads, thereby actually recutting the threads. Of course it may become necessary to try a number of nipples before the right size is found, but a bit of preliminary measuring with a vernier caliper will give you a pretty good indication as to the size of the

If a nipple is slightly over-sized for your caps, it can be polished a bit, either with a Dremel Moto-Tool and suitable polishing head, or by placing the nipple into a small bench vise and polishing it with a strip of emery cloth. When locking nipple into vise, be sure not to damage the threads, but lock the nipple into the vise on the shoulders where the nipple ↓ wrench engages.

nipple. Should the No. 11 caps fit too tightly, the neck can easily be polished down by chucking it either into a drill press or a Dremel Moto-Tool and polishing it down a bit with emery cloth.

Turner Kirkland, who heads up Dixie Gun Works, found that the old Colts had two different length nipples, and conjectures that American guns used the short one, while the British Colts came with the long nipple. Since there are some variations in sixgun nipples – a total of three different size revolver nipples have been noted – you must measure the original nipple before you can order suitable replacement nipples for your old sixgun.

The question of repairing an old gun, and the difference between repair and restoration is an often hotly argued point. Adding a spring or new nipples to an old gun that has some collector value is usually

Shooting the Muzzleloaders

Uncle Mike's stainless steel nipple at far left for rifle and at far right for pistol are typical of the available replacement nipples offered. Many shooters use a brass nipple for display, replace it with another nipple for shooting. Note the three different rifle and two pistol shapes and sizes.

considered permissible, providing the repairs and replacements are made with old but serviceable parts. Of course, using new nipples for shooting is something else since they can be removed in case the gun is sold, and the original nipples can be re-installed.

But when does gun repair become a restoration? And how does a restoration job affect the value of the gun in comparison to the value of the same model in original condition?

A complete restoration of a clunker, with original parts, is usually considered taboo among collectors. Of course, if you only want a shooter and money is no object, this is quite permissible, providing you tell the next owner of the gun just what has been done with it. On the whole, skillful restorations cost too much in relation to the cost of a replica, but repairs, such as replacing a broken spring or worn hammer, are worthwhile.

Many of the older black powder rifles have sadly neglected barrels. A thorough cleaning is, of course, the first step after removal of a live charge if there was one in the gun. Some barrels can be salvaged by recutting or even lining, but this is a job for the professional gunsmith who specializes in black powder guns. Since the bore of such a barrel will be somewhat larger than the original size, you will have to get a mold for the larger projectile. However, do not order the new mold or have your old one altered until you have determined the precise caliber of the restored barrel.

Shooting the Muzzleloaders

Chapter 3 BLACK POWDER

As already mentioned, there seems to be strong evidence that gunpowder or black powder came originally from the east. On the other hand, there appears to be just as much reliable information on hand indicating that gunpowder was discovered, perhaps accidentally, by Friar Berthold Schwarz or *der schwarze Berthold* because of his interest in black magic. Constantin Anklitzen took the Church name of Berthold when he became a Franciscan monk in Freiburg. Although documents about Berthold disappeared even before the Reformation, one historic fact is certain: Freiburg was the hub of a very active cannon casting center and was also famed for its gunnery school during the 14th and 15th centuries.

GREEK FIRE AND ROGER BACON...

In the year 670, Constantine the Bearded ordered ships to defend Constantinople from the anticipated attack of the infidels, these ships to be armed with Greek Fire. When the composition of this and the later gunpowder are compared, there is little doubt left that the inventor of black powder was conversant with Greek Fire.

Greek Fire consists of sulfur, sarcocolla, tartar, pitch, melted saltpeter, petroleum oil, oil of gum, all boiled together. Flax tow was impregnated with this mixture, and once ignited, it was found that neither sand nor water would extinguish the violent flames which burned for a surprisingly long time.

A somewhat different mix of black powder resembles the original formula even more closely, and even the wood – grapevine or willow – is specified as sources for charcoal. This formula called for one pound of pure sulfur, two pounds of charcoal and six pounds of saltpeter, all of this to be ground down and mixed in a marble mortar. Roger Bacon not only continued experimenting, but he also recorded in some detail his findings and formulas.

Over the years, as guns and ignitions systems changed, and as the technique of making black powder for various uses also changed, the formulas for black powder also varied somewhat. Between the 8th and the 18th centuries, these compositions were used:

Saltpeter	37.5 – 75.0 per cent
Charcoal	12.5 – 33.3 per cent
Sulfur	7.7 – 31.25 per cent

In 1915, the 10th edition of H. M. *Treatise of Ammunition* listed the composition of black powder thusly:

Saltpeter	75 parts
Charcoal	15 parts
Sulfur	10 parts
Moisture	.7 – 1.5 per cent

From the above mix, several other gunpowders evolved. The brown or cocoa powders contained somewhat more saltpeter, straw charcoal and moisture, and less sulfur. These mixes burn a little slower and are also more difficult to ignite. Although brown powder is now obsolete, it is interesting to note that a priming charge of black powder was needed to ignite the brown in a cartridge case. The sulfurless powders were introduced in England since it was believed that the sulfur content of the powder igniters in cartridges adversely affected the stability of the cordite. In this gunpowder, the mix consists of 70 per cent saltpeter and 30 percent charcoal, plus traces of moisture.

WHEN IT BURNS...

Two ounces of black powder will propel an iron ball weighing 1088 ounces (68 lbs.) a distance of 100 yards. Gunpowder burns rapidly, but combustion is by no means as instantaneous as it appears to the eye. In considering the chemistry of gunpowder, it helps to understand its components and the actions of these components once the mix begins to burn.

Saltpeter, also known as nitrate of potash or potassium nitrate, is a chemical compound that results from the reaction of nitric acid and a potassium base. Nitric acid contains six parts of oxygen to one part of nitrogen, and when exposed to heat levels in excess of 800 degrees, saltpeter begins to disintegrate chemically, the nitrogen is liberated, while the oxygen reacts with the potash to produce potassium oxide.

But if there is a combustible substance present when the saltpeter is exposed to the heat, all sorts of interesting things begin to happen. Just as bluing a gun barrel is, chemically speaking, a rusting process, the burning of any material is essentially an oxidation process. The more oxygen is present, the more complete the burning and the faster the chemical reaction takes place. The sulfur and charcoal are the non-chemicals in this reaction, but the chemical components of these react with the liberated oxygen. Sulfur, for instance, permits lowering the temperature of combustion; the charcoal appears to contribute the

crystalline structure to the black powder; and there are several other inter-reacting chemical steps taking place as the gunpowder burns.

Unfortunately, gunpowder in the unburned condition is somewhat hygroscopic. In other words, it attracts moisture. The chemical compounds of combustion that form after gunpowder has burned are also hygroscopic, and a bit more so than unburned gunpowder. It is because of this ability to attract and hold moisture that storage of gunpowder must be undertaken with care, and that black powder guns must be cleaned thoroughly as soon after shooting as possible. Moisture invites rust, and once the first spot of rust appears, you can look forward to a prolonged cleaning session, since rust begets more rust at a faster rate than a cat can have kittens.

GUNPOWDER GRANULATION

When black powder was still mixed by hand in a mortar, it soon became apparent that this was not a homogenous mix, but that powder particles came in many sizes and shapes. So it was ground a bit finer, and when it reached the approximate consistency of coal dust, it became known as Meal or Serpentine powder. Because the process of breaking down the particles was a mechanical one, the particles on prolonged standing or a fair bit of handling tended to sift out, with the smaller pieces going to the bottom of the container.

But this did not help the burning rate of the gunpowder, and so someone discovered that the ground gunpowder could be mixed with water until it

Woodcut dating to about 1630 shows how black powder was mixed, then ground together. At right, the moistened mix is forced through a sieve, thus becoming granulated.

formed a paste, which was then forced through a sieve to form the granules. Such Corned or Granulated powder did not separate, the particles did not travel to the bottom, but the paste was a mess to handle. So it was pressed into cakes which were dried, then crushed in a mill until all particles were more or less the same size. During this crushing process, the powder was passed through several screens, and the particles passing a given screen were lumped together. Now we have four major granulation sizes.

GUNPOWDER DESIGNATIONS...

The manufacture and sale of black powder is very strictly regulated in Europe. In Germany, for example, the famous RWS Dynamit Nobel line of powders, once numbering six or more different sizes, has been reduced to one. This was made necessary by the extreme cost of licensing for *each size* of powder manufactured. Following is a table minimum and maximum dimensions for each size of powder once offered by Dynamit Nobel:

Size // 00 0.1 - 0.4 mm; 0 0.3 - 0.6 mm; 1 0.6 - 1.2 mm; 2 0.7 - 1.3 mm; 3 0.3 - 1.2 mm; 4 0.3 - 1.5 mm.

The coarsest of the currently available powders for muzzleloaders is FG, sometime also marked Fg, with the next finest being FFg or two Fg, then comes FFFg or three Fg, while the finest is FFFFg or four Fg. The latter is sometimes hard to find, and is used for priming the flintlocks or flinters. The size of the granule determines its designation, and the particles are passed though a series of screens with a go and no-go system.

If you decide to participate in International Championship Shoots, as the one held in Germany in late 1974, you will encounter some slightly different granulations. But despite the slight differences in granule size, the designations and approximate uses remain the same.

Thus, our Cannon powder passes a German 336 mm screen, but does not pass a 168 mm screen; Musket powder 1.41 – 0.71 mm; FFg 1.19 – 0.59 mm; Shell 1.19 – 0.29 mm; FFFg 0.84 – 0.29 mm; Fuze 0.42 – 0.149 mm; and FFFFg 0.35 – 0.105 mm.

The black powders available to the American muzzleloader vary somewhat in size with manufacturers, and though the granule size does affect the burning rate and hence the ballistic efficiency of the powder, shooting tests indicate that the differences are minor, hence can be disregarded. It must be pointed out, however, that there have been some reports in the black powder literature which indicate that those differences in granules can become critical when working with maximum loads. As with handloading rifle and handgun ammo, shooting maxi-

Fg passes through 10 mesh/in. screen, does not pass 14 mesh/in. screen
FFg passes through 16 mesh/in. screen, does not pass 24 mesh/in. screen
FFFg passes through 24 mesh/in. screen, does not pass 46 mesh/in. screen
FFFFg passes through 46 mesh/in. screen, does not pass 60 mesh/in. screen

mum loads each and every time only burns up more powder, increases recoil, and with muzzleloaders only thickens that cloud of smoke that goes with shooting black powder. Maximum loads are not necessarily the most accurate ones, and although black powder is a forgiving propellant, there are limitations. Later on, in the ballistics chapter (Chapter X), some of these points will be covered in detail.

As a rough guide, here are the powder granulations and their uses in muzzleloaders.

FFFFg – for priming flintlocks, and for small bore rifles an handguns, although not very efficient in them. May be hard to find, and some old-timers still call this "Super-Fine".

FFFg – ideal for small bore rifles up to .45 caliber and for handguns. Can be used as priming powder for flinters if the finer grain is not available.

FFg – a good choice for the larger bore rifles, from .45 up to .58 caliber, for shotguns from 12 gauge to 20 gauge, and can also be used in the large bore single-shot pistols with good results.

Fg – primarily used in the large bore shotguns, such as 4 bore to 10 gauge. Since there is little demand for powder of this granulation, you may find that the local dealer does not stock it.

AVAILABLE POWDERS

Some years ago, the DuPont black powder plant went up in smoke – with a loud boom. Since then, Gearhart-Owen Industries has taken over the manu-

Small lots of the old DuPont powder are still around, Meteor and Shurr-Shot are currently imported from Canada, and at far right, a can of Gearhart-Owen powder, which is at present the most widely distributed gunpowder. Burning rate of this powder is very similar to the rate of the old DuPont product.

facture, and the G-O powders are, for all practical purposes, identical to the old DuPont powders. Once in a while you may find some of the DuPont powders, and if the stuff has been stored properly, it can be used without making load adjustments. Another domestic black powder maker sells his wares under the Western Industries label, and the rest of the black powders are imported, notably from Canada and Scotland. C-I-L and Shurr-Shot are powders of Canadian origin, while Hodgdon's private brand and Curtis & Harvey powders come from Scotland. Other labels will be seen from time to time,

and most of these carry proprietary brand names, such as that seen on the Hodgdon powders.

It is true that the early pioneers were sometimes forced to make their own powder, and while any chemistry student can give you the precise formula and method for making the stuff, the best advice anyone can give you is: DON'T!

Making gunpowder is neither complicated nor costly, but it is DANGEROUS ! NEVER, NEVER ATTEMPT TO MAKE YOUR OWN POWDER OR PERCUSSION CAPS.

All of the different brands of black powder on the market today have a fine graphite coating that gives gunpowder that shiny black appearance. However, the graphite is not added for the sake of appearance, but to make the gunpowder flow more smoothly out of flasks and horns. Graphite has also been shown to have anti-static-electricity properties.

Black powder has a specific gravity of 106 pounds per cubic foot – this bit of physics information is not vital to the shooter, but it is to the manufacturer of gunpowder. When the specific gravity of the mix drops below that figure, existing powder measures and flasks will not be able to deliver the required volumetric amount of powder – another reason why you should never attempt to make your own gunpowder. Even if you survive the experiment, the product will have totally unknown chemical properties and burning characteristics.

Unless the moisture content of gunpowder is held to a carefully determined maximum, the powder granules will clump. Again, measuring charges then becomes uncertain and a matter of guesswork, and of course the burning rate, hence the ballistic performance, of the projectile will be affected.

HANDLING GUNPOWDER...

Just how dangerous is gunpowder? Fairy tales prevail when it comes to accidents allegedly due to gunpowder, and even smokeless powder comes in for its share of bum raps and bad publicity. By chemical definition, most everything that goes boom is considered explosive. This, of course, includes all propellant powders, smokeless as well as black, and the class of explosives is further broken down into high and low explosives. Black powder is a low explosive, while TNT and dynamite are high explosives. But, and here comes the kicker, gasoline also goes boom with a lot more flash and noise, and nobody thinks of it as an explosive.

Black powder is fairly stable, both chemically and mechanically. Chemically, it may absorb moisture if not properly stored, but seldom does it lose moisture. Either will affect the performance of the powder, and although here and there in the literature someone will make recommendations about drying out powder or adding moisture to it, the best way is to prevent such changes. Keep powder canisters closed at all times, and don't break the original closure until you are ready to fill a powder flask or horn, or to begin weighing out charges. Then close the can tightly and store it where you keep the rest of your supply of black powder.

Handle the cans of gunpowder with care: that is, don't drop them or toss them around. Violent shaking is not recommended for two reasons. First of all, the particles rubbing against each other will, if agitation is prolonged or repeated, produce dust which will sift to the bottom of the can. This means that the burning rate of the powder will not be the same as it was originally and, of course, this affects the ultimate performance of your gun. Violent shaking of the can should be avoided, not only because of the dust problem, but also because a series of circumstances, such as an accidental sparking between metal and metal or metal and stone, could set off the fireworks.

When handling gunpowder, avoid all open flames, do not smoke, and stay away from pilot flames. Essentially, the precautions needed for handling black powder are similar to those you use when handling a five gallon can of gas for your lawnmower.. except that the gas fumes are a bit more dangerous.

STORAGE TIPS...

Do not open a can of gunpowder until you are ready to start filling your powder horn or flask or to weigh charges. As also mentioned before, keep the lid – that is, the screw cap – on, and when you are finished pouring whatever amount of powder you need, close the can tightly. During the humid summer months, a strip of elastic electrician's tape around the screw top of the can will help to keep moisture in the atmosphere from getting to your powder. Remember that black powder attracts moisture.

If at all possible, store your black powder outside the house. A corner in the garage, toolshed or any such place is suitable, as long as it can be locked up and is not open to the weather. You can still find GI ammo boxes with rubber gasketed lids in surplus stores and even some gunshops. Since you won't

have more than two to four cans of powder on hand at any time, a small ammo box will do just fine. There is little sense in stockpiling the powder and although it does not deteriorate materially during storage, it does not improve with age.

A specially designed portable storage magazine – a steel box on four 2" casters with a 3/8" non-sparking wood liner and two locks – is a good investment. Your dealer can order such a portable magazine from C&M Gun Works (2603 41st Street, Moline, IL 61265). The box meets all federal requirements for powder storage, and your insurance agent and the company handling your fire insurance won't give you any static about having a couple of cans of gunpowder in the garage if you use such a storage magazine. But no matter what kind of container you use to store the black powder, don't stick the percussion caps in the same can or box!

POWDER CHARGES...

Because black powder dates way back into the days of hand-made guns, and because the powder flasks and horns of the early days did not have powder measures in them, a great many old wives' tales about charges are still passed along as gospel.

The one with the greatest longevity and the least amount of truth in it goes like this: Place a ball for your rifle in your palm, then pour powder over the ball until it is completely covered with gunpowder. After trying this some years ago, with all charges being carefully weighed by two reloaders, it was found that charges varied too much for continued good health. For instance, one tester cupped his

hand, the other did not, and the difference in charge weight was almost 20 grains of black powder! Moreover, the hand size, and hence the palm size, varies not only between individuals, but your own right and left palm vary, at least to a degree. So much for this way of doping out the charge for a muzzleloader!

A somewhat more reliable method is to say that the charge should weigh between 33 to 40 per cent of the weight of the ball. Somewhat similar is the 3:7 rule which says simply that you use three grains of powder for every seven grains of the weight of the round ball. Yet another suggestion says 1 1/2 caliber when under .40 caliber, but 2 calibers when over .40 cailber. However, some tests with replicas has shown that this gives you some fairly stiff charges, and that these loads are especially suitable for long-range shooting.

Considerable testing has been done to determine the "best" way to figure out a load for any rifle, and it seems that the "grain to caliber" rule works best. Let's say that you want to load for a .36 caliber rifle, so you use 36 grains of powder. For a .57 caliber gun, you would then use 57 grains of powder. This will give you a good medium and short range load which is neither hotter than the hinges of hell, nor a pipsqueak load. If accuracy is not all you want or expect, increase the charge by 2 grain increments, being cer-

tain to shoot each of the newly worked-up loads at a target and never fire less than three – and preferably five – shots at one target to check for grouping.

In sound replicas, you can increase the charge up to 1 1/2 caliber, so that a .50 caliber gun could be loaded with up to 75 grains of powder. This would be a long-range load, and is certainly very close to, if not slightly exceeding, the maximum charge for this gun and caliber. More about maximum loads and pressure in Chapter X.

The correct charge burns a lot cleaner than one in which too much gunpowder is used, and rather than a boom, the sound of the rifle changes until the crack is somewhat like that of a medium caliber centerfire rifle.

As is the case with centerfire guns – rifles, handguns as well as shotguns – each muzzleloader is a law unto itself. The load that shoots well in one rifle may very well be a miserable failure in another gun of like caliber. Barrel length and twist, the condition of the bore, patching material, size of the projectile, the condition of the firing mechanism, including the needed clear passageway into the main charge – all of these play an important role in working up good loads. In contrast to handloaded centerfire ammunition where one load is usually suitable for shooting over all distances, you can, without too much effort or trouble, work up specific loads for your muzzleloader. For instance, you can easily develop a load for 25 yard plinking and small game hunting, and with a stiffer charge and perhaps a bullet rather than a ball, use the same rifle for long range shooting.

And don't let anyone tell you that black powder rifles have a maximum range of 100 yards! Every year, at the national shoots as well as at regional

A replica of the Colt Dragoon sounds, off on an indoor range. Note the sparking from the percussion cap and the large muzzle flash which supplied enough light to take this picture.

matches, all held under the auspices of the NMLRA, 200 yard groups are fired that would make many a centerfire rifleman turn green with envy.

Although the matter of patches will be covered in Chapter V, a few words about them are in order, since they too affect the performance of your gun. If you have developed a load that is satisfactory in all respects, and then change the patching material, perhaps to one a bit thinner or a shade heavier, you will immediately alter the ballistics of your load. Here is one tip that is based on sad experience – when you work up a good load, make sure to collect enough of the same patching material that you used in working up your load to last you for some time.

If for some reason you change molds, switch either to a heavier ball or conical bullet, or simply get a new round ball mold that delivers a ball not identical in size and thus not of the same weight as the original, then you have to start working up new loads. Fortunately for those who don't like to experiment around too much, here the load change is probably going to be a minor one, and one or two range sessions should take care of the load development time.

Simply cast an adequate number of balls, take a can or two of powder, a box of caps, your cleaning equipment, and you can do your load development right at the shooting bench. Of course, you should do all your testing over sandbags or some sort of rest, and later on you will find out how to load your gun accurately so that the human element of loading becomes a negligible factor that won't affect accuracy.

Shooting the Muzzleloaders

The following loads have been found safe in replicas in good working condition. However, neither the publisher nor the author can assume any responsibility for the use of these data, since condition of gun, loading techniques and other factors not under the control of either the publisher or the authors affect the performance of the loads, and possibily also the safety of the shooter.

RIFLES AND MUSKETS

Gun/Caliber	Ball/Bullet	Powder	Charge/ Grains
.36	RB1 .350–.355	3 Fg	35–45
.36 H & A	RB .349–.351	3 Fg	41
.40 Dixie F2, P3	RB .395	3 Fg	65
.44	RB/MB4 .429–.435	3 Fg	45–65
.44 Kentucky	RB .434	3 Fg	58
.45	RB .440–.445	2 Fg or 3 Fg	50–68
.45 T/C	RB .445	3 Fg	60
.45 H & A	RB .445	3 Fg	68
.45 Kentucky	RB .450–.452	3 Fg	66
.50	RB .490–.495	2 Fg	70–90
.50 T/C	RB .490	3 Fg	80
.50 Maynard, issue	RB .517	3 Fg	50
.52 Sharps, issue	RB .535–.555	3 Fg	60
.54 Gallager	RB .535	3 Fg	54
.577 Enfield	RB .570–.575	2 Fg	60
.58 Rem. Zouave	RB .570–.575	2 Fg	60
	MB	2 Fg	57–59
.70 Brown Bess	RB .663	Fg	70

1 – RB – Round Ball
2 – F – Flintlock
3 – P – Percussion
4 – MB – Minie Bullet

SINGLE-SHOT PISTOLS

.40 Dixie F2, P3	RB1 .395	3 Fg	25
.54 U.S. pistols	RB .535	3 Fg	35
.58 U.S. Springfield M 1855	RB .570–.575	2 Fg	40
.45 T/C	RB .440	3 Fg	26–35

1 – RB – Round Ball
2 – F – Flintlock
3 – P – Percussion

As can be seen from the above data, the grain/caliber rule does not hold true when loading single-shot pistols. Turner Kirkland, who heads Dixie Gun Works and is one of the prime suppliers of black powder guns and accessories, suggests this: for best accuracy, use the lightest possible load that will deliver the ball to the target without a rainbowlike trajectory.

CAP AND BALL REVOLVERS

.31 Colt Rem. Pocket Revolvers	RB1 .321	3 Fg	8–14
.31	RB .310	3 Fg	8–11
.36	RB .376	3 Fg	19–22
.36	RB .375	3 Fg	15–19
.44 Dragoon replica	RB .451	3 Fg	38–40
.44 Replica	RB .450	3 Fg	28

1 – RB – Round Ball

When loading for an original gun, after ascertaining that the revolver is in good shooting condition, work up your loads slowly. Thanks to modern steels and foreign proof laws, most replicas can handle somewhat stiffer charges than their original counterparts.

Shooting the Muzzleloaders

SHOTGUNS

Gauge	Powder	Charge/ Grains	Shot/Ounces
.410	2 Fg	34–41	1/2
		41	5/8
32	2 Fg	41	1/2
		41	9/16
38	2 Fg	48–55	5/8
20	2 Fg	55	3/4
		61	7/8
16	2 Fg	61–69	1
12	2 Fg	76	1 1/8
		82	1 1/4
10	2 Fg	102	1 1/4
		109	1 1/2

For 10 and 12 gauge guns, some shooters prefer to use Fg powder, but little is gained by the use of such a coarse powder, and neither velocities nor patterns showed statistically significant changes or improvements.

REMEMBER, HANDLE BLACK POWDER WITH CARE, AND KEEP IT AWAY FROM OPEN FLAME. AVOID UNDUE EXPOSURE TO MOISTURE. NEVER ATTEMPT TO MAKE YOUR OWN POWDER OR CAPS. If you follow this advice, you will be able to enjoy black powder guns for many years to come.

THE MANUFACTURE OF BLACK POWDER

While most shooters today, especially those engaged in the muzzle-loading sports, tend to think of black powder as an ancient and outdated propellant, the truth is that it continues to play an important role in the field of modern pyrotechnics. The development of nitro-cellulose powders and higher orders of explosives such as dynamite have not been able to drive it into obsolesence simply because black powder provides some unique ignitional and propellant properties that remain unparallelled. It continues as a primary propellant – a pushing force – whereas contempory explosives are principally detonating and destructive. Whenever, and wherever a controlled but rapid expansion of gases is required to exert a precalculable propellant energy its ease of ignition and sensitivity is certain to be scrutinized, even among those engaged in military pursuits.

Interestingly, the present-day formula for black powder does not differ appreciably from the recipe concocted by Barthold the Monk in medieval times: it consists of saltpetre, charcoal and sulphur (percentagewise, 75–15–10, in that order.) However, it is no easier to manufacture, today, than it was when Barthold made it. In the fourteenth and fifteenth century black powder makers were thought of as men who had successfully negotiated a pact with the devil: who else of sound mind would attempt such a treacherous undertaking? Indeed, the frequency of medieval powder-plant mishaps were such that sovereigns felt obliged to intervene by establishing standards for production and safety. Over the years those who set out to develop improved manufactur-

A black powder granulating device. Spiralled column at left is a form of elevator that lifts powder to the feed board of the machine.

37

Modern black powder plants consist largely of wood frame structures set in earth-mounded bunkers and connected by wooden walkways. When reinforced concrete is employed in a given structure it is roofed lightly to channel explosive forces skyward in the event of an accident.

Quality controls start with the arrival of raw materials; powder chemists check each lot in the laboratory and every subsequent phase of production is likewise repeatedly examined and regulated. Every tool, machine, transporter and waste receptacle is cleaned and checked repeatedly during each shift. Waste, incidentally, is especially hazardous when it takes the form of fine dust. In view of the foregoing, one can readily appreciate the time-consuming nature of powder-making.

When raw materials have been examined and approved they enter the first stage of production – pulverization. This is accomplished in a mill where huge, plastic-covered bronze (spark-proof) wheels crush two of the components. The third – potassium nitrate – is powdered in a special punch-mill. Following pulverization the milled material is passed through a sieve to remove any contaminating foreign substances. From here, the dry powders are taken to a stone mill where they are pressed, mixed and blended under the pressure of large stone rollers. The material lies in a "dish" where it is moistened with a mix of water and alcohol and where it is continuosly "ploughed" and "scraped" since the uniformity of the mix is of paramount importance. The 10% moisture content at this stage serves two purposes: it stabilizes the ingredients by reducing sensitivity (simultaneously reducing the dust factor) and it

These huge powder forming rollers weigh approximately 12,000 lbs. and are suspended above the floor of the pan.

ing techniques were inevitably frustrated, discovering that they could add only more exacting practices to an already painfully tedious process. Safety and ease of production were not the only criterions, of course, the quality and uniformity of the finished product were obviously vital considerations.

induces the charcoal to absorb the potassium nitrate, thereby intensifying potential explosive properties.

The millstones weigh approximately 12000 lbs. and are suspended in such a way that they do not contact the base of the dish. They simply compress the powder as it is being blended, completing a given batch in eight or nine passes.

Ploughs and scrapers are also made from non-sparking bronze and the entire mill is carefully grounded to eliminate static electricity.

When blended and compressed the finished mix is removed in cake form. These are next shredded by degrees, to result in granulations ranging from 0.1 mm to 1.5 mm's in size. Another cleaning follows before the "green powder" moves to the drying room where warm air is forced through the gently agitated granules. When dry, it is cleaned for the third time and loaded into drums where it is mixed and tumbled with graphite which coats the individual grains, turning them black. This graphite coating also serves to prevent any subsequent caking of the finished powder.

Powder mill safety precautions are exceptional – "extraordinary" would probably be a better word. Not only are structures and machines designed and maintained with infinite care, but every laborer and technician must be trained, methodically, in the painstaking powder-handling routine. Needless to say, job applicants are very carefully screened to determine if their temperments are suited to such regimented work.

One of the problems that has continuously stymied powder-makers from the beginning, is that witnesses rarely survive to explain the cause of an accident.

A powder scale and loading machine.

After a mishap, all manner of experts are consulted in an attempt to pin down the fault. Grisly as it may sound, a human body is usually the best source of information since it absorbs flying fragments. The unfortunate victim can usually be traced to one location and the direction and force of the fragments

Another form of scale measures canister lots and loads them into small containers.

measured from that point. With this information, experts can frequently track down the point of origin.

On one of the rare occasions when a victim survived long enough to talk to his would-be rescuers he related that a co-worker had simply pushed a broom into a basket of warm powder. The broom, obviously, had generated enough static electricity in its bristles to effect ignition.

Through most of its history black powder was made by technicians who worked in close proximity to the powder-fabricating machines. Later, when electrically driven equipment was employed, switches were added so that everything came to a stop when the door to the fabricating room was opened. One directive of early concerned sovereigns is followed to this day: no more personnel than absolutely necessary will be permitted to occupy a given production area. Mills still try to limit work forces to one man per site and each stage of production is widely separated from others.

Modern powder plants have also separated the operator from the machine, placing him behind a heavy, reinforced concrete barricade where he watches the equipment through a small, heavily glassed, sight slot. Remote controls and emergency cut-off switches occupy a panel before him.

While many sources of trouble have been eliminated in modern powder factories there will always remain some danger in feeding and clearing the various machines.

Strange, isn't it, that three such innocuous substances can prove so devastating when combined?

The following excerpt, translated from a document that originated in Augsburg (Germany) in 1529, graphically illustrates the prerequisites for a powder-making apprenticeship in medieval times:

"He who would make gun powder must honor God more devoutly than other men and live close to Him for all of his days for in his hands he will grasp the Devil.

He must be a man of courage, moderate ways, and an individual of strong confidence.

He must be a master of the sciences and one who both reads and writes, or he shall not know his measure nor understand his formulas.

To these three things he must devote his mind and his efforts: the substances, the measures and the mix, if he would put them all together.

He must be a man of gentle nature, sober, and keen not to fall drunk…!"

Fortunately for the black powder enthusiast, the greatest perils of black powder are found in its manufacture. The finished product, safely delivered into the hands of the sportsman requires only some basic safety precautions:

1. Do not expose black powder to flame, excessive heat, electrically charged atmospheres, nor sudden and violent forces.

2. Keep all canisters tightly closed when not in use and store cans out of the reach of children.

3. Don't smoke in close proximity to stored powder.

Chapter 4 THE PROJECTILE

Rifled muzzleloaders use two different kinds of projectiles – round balls or bullets. The smaller calibers are loaded with balls, the larger ones can be loaded either with balls or bullets of one kind or another. Let's consider the round ball first.

Round balls are loaded patched – that is, the ball is partly encased in a piece of material, in most cases, linen. Patching material (see Chapter V) comes in various thicknesses, and the relationship between bore diameter and ball diameter will govern the thickness of your patching material. If a ball is undersize, a somewhat thicker patching material is used. Conversely, a tight fitting ball calls for a thinner patch. Just as an undersized ball and a too-thin patch won't perform well, a ball that is oversize and patched too heavily will present some difficulties, the least being the seating of the ball on the powder charge. More than one hickory ramrod has broken under such conditions, the sharp wood splinters in the shooter's hand reminding him of his mistake or carelessness in loading.

Cap and ball revolvers are usually fired with lead balls, but no patch is used. In the large calibers, both handgun and rifle, the ball may be replaced by a conical bullet that is either lubed, or in rifles is equipped with a paper patch.

BALL SIZES...

Because of the relatively shallow rifling in black powder barrels, only pure lead projectiles should be used. The projectile has to engage the rifling within the barrel for the sake of accuracy, and pure lead is best suited for this. Moreover, because of its softness, pure lead does not create undue friction, hence

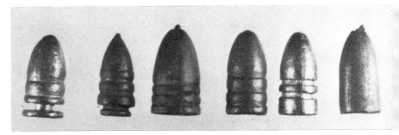

Six types of muzzleloader bullets that saw use during the Civil War. At far left, the Williams bullet, also known as the .58 caliber clean-out bullet, and at far right, the .577 Pritchett bullet, the only one of its period without grease groove.

barrel wear seldom becomes a problem.

In recent years, a few advanced black powder technicians, who not only build their rifles but also rifle their own barrels, have reported that in bench-rest matches with extra heavy rifles and custom barrels a lead alloy rather than pure lead has given promising results. This is especially true at long-range matches, and perhaps a somewhat harder projectile may be the answer for extreme accuracy in large bore rifles when premature barrel wear is less important than group size.

If the ball fits too tightly, the force and pounding exerted by the ramrod while seating the ball and patch on top of the powder charge will deform the forward part of the ball. This, in turn, prevents the ball from flying true, and accuracy will suffer. Although most replicas are marked with the caliber, manufacturing tolerances and rifling variations are just great enough to make it almost essential that you slug your barrel before buying a mold.

Remove the barrel from the gun, and with the help of a breech plug wrench, unscrew the breech

41

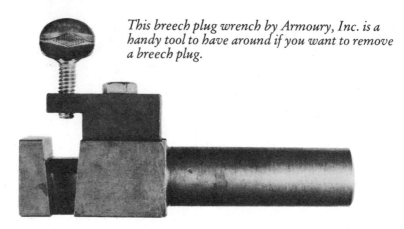

This breech plug wrench by Armoury, Inc. is a handy tool to have around if you want to remove a breech plug.

plug. Be sure to pad the jaws of your bench vise so that the barrel won't be marred or damaged. Using a pure lead slug that is 0.01" or so larger than the bore, drive the slug from the breech and right out the muzzle. Use a good solid rod for the job, and if you are careful not to drag the rod across the lands, you can even use a length of drill rod. Instead of a hammer, use a rawhide mallet for the pounding. For a slug you can use either a larger lead bullet whittled to the approximate caliber with a knife, or a piece of scrap lead roughly formed in your bench vise. The slug that comes from the muzzle will carry perfect land and groove markings. Now measure the groove and bore diameter as engraved on your slug.

Let's say that the groove diameter of your rifle miked .4653" and that the bore diameter miked .450". Subtract bore diameter from groove diameter, then divide by 2, which gives you the groove depth. In the example here, this would be .00765" and rounding this up gives you .008". Therefore, the patch thickness must be a bit greater than .008", and the size of the cast ball must be a bit under .450".

In measuring patching material, be sure to close the micrometer fairly tightly. When you think the material is held tightly enough in the mike, tug on it hard – if it comes out, you have not tightened the mike up enough. Any material, and that of course includes the material from which the patch is made, is compressed even more when it is wet, and patches are lubed with spit or a lubricant when the ball is seated with the patch.

As a very general rule of thumb, barrels designed to handle round balls have a somewhat slower twist and somewhat deeper rifling than those made for conical bullets. Hollow-base Minie bullets should fit the bar-

Special molds for black powder shooters are offered by Lee Engineering, Shiloh, and Lyman. Not shown are the new RCBS molds, which are very much like the Lyman molds.

rel so that the bullet slides down the barrel. Once the Minie bullet is on its way up the barrel, the skirt of the bullet spreads, thus giving a better gas seal and allowing the bullet to engage the rifling. A faster twist tends to stabilize the conical bullet better than a round ball which invariably weighs 1/2 – 1/3 less than a conical bullet, but the faster twist also produces barrel fouling more rapidly, and the degree of fouling is more severe.

Once you have the patching material that is theoretically the right one, you should also try other patching materials, both a bit thicker and a bit thinner. Somewhere among the patching material you try, you will find that perfect one – but you have to do your own experimenting and testing, and accuracy is the basis of comparison. Of course, in the testing of the patching material – as with all other testing – change only one variable at a time. Thus, if you are testing patching, keep ball size and weight, caps and charges identical; if you are testing charges, keep all other variables constant.

BULLET SIZES...

Most manufacturers and importers of replicas also offer suitable molds for their muzzleloaders. The replica molds are made from brass, and this metal makes a handsome display mold which unfortunately, is not very suitable for casting balls or bullets. Brass is an excellent conductor of heat, and the small handles are awkward when manipulated with heavy gloves. A few manufacturers specify a mold maker and the size or number of a mold, and these recommendations are usually based on actual tests, thus can be followed. If you only know that the rifle is such-and-such a caliber, you should slug the barrel as already outlined.

Minie bullets should just slide down the bore, while solid or hollowbase bullets should be slightly over-bore diameter so that when seated, the land and groove marks will be engraved on the soft lead of the bullets. On looking over a solid conical bullet, you will note that the upper or top band of the bullet appears to be a shade wider than the base of the bullet, and when you mike it, you will be able to confirm this. This band offers the barrel seal needed, while the base of the bullet will measure the same as the bore diameter.

The ultimate bullet performance depends on a number of factors, such as rate of twist, number of

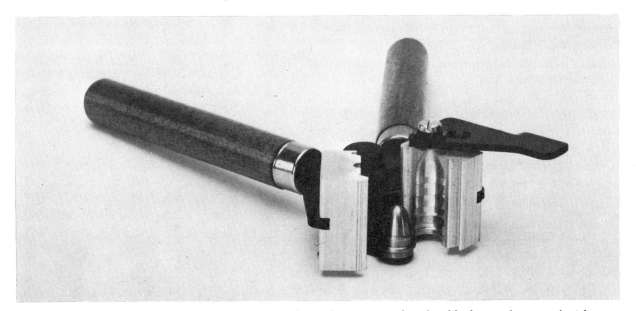

Aluminium block Lee molds are lightweight for prolonged casting comfort, but block must be treated with special care to avoid damage.

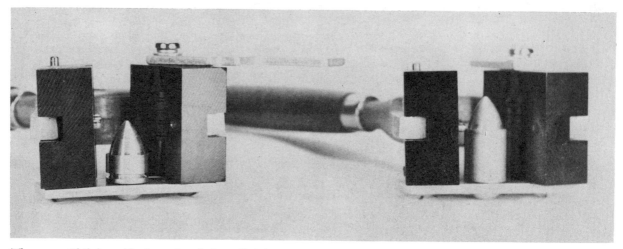

These two Shiloh molds show clearly how Shiloh overcame the hollow base pin problem which makes a mold more expensive and also more difficult to handle. These are excellent molds, available for black powder projectiles only.

grooves and depth of rifling, the velocity at which the bullet is driven, and of course, bullet design. One other factor is often overlooked, but a series of tests recently confirmed the role played by the amount of barrel fouling. As fouling increases, the soft lead bullet not only does not engage the rifling adequately, but excessive fouling also will seriously affect the bullet's preformance.

As is the case with centerfire rifles, one bullet may perform somewhat better than another one in a muzzleloader. Once you have mastered the mechanics of loading and shooting your muzzleloading rifle, you may want to try some other bullet design. For instance, one rifle does very well with a bullet cast from a Lyman mold, but another rifle, of the same caliber with almost identical rifling specifications, simply will not group with the Lyman bullet, but does extremely well with one cast from a Shiloh mold. Try several molds, such as those made by Shiloh, Lee, RCBS or Lyman. Often a local shooter, who has a gun in the same caliber as yours, will either cast some test bullets for you or will lend you the mold before you invest money in yet another mold.

What about bullet sizing? The vast majority of dedicated black powder shooters prefer to cast a bullet of the correct size, thereby eliminating the need for sizing. Only Shiloh offers a special and very clever bullet sizer, and sizing becomes essential only when a suitable size mold is not available and a standard size bullet has to be reduced in diameter.

CASTING YOUR OWN...

If you have been casting your own bullets for centerfire rifles and/or handguns, you only need a mold or two to cast balls or bullets of suitable diameter for your muzzleloader.

If you have never cast a bullet before and have been bitten by the black powder bug, you should consider casting. A great many companies offer cast bullets and balls, but not every gun shop stocks them and because of the weight, shipping cast projectiles can become expensive, especially if you will be doing a great deal of shooting. But there is one way you can avoid casting, and still get your projectiles locally. Nearly every gun shop or sporting goods store has the name of a local bullet caster, and quite a few of them have added suitable molds so that they can custom cast for anyone who is inclined to spend the money for it.

If you decide to go this route, be sure, that your custom caster understands that you want pure lead balls or bullets. Commercial casters usually work with a hard alloy, casting many .38 and .45 bullets for handgunners, and here the rule is the harder the better. You may have to furnish the lead, and one of the large plumbing supply houses is a good source for pure lead. Junk yards always have lead on hand, but you may have to clean it, or at least rub it down with steel wool. Lead cable and wire sheathing from the local telephone company, the radiology department of your hospital, and house wreckers who sell

The easiest way to bring a mold to casting temperature is to perch it at the edge of the electric pot.

A complete description of the bullet the mold casts can be found on the mold box, a good reason for saving either the box or the front panel of the box, storing it along with the mold.

scrap of all kinds are often totally untapped sources for good lead.

If at all possible, you should do your own casting since it saves you money in the long run, allows you to try a borrowed mold, and to control the purity of the metal you convert into projectiles. The needed casting equipment is basic, and aside from lead and molds, you won't need to add to the equipment in later years.

A melting pot is the first consideration. You can either use a bottom spout electric pot such as offered by Lyman, SAECO or Lee, or a pot that uses gas, most often propane. This type is available with a bottom spout from RCBS, and a number of other such pots are used in conjunction with a casting ladle or dipper. If you are certain that you will never have the urge to shoot a big caliber muzzleloader, the small pots using gas heat and a dipper will prove more than adequate. But if you want to cast some .50 or .54 caliber bullets, you may suddenly find that such a pot is too small, and that either the ladle or the spout does not deliver enough molten lead to fill the large mold cavity. If available, an old-fashioned plumber's furnace, pot and ladle are nearly ideal for casting large quantities of the big bullets, and operating costs for an electric pot and a gas or propane unit are almost identical, with actual costs varying somewhat with localities.

A large blanket, a wooden box for sprue waste and scrap bullets, a retired slotted mixing spoon from

This propane-heated pot has just been fluxed with a mixture of beeswax and grease – note the cloud of smoke which results from the burn-off of fluxing material used here.

45

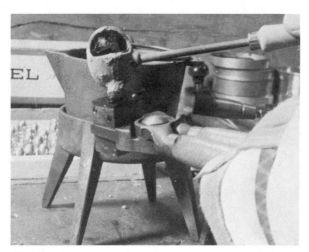

Mold and ladle have been turned 90 degrees to the left, and lead is being poured into round ball mold.

The flow control handle of this electric pot has been released, cutting off the flow of molten lead.

the kitchen, plus a rawhide mallet takes care of the tool question.

The blanket, folded several times, will serve to catch the newly cast bullets or balls as they come from the mold. The wood box, or even a large flat tin can, catches the sprue as it is knocked off the sprue cutter, and of course, all of the spoiled, uneven or badly cast bullets are also dumped here, to be remelted when the pot needs more metal. The slotted mixing spoon should be used to lower additional lead into the pot. NEVER DUMP COLD METAL INTO MOLTEN LEAD. Liquid metal will splatter, and hot lead causes painful and often serious burns.

For this very reason, get some heavy welder's gloves and use them while casting or handling the hot pot, liquid lead or any other such job. When casting, always wear a long-sleeved shirt and boots, since low-cut oxfords could allow hot lead spatter to fall into your shoe or onto your ankle. When casting, be sure that your pants legs are outside the boots, and wear protective glasses or safety goggles.

The rawhide mallet is a better choice than a stick of hardwood or an old hickory hammer handle. Extensive use of such a handle will shortly begin to fray the wood, and then wood chips and splinters end up in the sprue box, and later in the casting pot where they either burn off with odor and smoke, or have to be fished out with the slotted spoon.

Begin your first casting session by laying out all your needed gear, then clear the bench of all unessential clutter. If you are casting only pure lead, you

can, at the end of the session, simply turn off the heat source and let the lead harden in the pot. If you also cast hard alloy bullets, you may want to get a couple of ingot molds so that you can clear your pot of pure lead. Never handle a freshly filled ingot mold with anything but a pair of pliers – cast iron molds heat quite rapidly and are relatively slow to lose their heat.

Fill the pot with unmolten metal, start the heat source, and select the mold you want to use. Perch the mold at the edge of the pot. Only the Lee aluminum molds can be pre-heated to casting temperature by sticking a corner of the mold into the molten metal. If the mold has not reached casting temperature, the metal poured into the cavity will cool prematurely, the cavity will not fill completely, or wrinkles and bubbles will appear in the newly cast projectile.

If you use a bottom spout pot, you simply hold the closed mold, with the sprue cutter all the way to the right, under the spout and operate the handle. When a couple of drops of molten lead appear on the cutter, release the flow handle and remove the mold. Now hit the leading edge of the sprue cutter with the rawhide mallet, dumping the now-hardened sprue into the box. Open the mold and dump the newly cast ball or bullet onto the blanket. Should the bullet not drop readily from the mold, tap the hinge pin of the mold handles once or twice, but never hit the mold itself. Banging a good mold

Rawhide mallet is used to knock aside the sprue cutter. This severs the sprue from the mold, allows opening of mold and dropping of projectile.

if your pot is to be used for making bullets with another alloy, pour leftover lead into ingot molds. Ingots like these store easily and melt more readily.

around like this is the fastest way to ruin a precision piece of equipment.

When dropping a newly cast bullet from the mold, be sure that it does not make contact with a previously cast projectile. Newly cast lead balls and bullets are soft, hence can be damaged all too easily by having them bang against one another. Close the mold, tap the sprue cutter back in place and cast your next bullet.

If you decided to use a ladle or dipper, preheat the mold as before, and immerse the dipper in the melting lead and leave it there. If you attempt to pour lead from a ladle that is not heated properly, the metal will solidify in the pouring spout, and you almost certainly will not be able to fill the cavity of the mold.

Fill your dipper with hot molten lead, and hold it in the right gloved hand. The mold is held in the left hand, which is also gloved. Keep the dipper in the hot metal to prevent cooling of the lead. Now bring the hole in the sprue cutter plate in contact with the pouring spout of the ladle as it is lifted clear ot the pot. Turn the mold to the right until contact is made between the hole in the sprue cutter plate and the pouring spout, then turn the ladle down to the left until the mold once again is horizontal. When the molten metal has filled the cavity of the mold and the first few drops of metal show up on the sprue cutter, remove the ladle and return it to the pot to keep it hot. By now the drop of molten metal on the sprue cutter has hardened. Open the

sprue plate as above, dump the sprue into the sprue box and remove the bullet. You are now ready to cast the next bullet.

If you are going to cast a fair number of Minie bullets, get the largest lead dipper you can find. These bullets require a fair amount of lead, and some of the smaller ladles do not hold enough molten lead to fill the cavity of the mold. Refilling the ladle is not the answer since the base of the bullet in the mold would have cooled quite a bit before more metal could be added, and the resulting bullet would certainly be defective.

Lead as you buy it is, in most instances, fairly pure, but all foreign substances should be removed. This is accomplished by fluxing the molten metal. It seems that every experienced bullet caster has his pet flux, and anything from beeswax to bullet lube has been used and recommended. The great majority of these preparations are good, but have the drawback that they tend to smoke and smell up the place. Some housewives don't take kindly to the odoriferous smoke billowing up the basement stairs, and they may insist that you move your base of operations to the garage, chicken coop or the like.

Marvelux (Marmel Products, Box 97, Utica, MI 48087) is an excellent fluxing agent that neither smells up the place nor creates large clouds of smoke. Best of all, a little bit of the stuff goes a long way. Flux the metal in the pot when it becomes gray and cruddy looking, and before fluxing, see if you cannot skim off the dross with the slotted spoon. Drop a

47

Bullet boxes made from scrap lumber are the best and also the least expensive way to store cast bullets.

Hollow base plug with bullet, mold and sprue. Filling the cavity of such a mold takes practice since it has to be done rapidly.

small hunk of Marvelux into the pot, stir, and again skim off dross, if required.

Once the bullets or balls have cooled so that they can be handled, inspect each one. Imperfect castings are dumped back into the sprue box to be remelted some other day. Experienced casters, and it does not take long to get the hang of it, often use two different molds which cast different projectiles. Now such a caster must segregate the two different types of castings, and store them some way.

Probably the easiest way to go about the storing is to make up a dozen or more small wooden boxes from scrap lumber. All you need is some 1/4" ply-score wood and some wood strips, either 1x1, or 1/2x1, or anything similar that you can run through a rip saw and make up. Prepare labels that identify each mold and projectile, weight of bullet or ball, and then collect each type of casting in such a box. The boxes stack easily on shelves, and it's a simple matter to check on your supply of ready-cast bullets this way. If you are serious about your shooting, after culling the badly deformed bullets, you should weigh each bullet unless you just want to plink and accuracy is not important. A variation of a grain or two won't affect the performance of your rifle to any noticeable degree, but weighing the bullets, especially the larger ones, will immediately reveal those that have an air cavity which is due to pouring the metal too slowly.

Wrinkles, rounded rather than sharp edges, and air cavities are casting faults. If either the mold or the

metal has not reached casting temperature, wrinkles and rounded edges occur, even with the most experienced casters. As a matter of fact, some long-time casters prefer to heat their mold by casting bullets which they know will end up in the scrap box, but they also feel that the mold is brought to casting temperature more evenly and that this is the better way to treat a good mold.

If bullets take on a frosty appearance, the casting temperature was too high, and either the mold or the metal was too hot. While too low a temperature produces imperfect bullets, and these should be scrapped since they won't shoot true, the frosty look is merely a cosmetic matter. A steel mold can be cooled off by sticking it quickly into a bucket or can of cold water, and removing the mold from its bath just as quickly. Continue casting, and if the cooling was done quickly enough, the mold will deliver unfrosted bullets or balls, without having lost much of its temperature.

Molds casting small balls or bullets present no problem when it comes to filling the mold cavity. The big molds casting hollow base bullets of the Minie type sometimes seem to present insurmountable difficulties to the beginning caster. As the liquid lead flows into the mold, the air must be able to escape from the mold cavity. Thus, the spout cannot occupy the entire sprue hole in the sprue cutter of the mold, yet the flow of the metal must be rapid enough to fill the cavity before either the

Hollow base plug in mold at left has been rotated so that half-moon retaining washer is locked under screw head; other is unlocked.

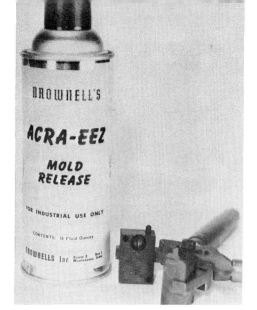

Brownell's Acra-EEZ mold release agent, sprayed on mold after it has cooled, is a good way to prevent rust between casting sessions.

metal or the mold can cool off too much. The Lee and Shiloh molds have hollow base plugs as integral part of the mold, and are therefore a bit easier to cast than the molds using a base pin.

The base pin has a metal disc that must be rotated to lock the pin in place while casting the bullet. Because of the size of the bullet and the size of the base pin handle or knob, such a mold may not fit under every bottom spout pot, and it is best to use a large casting dipper or ladle for such molds. Some casters fill the cavity of the mold with lead, knock away the sprue cutter and sprue, open the mold and gently lower base pin and bullet on the blanket or padded surface. Others prefer to remove the base pin manually by rotating it so that it disengages from the locking screw, then knock aside the sprue cutter and open the mold. While this method has some merit, be sure to replace the base pin and lock it in place before casting the next bullet.

MOLD CARE...

All steel molds are either treated by the manufacturer with some rust inhibitor or are coated with a fine oil. Either must be removed before casting. While it is possible to burn out the rust inhibiting gunk that was used, the resulting smoke and odor may lead to some unkind comments about casting. It is best to "wash" the molds, and this can be done with a cleaning patch, using either acetone or dena-

tured alcohol. Both of these liquids are flammable, so keep all open flame away, and don't smoke while washing your molds.

It has long been tradition to retain the last cast bullet in the mold, complete with sprue. This is supposed to forestall rusting of mold cavity and faces, but it does not prevent the outside of the mold from rusting. Moreover, if you want to look at the inside of the mold, the old bullet has to be removed and this supposedly leaves the mold unprotected. If you decide to spray all mold surfaces with one of the commercial rust inhibitors, you will have to wash the mold or molds before the next casting session, especially since some of the new anti-rusting agents won't burn off readily.

The far easier way of keeping molds rust-free is to spray them with Brownell's (Route 2, Box 1, Montezuma IA 50171) Acra-EEZ mold release agent. This stuff is sprayed on the mold after it has cooled completely, and need not be removed before the next use. Simply bring the mold to casting temperature and you'll be able to cast a perfect bullet. When finished casting, and after the mold has cooled sufficiently, re-spray with Acra-EEZ and you won't need to worry about rust and humidity during the summer months.

It happens even to the most experienced casters – lead splatters and then there is hardened lead on the face of the mold, thus preventing proper closure of the blocks. There may even be casting metal on the bars of the handles where the mold is fastened

49

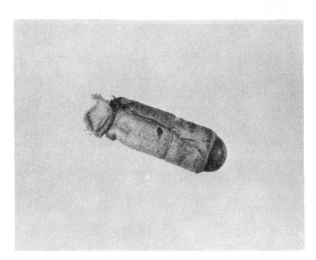

Confederate .69 caliber musket cartridge wrapped in canvas – an intermediate development between pouring the charge down the barrel and seating a ball atop it, and the self-contained metallic cartridge.

to the handle. Never attempt to remove hardened casting metal from the mold with a metal tool. There is only one safe way to get these splatters off the mold – carefully bring the mold to casting temperature and then a bit beyond that point. When the mold is hot enough, that extra lead will simply drop off the mold, handles, hinge pin and all other spots where metal splattered.

Remember at all times that a casting mold is a precision piece of equipment, and treat it accordingly. Never attempt to remove a sticking bullet or ball by pounding on the mold itself with the rawhide mallet, nor try to pry a sticking bullet out of the mold with an awl or similar instrument. Again, bring the mold to casting temperature and if need be, a bit above that, and the bullet will fall out of the mold thanks to gravity.

The Lee molds are made from aluminum blocks, and thanks to their light weight, a great many casters prefer them. They cast excellent bullets, but extra care must be taken with the aluminum mold blocks since they are all too easily damaged.

Now before you dump the first batch of lead into your casting pot, here is one more reminder. When adding metal to the pot, the pot temperature will be reduced. The same thing happens whenever cold metal is introduced, either in the form of the casting dipper or a mold. Lowering the temperature of the casting metal even a few degrees affects the pourability of the metal, and badly cast bullets will be

the result. The pot should always be slightly more than half full, and when the level of the liquid metal drops to the half-way mark, add more ingots or bullets and sprue from the scrap box. When adding lead, lower it gently and carefully into the hot metal in the pot to avoid splattering. Add only one or perhaps two ingots at a time, and when they have melted, stir the metal in the pot to effect a good mix and to bring all the dross to the surface for skimming off.

When buying molds, you will find that some come with integral handles, other have detachable handles. The latter come in a small and a large size, suitable for specific mold sizes. Molds casting Minie bullets and related large projectiles always take the large handles. Interchanging of mold blocks takes only a minute, and if you use the two-mold system while casting, you may want to invest in two small and two large handles.

The detachable molds are easier to store than those where the handle is an integral part of the mold. Blocks can, after being treated with Acra-EEZ, be wrapped into small plastic bags, and a piece of masking tape can be used to fasten mold information to the outside of the bag. A parts cabinet with good-sized plastic drawers will do fine for mold storage. If you acquire molds with integral handles, wrap the mold in a small plastic bag and fasten it in place with a rubber band. The mold data, of course, should go on the bag as above, or can even be written on the bag with a felt marking pen.

Many a novice, after looking over the size of the ball or bullet he wants to cast, makes a mistake in judgement. He buys too small a pot... buy the biggest one you can afford. It does not make any difference whether it is an electric one or one heated by gas. This way you won't have to add metal to the pot as often, and when casting large bullets, it becomes essential to have enough molten metal in the pot to cast a dozen or so bullets before ingots or scrap have to be added again.

Casting your own bullets or balls is neither difficult nor hard to learn. And the nice thing about any mistakes you make is that you can melt them in the pot and nobody will be the wiser.

Chapter 5 ACCESSORIES

Now that powder and projectile have been covered in some detail, we must consider some of the other essentials for shooting the muzzleloaders. The nice thing about black powder shooting is that you can get along with a minimum of equipment, and that much of the needed stuff can be home-made and therefore look more authentic, or can be improvised if you don't have the time and skill to whittle your own equipment.

FLAKES AND MEASURES...

Originally, the small powder horn was used for the priming powder, the large one for the coarse powder that goes into the barrel. Antique powder horns, often with parts missing, fall into the same collector class as an original Colt Dragoon in mint condition — you leave it at home, under glass, and use a substitute. Excellent replicas, complete with handcarved decorations and scenes depicting early frontier life, are now available, but at relatively high costs.

Dixie Gun Works, as well as other suppliers, offers a wide choice of powder horns, with and without measure or spout, and Dixie can even sell you a do-it-yourself kit in addition to components for powder horns.

The metal flasks can be bought in many gun shops and are available from nearly every replica maker or importer. Some are good reproductions of the originals, while others are figments of someone's imagination as far as design is concerned. Powder flasks are usually classified for pistol or rifle, the larger ones being of course for the long guns, since

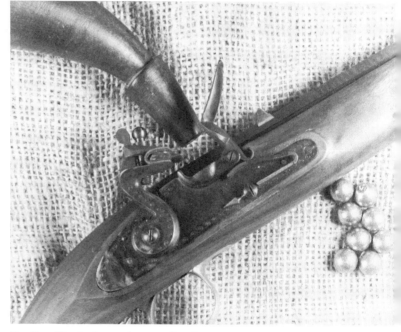

Replica flintlock pistol is usually charged with an antique powder horn that delivers a small charge of 4Fg into the priming pan.

Authentic powder horn is flanked by two replica flasks which are good copies of the originals.

51

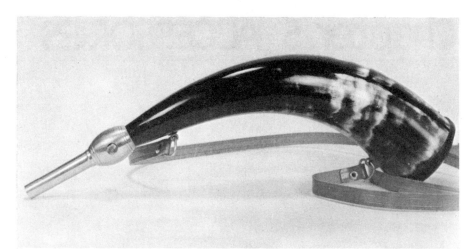

This replica powder horn, sold by Dixie Gun Works, is typical of the horns that can be bought, ready for use. Various size powder charge tubes are available, and choice of modern horns is wide enough for even the most sophisticated black powder shooter.

← *Colt Paterson flask charges the five chambers simultaneously, after flask is seated on chamber mouths. This means that cylinder must be removed for charging, and the question has often been asked: Is this really an efficient way of charging the Paterson cylinder?*

larger powder charges are needed, and the shooter must, by necessity, carry more powder with him. Flasks come with interchangeable spouts or measuring tubes. In the neck, most of them have a spring-operated closure. In use, the flask is inverted and the pad of the thumb is used to close off the opening of the spout. Move the spring-operated lever aside and let the powder run into the spout, release the lever and you are now ready to drop a measured charge into your gun.

A word of caution is in order about the use of powder flasks and horns. On occasion some glowing embers will be left in the chamber of a rifle or shotgun and when dropping a new charge from the powder horn or flask directly into the barrel the smouldering residue will ignite the new charge. This, in turn, will ignite the powder granules left in the charge tube and also the powder in the flask

or horn. Experienced black powder shooters have made it a rule to use either the flask or horn as a means of carrying the powder supply, metering each charge into a smaller measure or scoop. This effectively reduces the amount of powder near such a hot barrel and prevents accidents.

If you don't want to go to the expense of a powder flask or horn, you can get a small plastic powder flask designed to deliver either 20 or 25 grains of powder. The spout can be filed down until the amount of powder held in the spout can thus be controlled. Or you can go to the local hardware shop and buy one or more of the plastic squeeze bottles sold for mustard and ketchup. Although you won't have the advantage of the adjustable spout, such a container will do very well with a home-made powder measure.

To make your own powder measure, weigh out the desired charge of black powder and dump the charge into a cartridge case. Then mark the level of the powder on the outside of the case, dump the powder back into the container, and cut off the case at the mark. A small tube cutter will cut a case cleanly and quickly, and then you need only solder a wire handle onto the case, and your custom measure is ready for use. If you make up several such measures, be sure to mark each as to its capacity You can buy powder scoops from Lee Engineering or Thompson/Center which packages Lee measures

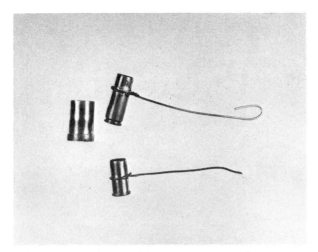

There is no trick to making your own powder scoops or measure, as described in the text.

If you don't like the replica powder flasks, you can use the less expensive plastic powder measure which is every bit as reliable and accurate as the flasks, but has less eye appeal.

suitable for black powder. In using any black powder measure, just fill the measure to the top, but do not tamp the powder level down.

A number of brass powder measures are also available. Some deliver a fixed amount of powder, while others are adjustable and can be used with FFFg or FFg powder. An adjustable measure, complete with funnel that makes dumping the powder down the barrel easy, comes from the Armoury, while other measures are sold by Lyman, Uncle Mike's, Dixie Gun Works and others.

If you enjoy working with wood and want to try your hand at whittling, you can make your own powder measure that also holds a patched ball. Start with a piece of hardwood that measures 2"x2" and drill it out, but don't bottom out with the drill. If you know the final diameter of your patched ball, drill a hole in the bottom that is one or two thousandths smaller and will hold the patched ball securely. Now fashion a wooden plug for the open end, then whittle the whole thing into the round, adding whatever decorations or carving you feel are appropriate. Stain it dark and apply a couple of coats of paste wax, attach a rawhide lanyard, and you are ready.

In practice, the measure is filled, with the patched ball seated in the bottom of the measure. When it is time to reload, remove the whittled plug, pour the powder into the barrel, and then seat the patched

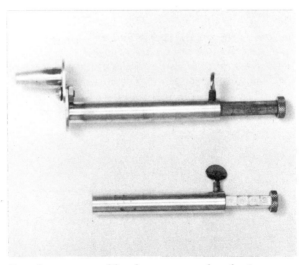

Powder measures like these are very handy since they are adjustable. Upper measure also has a powder funnel that makes it easy to dump charge into barrel. Lower measure lacks this feature, was found to be very reliable. These measures are sold by the Armoury, as well as by others.

Handcrafted powder measure with patched ball in bottom that allows quick reloading of a caplock rifle. Home-made leather capper holds ample amount of caps, and each cap is held securely in leather, yet this design allows quick seating of percussion cap on nipple.

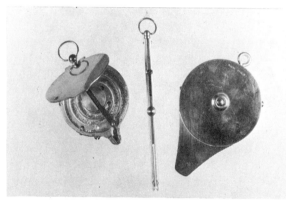

The capper at left is designed for the Paterson revolver, a straightline capper is in the center, and a musket capper is at right. Each capper delivers only one cap at a time and on cold days, a capper is a most welcome addition to the black powder shooter's gear.

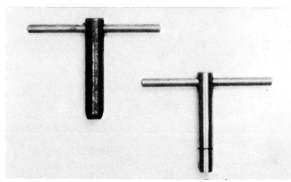

Nipples come in several shapes and sizes, and a suitable nipple wrench for each is a good investment since these tools make removal of nipples very simple without a chance of damaging the nipple.

ball by placing the measure over the muzzle of your rifle. With the help of the ball starter, move the ball down the barrel until you can use the ramrod for the final seating of the ball atop the charge. To facilitate aligning ball with muzzle, you can counter-sink the base of the measure slightly, but be sure to mark the inner and outer circumference of the muzzle carefully so that you will seat the ball in a straight line.

If you don't want to whittle your own, here is one way you can carry a measured charge and an unpatched ball with you. Take two small pill bottles, and using white glue, glue the bases together. In one, you dump the measured powder charge, the other one holds the ball and maybe even the lubed patch.

The pill bottles cost only pennies each, and you can make up as many of these paired bottles as you need, and carry them afield either in a shooting pouch or your jacket pocket.

Measures for priming the pan of a flinter as well as nipple primers, both made from solid brass, can be ordered from Dixie Gun Works. Both are spring-operated, and the nipple primer is said to have found favor with hunters. The measure delivers a small quantity (1/4 oz.) of fine powder directly into the nipple, thus supposedly insuring certain ignition.

The gadget works alright, but few hunters bother with priming the nipple, relying rather on protecting the firing system and lock area from inclement weather.

A hand-carved beaver ball starter and two commercially available ball starters.

CAPPERS AND NIPPLE WRENCHES...

Unless you are overly clumsy, you should not find it difficult to seat a percussion cap on the nipple or nipples of either a rifle or shotgun. Placing the percussion caps on the nipples of a sixgun is a bit more tricky since there is not much space for you to get two fingers and the nipple into the recessed cut in the cylinder. When the weather gets nippy and fingers stiff, putting a cap on a nipple becomes a challenge. Cappers have been in use since the invention of the percussion nipple, and there are three types of commercial cappers, plus any number of home-made ones. The round musket capper operates on the gravity feed system, while the Paterson and the straight-line, also called inline, cappers depend on a spring to move each cap into position. A capper may not be essential at first, but it is recommended for hunters and match shooters. Even if you only plink with your muzzleloader, a capper will come in handy.

The home-made capper is made from two thick pieces of sole leather, and the upper layer has holes punched into the edge to hold each cap securely. A small slot cut into the edge of the leather facilitates seating the caps on the nipple.

A nipple wrench is an inexpensive accessory worth its weight in gold. You'll have to remove the nipple to clean your rifle or shotgun, and nipples get damaged and have to be replaced. Without a nipple wrench, such a job could become a chore. When buying a nipple wrench, it is best to take a spare nipple along to be sure that the wrench fits the base of the nipple. If this is not possible, either be sure of the model and make of your gun, or order the wrench from the place where you got your gun — and when the wrench comes, make sure it fits.

Equally as important as the nipple wrench is a nipple pick, and this item of black powder paraphernalia is best carried with you afield and on the range. When dirt and residue clog the small hole in the nipple, the nipple pick will clear the passage. Stainless steel piano wire is most often used for the job, and a two- or three-inch length of it will suffice. You can buy nipple picks or make them yourself, and if you cannot find piano wire, other wire such as copper will do in a pinch. Since nipple picks are small and therefore easily lost, it is best to have several of them on hand. If your gun has a patch box, that's as good a place as any to carry your picks.

BALL STARTER...

The fit of the bullet or ball in the rifle barrel should be fairly tight, and seating should be done so that the soft lead projectile will not be damaged. In the next chapter, the loading steps will be described in detail, but in case your gun did not come with a ball seater or starter, you can either buy one, or make one. The round ball handle on commercial models is made from hardwood, and since turning such a ball calls

55

Hartford English Dragoon in the Original-Case.

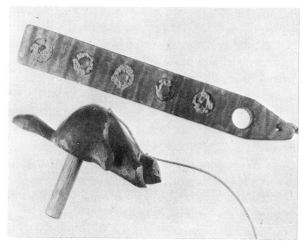

Six patched and lubed balls are held securely in this loading block. Attached to block is a ball starter.

for a lathe, you can go to the nearest automotive store and buy the round knob that goes on the stick shift handle. Take hardwood dowelling of the suitable size for the caliber of your gun, and cut off two lengths – one should project from one side of the knob about 1/4"–1/2", while the longer one, about 4"–5", projects from the other side. Once the patched ball is seated atop the muzzle, the short starter is used to move the projectile down the barrel. This is done with a whack of the hand on the ball, and once the bullet has been moved down the barrel a bit, the other length is used to seat it farther down the barrel. Final seating is done with the ramrod, but attempting to seat the ball from the muzzle with the rod almost always means a broken rod.

Again, many devotees of the muzzleloaders make their own starter, carving it artistically from hardwood. Carving such items as starters, powder measures, loading blocks and other gear is fun and you can improvise, improve or alter as much as you want. All such projects call for the use of hardwood, and since many black powder shooters make their own guns, many of them have scraps of wood left over after they get through stocking their guns, and most of them are happy to share their scrap box with you.

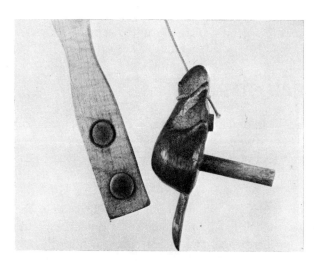

This loading block holds two patched balls, and the ball starter has two short pieces of hardwood dowel – the short one starts the ball, seating it just below the muzzle, the longer pushes the ball down farther, until a ramrod can be used with ease and safety.

LOADING BLOCKS...

For the man who shoots a caplock rifle and uses a patched ball, a home-made loading block will be a tremendous help when it comes to loading his rifle quickly and efficiently. As will be shown in Chapter VII, seating the ball with the patch is critical for good accuracy.

Made from hardwood, a loading block can accomodate two to eight patched balls, is carried on a leather or rawhide lanyard on the belt, often with a ball starter attached to it by yet another piece of rawhide. In making up a loading block, it is better to make it for one row of patched balls, plus about 1/2" of wood on each side of the hole that holds the patched ball tightly. If the board is made up too wide, it becomes unnecessarily difficult to place the ball directly over the muzzle of the rifle and if not properly centered over the bore, a hard push with the ball starter could damage the soft lead missile.

To determine the precise hole needed in the board to hold the ball with the lubed patch tightly, either take a precise measurement of the bore, or take the needed measurement this way: Take a slightly larger-than-normal piece of patching material and lube it. Place the suitable size ball in the center of it, and bring the edges up around the ball, twisting the material tightly over the other end, preferably the sprue side of the ball. Now use a micrometer to determine the diameter of the holes needed in your loading block. Stain and wax the finished block, and

if you shoot a number of muzzleloading rifles in different calibers, by all means make up several blocks. However, make each of them a bit different so that you can tell at a glance what caliber patched ball you are loading. If you are not a do-it-yourselfer, you can buy loading blocks and stain and wax them yourself, or even use them as they come – unfinished.

PATCHING MATERIAL...

That hunk of linen, pillow ticking, denim – and at one time tanned hide – called the patch, serves several important purposes. If an unpatched round ball is inserted into a rifled barrel, the ball would ride on the lands only. This means that it would not take on the rifling, or would not be engraved, hence accuracy and ballistic performance would be sadly lacking. Moreover, since there would be no seal between ball and the rifling of the barrel, gases of the burning powder would escape around the ball and this, too, would contribute to poor ballistics.

The lubed or greased patch takes up the space between barrel wall and the ball, therefore seals the gases behind the ball. The lubed patch also stabilizes the ball during its travel from breech to muzzle, and a stabilized ball has better flight characteristics, hence improved accuracy. Last, but certainly not least, the lube on the patch serves to keep powder

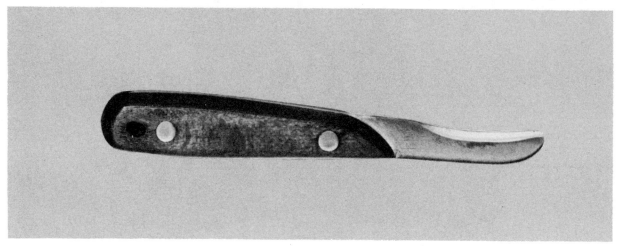

This patch knife, sold by Lyman, does the job of trimming the patch quickly, and keeping it sharp is very easy.

fouling soft, and reduces fouling so that loading is easier, cleaning is not required so often.

Thanks to the lube used, the patching material is softened, hence can be fitted more snugly around the ball. A lubed piece of patching material can also be compressed more than a piece of the unlubed material. As pointed out before, the thickness of the patching material selected is governed by the actual bore measurements.

If you cannot "liberate" suitable cotton or linen material from the rag bag, you may want to buy some at a fabric store. Stay away from synthetics or synthetic and cotton blends, since they have a very low melting point in most instances. New material usually contains a good deal of sizing and this must be removed by several launderings. If the sizing is not washed out, the material will be stiffer, and even a thorough lube application will not soften the patch enough to make it fit the ball and bore as smoothly as it should.

The matter of determining patch material thickness has already been discussed. It was also pointed out that the material selected should be three or four thousandths thicker than your calculations indicate, since the lubed patch can be compressed more. Theoretically, this should give you the correct thickness for your patching, but experience has shown that a little bit of testing, with material a bit thicker or thinner, heavier or lighter, might well give you even better ballistic performance. Before there is a chance of confusion arising, it must be pointed out that the

cleaning patches, used for actual gun cleaning, are not suitable ball patching material.

Whether you use material salvaged from the scrap bag or buy new, acquire more than just a foot or two. If the material you selected works out perfectly for you, and it might well do just that, you will find that the patching material disappears quite fast.

PATCH KNIFE...

As can be seen in the pictures of the loading blocks, the patch containing the ball is cut flush with the level surface of the board. If you seat the ball and patch directly into the muzzle of your rifle, the patch also has to be trimmed. Pioneers and mountainmen carried razor-sharp knives and usually used their belt knife to trim the patch. Modern black powder shooters now use a special patch knife, and one can easily be fashioned from a hacksaw blade. However, getting the right temper into the steel so that the blade will hold an edge may be difficult, so it is best to buy a patch knife. Lyman, Dixie Gun Works and others offer such a tool.

The patch knife is held level and flush with the muzzle while trimming the patch, and the commercial knives have one side that is perfectly level without a cutting edge on that side of the blade. The slight curvature or hook near the usually rounded tip is kept sharp on the upper edge only, and a slicing motion is used to trim away the excess material of

These are only a few of the commercially available lubes. All of the commercial products are good and have been designed especially for black powder shooting.

the patch. Since all black powder shoots are held in replica costumes of the period when the American frontier was being opened, some black powder shooters use copies of the knives carried at that time. But just as many are content to hang a modern knife on their belt.

The modern patch knife therefore does not have a sharp point and the one cutting edge is well protected, hence accidents are unlikely when the shooter carries the knife dangling from his belt. Patch knives are carried without a sheath because the shooter has enough paraphernalia that is tied on or hitched to belt, hunting pouch or whatever, and a sheath would be just one more thing to get in the way. Of course, those shooters using replicas of the original woods and fighting knives of the black powder era carry their blades sheathed.

SPIT AND LUBE...

The spit or saliva patch is still in use today, but its use is pretty much restricted to the range when the shooter knows that he'll touch her off within minutes. The spit patch can also be used while hunting, but is now limited to emergency uses. A properly seated ball rests right atop the powder charge in the chamber of the rifle. A spit patch - and saliva is mostly water- that remains in the gun for a prolonged period is an almost certain invitation for rusting and

later pitting, which may call for professional repair or possibly even replacement of the barrel.

Lubed patches are better by far than the spit patch, and thanks to the use of a loading block, the muzzle-loading rifleman can have several properly prepared balls, complete with trimmed and lubed patch, ready for loading. Lard and bear grease were at one time popular, and although few shooters can agree as to which of the commercial lubes is best, tests have shown that all of them are good, but that some guns do just a shade better with one lube than with another. It is not so much what brand of lube you decide to use, but just how well it is applied and worked into the patch.

Whether you buy pre-cut patches, or cut your own with the help of a patch cutter, or use a pair of scissors to cut the patching material into a suitable shape, the lube is best applied by hand. Dip your index finger into the lube, then rub the patch between that finger and thumb until the lube is well worked into the material. To assure complete penetration of the lube into the fibers of the patch, it is best to let the freshly lubed patch rest for a day or two.

For cap and ball revolvers, another type of lube or grease is recommended. In the next chapter, you will learn how to load a cap and ball revolver, and the reason for the grease will be discussed in some detail, complete with some historical events. Suffice it to say here that the space left in the chamber of such a revolver, after the unpatched ball has been seated on

59

Caps, imported or domestic, come in four basic sizes, although a number of odd-ball sizes are encountered once in a while. Note the size of the musket caps in contrast to the other caps shown here.

the powder charge, must be filled with grease to prevent "chain-firing". Hodgdon's Spit Ball or Beare Grease by Caution are good choices for this. But here again, most confirmed pistoleros have their own pet lube, and these include Crisco, petroleum jelly and numerous other such products. The advantage with the commercial products is that they come packaged so that the tube or bottle has a small spout to permit easy application of the stuff into the chamber. A small cake decorator filled with Crisco or similar lube will do just as well, and in the long run, it does not seem to make too much difference what you use, as long as you don't forget to use a lube.

Benchrest muzzleloading rifles, at least one type, are fired with a conical bullet. This bullet is paper-patched, and for this a tough bond paper, miking .003" –.005", is used. These shooters stamp out their "patches" either in cross form or in strips, placing two strips crossways before seating the bullet.

PERCUSSION CAPS...

Domestic and foreign caps are on the market, and if you ask three black powder shooters which one they prefer, you'll get three different answers. There are two important points to consider: Certain ignition and proper fit of the cap on the nipple.

The musket caps, sometimes also called "top hats", are the largest ones of the lot and will fit only on the

musket nipple. The other nipples come in many sizes, with 10's, 11's and 12's being the most widely used sizes. The lower number designates a small cap, the large number a larger cap. In selecting a percussion cap – and most manufacturers and importers specify the suitable size in their product brochures – be sure that the cap fits snugly on the nipple. It should reach the bottom of the nipple base without splitting, but should not be too long for the cone of the nipple.

Deliveries of foreign caps are sometimes uncertain and you may have switch to a different make cap if there is a shortage of your pet make. Of course, one way to prevent running out of caps is to buy 1,000 caps at one time, and storage of caps is no different than storing primers. Since percussion caps contain a detonating charge, they should be handled with care, but there is no reason why anyone should shy away from shooting black powder guns because the caps contain a small explosive charge.

WORMS AND PULLERS...

A worm is often included with the gun, and many shooters buy not only an extra worm of two, but also ramrods, topping them off with a worm at one end and a bullet seater at the other end. Worms are most frequently used to hold a cleaning patch during the cleaning or wiping of a barrel. Worms can also be

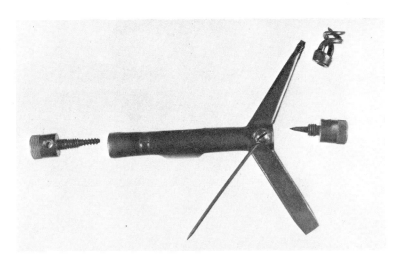

This combination tool, supplied with the Enfield sold by Jana International, is typical of the better combination tools available to the black powder shooter.

used to pull a ball from the barrel, but a ball puller is by far the better choice for this job.

And why should you or anyone else want to pull a ball from a rifle? It happens to the most experienced black powder shooter – you swab out the barrel, forget to dump a powder charge down into the chamber, then carefully seat a ball on nothing. If you decide to add a spare rod to your shooting kit, get a long, well-tapered self-threading sheet metal screw and weld or braze it to the bullet or ball seater. This allows you to lower the rod with some force into the ball, and the self-threading screw will easily enter into the lead ball. Since the fit between ball and bore should not be too tight anyway, you will be able to pull the stuck

ball out without difficulty.

Should the ball come only partway up the barrel and then become disengaged from the screw or ball puller, here is the easy way of getting the ball out. Unscrew the nipple and pour some fine powder into the chamber. Replace the nipple, and with the ramrod, bring the ball all the way back down to the bottom of the chamber. Place a cap on the nipple, point the gun down range, and fire. Chances are that the ball will come out, but remember to seat the ball all the way down. If the ball remains somewhere up in the barrel, this shooting-out will almost certainly ring the barrel and can even burst it.

SHOT POUCHES, BULLET BAGS...

An over-the-shoulder bag, usually made from tanned and decorated leather, is handy. You can make one, or buy any number of designs. Some bags are just a pouch with a large lid, others have a divider to keep things nice and tidy. Here, spare flints, caps, nipple pick, ball starter (if not carried on a lanyard around the neck) powder measure and powder flask, patches and the rest of the paraphernalia, ride. Each shooter must decide just how much gear he wants to

carry, and of course the hunter may even want to take along a spare nipple and nipple wrench.

Although only a few of the new replica muzzleloaders come with special combination tools, it is interesting to note that such suppliers as Dixie Gun Works offer a good selection of these tools. A combination tool may consist of a screwdriver, nipple pick, worm, and nipple wrench, and shooters who are skilled in metal working often design and then make their own to meet their own particular needs. Some of these tools have been modified from standard designs, while others remind you, only in shape, of the combination tools of a bygone era.

61

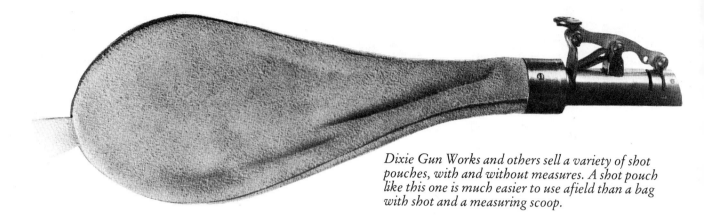

Dixie Gun Works and others sell a variety of shot pouches, with and without measures. A shot pouch like this one is much easier to use afield than a bag with shot and a measuring scoop.

FROM HEAD TO TOE...

Many of the dedicated black powder shooters, especially those participating in the various National Muzzle Loading Rifle Association events, dress in period costumes, each item of clothing carefully researched for authenticity and then copied with great care. Much depends on the type of rifle or handgun you shoot, and a wealth of information regarding dress is available. A number of dealers make and sell clothing directly to the consumer, others will furnish you with do-it-yourself kits for anything from shirts and pants to moccasins and pouches.

For the black powder shooter who enjoys shotgunning with a percussion smoothbore, carrying shot afield is made simple – use a shot pouch. Most of the ones available today are made from leather and come with some sort of charger. The charger either delivers a fixed amount of lead shot or is adjustable. A shot pouch with charger makes loading afield a lot easier with a muzzleloading smoothbore.

Of course, you can also use either a small canvas or leather bag and measure out your shot with a measure – or make your own measure as outlined for powder measures.

Bullet bags are small leather bags that are used to carry bullets or balls afield. These bags are usually carried in the hunting pouch or bag that is slung over the shoulder and that contains sundry shooting gear. Bullet pouches or even flasks, although according to some were used on the frontier, seem to be more gadgets than useful items. Basically, they are supposed to deliver one ball or bullet at a time thanks to a constriction in the delivery tube, the whole thing operating on the gravity feed system.

BAGS AND POUCHES...

Dixie Gun Works carries a large supply of authentic as well as replica clothing and gear, and with the help of this catalog, you can select the correct outfit for any and all black powder events.

A word of caution may be in order. Before you decide that all of this is out of your financial reach, and that you don't want to get dressed up to shoot a black powder gun – go ahead and wear whatever you feel like wearing. The idea is to enjoy the shooting. Dress and incidental gear can come later, and most of us have built up our wardrobe over a period of some years.

Chapter 6 LOAD AND LOCK!

Despite the fact that gunpowder is a relatively easy propellant to get along with – it is often called a "forgiving" one – a few general precautions must be taken at all times. Of course, some of these rules apply to all types of guns, no matter what the ignition system, action type, or whether the gun is loaded with shot, bullet or ball, metallic ammo or a home-made load. In addition to general gun handling safety rules, a few special conditions may exist which make it essential to be extra careful.

GUN SAFETY...

The basic mechanics of the different ignition systems have been discussed, and the mechanics vary but little from one system to the next. The flintlock's sparking must be certain and positive, or the priming charge won't ignite. This makes a large spark essential, and if you shoot your flinter on a public range where there is another shooter to your right, make certain that he does not stand next to the lock when you pull the trigger. Onlookers forever want to see how it works, want to watch as the spark ignites the priming charge. Do not discourage onlookers, but let them do their looking from a distance that is safe for them.

If your percussion rifle, shotgun or handgun is loaded but not yet capped and the range master calls for a halt in all firing, place your gun on the shooting bench with the muzzle pointing down range – the only safe direction. If the cease firing order comes after the gun has been capped, you will find that most range masters prefer that you carefully lower the hammer on a capped nipple. Thus, the hammer

cannot be dropped accidentally on the cap, nor can the hammer be readily dislodged from its half-cock position should a shooter slam a heavy object on the bench.

Any kind of black powder shooting calls for a number of accessories, one of them being a powder flask or horn. Never leave a container of black powder on your bench where it can be exposed to the heat and rays of the sun, or where a spark could make contact with the container. Should the loading cycle be interrupted for some reason, place your gun on the shooting bench, muzzle facing down range. Of course, you don't smoke when handling powder, be it black or smokeless, and if you do spill powder, clean up the spillage.

Before handling another man's black powder gun, not only ask for permission to do so, but also ascertain if the gun is loaded or capped. Remember, capped or uncapped, loaded or unloaded, the muzzle must always point down range, even while you hold the gun in your hand to inspect it. It is more important to consider the safety of others on the range than to be able to eyeball some fine detail on furniture, nipple or engraving.

Black powder burns quite rapidly and, as with smokeless powder, the burning rate and the amount of gases generated depends on the amount of powder, the granulation, and the space in which it is confined. Every so often it happens that small particles of black powder remain in the barrel or breech area, and these remnants, instead of burning with the rest of the charge, simply continue to glow like embers. The shooter who charges his gun with a powder horn or flask is thus exposed to the possibility that the charge being dumped catches fire from

63

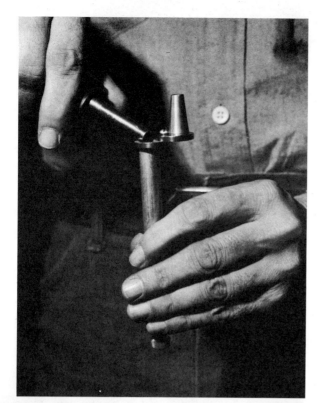

Powder charge is measured by pouring powder from flask into measure. This measure, by Uncle Mike of Oregon, has an integral powder funnel.

these embers. Savvy shooters, therefore, never use a full flask or horn, and many of them use a container or measure that holds only one charge. Cap and ball revolvers do not appear to be prone to retaining embers, are therefore charged with a suitable flask.

Ramming home a charge, bullet, or wad, or even wiping out the barrel to clear it of accumulated fouling, calls for the use of a ramrod. Instead of holding the ramrod like a broomhandle, manipulate the rod between thumb and index finger. Should there be an accidental ignition in the barrel, and should the rod suddenly become a projectile, handling the rod with only two fingers will prevent injury to the shooter's hand.

For the same reason that a ramrod or cleaning rod is held but lightly between two fingers when used, the muzzle of any black powder gun, loaded or unloaded, is always directed away from the face. When using the rod or the ball starter, tilt the gun away from your body. This safety precaution is practiced when the gun rests on the butt and your hands are busy at the muzzle.

When running a patch up and down the barrel of a caplock rifle or shotgun, be sure that the hammer is placed on the half-cock notch during the wiping. If the hammer nose fits securely over the nipple, as it should and does in most of the replicas, the hammer resting on the nipple creates a very effective vacuum in the barrel. Then, when the wiping rod is pulled from the muzzle, the patch is often sucked right back into the barrel thanks to the vacuum created by the hammer resting on the nipple.

Whenever you seat a round ball, it must be seated so that the point where the sprue cutter removed the sprue is uppermost and dead-centered in the muzzle.

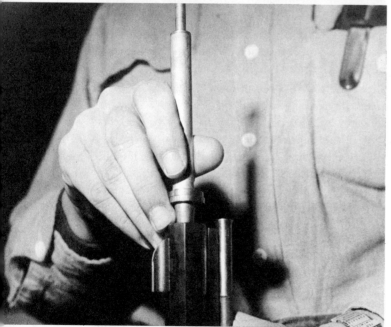

When charge has been measured, funnel is swung over the opening of the measure, the measure is inverted over the muzzle, and the powder charge is now in the chamber of the gun.

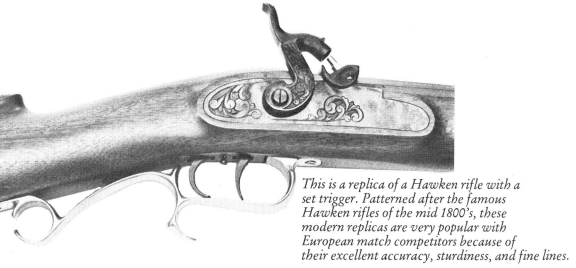

This is a replica of a Hawken rifle with a set trigger. Patterned after the famous Hawken rifles of the mid 1800's, these modern replicas are very popular with European match competitors because of their excellent accuracy, sturdiness, and fine lines.

↑Note how the gun leans away from the shooter while he uses the ramrod to seat a ball.

←←This is the way to hold the ramrod safely, and the thumb can be placed across the top of the rod to force the ball down the barrel.

←How not to hold the rod is shown in this posed photograph.

65

Properly seated flint in jaws with small leather patch assures good sparking.

These flints have been shaped commercially, are ready to be installed in flintlock guns.

If maximum accuracy is what you are after, you may even want to trim the sprue somewhat so that it is flush with the rest of the ball's surface. If the ball surface presented to the pushing gases is not always the same, the shooting results will vary, and loading the ball so that the sprue will rub against the rifling will also lead to poor accuracy.

LOADING THE FLINTLOCK...

The priming charge of the flintlock, be it pistol, rifle or shotgun, depends for its proper ignition on the performance of the flint. In motion, the flint scrapes small steel particles from either the battery or the frizzen, and these steel particles are glowing thanks to the friction created between flint and steel.

The flint must be of high quality and shaped properly. Flintknapping is a gradually dying art, and the edge of the flint must be flat on its upper surface and bevelled underneath at both ends so that there is an obtuse angle at one end and a perfect chisel edge on the other.

A new flint, properly shaped, will be good for 15 to 20 perfect ignitions. Once a flint wears somewhat, and the number of sparks is reduced to three or maybe four, ignition failure is almost certain. The new flint must be inserted into the jaws with the little piece of leather protective covering so that the flat side of the flint faces up. Positioning the flint in the jaws is not difficult, and is best done in the following manner.

Prepare the leather patch and insert the flint, flat side up. Tighten the screw just enough so that the flint won't fall out of the jaws, then bring the gun – unloaded, of course – to full cock. Close the pan

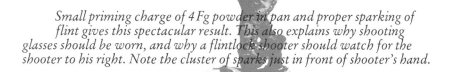

Small priming charge of 4 Fg powder in pan and proper sparking of flint gives this spectacular result. This also explains why shooting glasses should be worn, and why a flintlock shooter should watch for the shooter to his right. Note the cluster of sparks just in front of shooter's hand.

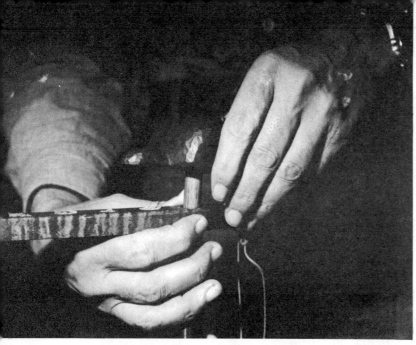

Loading block with already lubed and trimmed patch is placed over the muzzle of the gun, and the ball is started with this hand-carved ball starter.

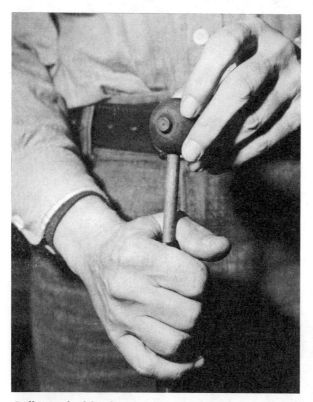

Ball is pushed farther down the barrel, about 4–5 inches, so that ramrod can be used with ease to push the ball down on top of the charge.

If no loading block is used, the patched ball is started, then the patch is trimmed flush with the muzzle. Special patch knife, such as sold by Lyman, is handy but not essential. Seat ball sprue up, trim patch close.

Plugging vent hole with sparrow feather prevents blowout of charge as ball is being seated.

cover, and slowly lower the hammer, holding it back with the thumb, until the entire length of the striking edge of the flint rests flat against the battery face, about three-quarters of the way up. Bring the gun to half-cock and tighten the cap screw without moving the flint. Bring the hammer to full cock and pull the trigger. The pan cover should open instantly, and there should be a shower of sparks in the pan. If there are not enough sparks or the cover does not fly open, the flint has to be retracted or perhaps moved forward, and you have to test the performance of the flint until it is perfect.

If you are using a loading block, you simply center the patched ball in the muzzle, and start it down the barrel with the ball starter after placing the correct amount and granulation of powder into the chamber of your gun. Never attempt to seat any ball or bullet right away with the ramrod. It is much easier, and also safer, to start the ball with the ball starter, at first seating the ball about 1/2" below the face of the muzzle. Then use the somewhat longer starter to push the ball down 4–5 inches. Now the ramrod is used to seat the ball atop the powder charge with a smooth stroke of the rod. Experienced black powder shooters make a mark on the ramrod that indicates the height of the powder charge, and yet another mark that indicates the combined height of the charge and the properly seated ball.

If no loading block is used, the lubed patch is placed over the muzzle and the ball, sprue up, is seated just deep enough so that the patch can be gathered and trimmed with the patch knife. From then on, ball seating is identical to the system outlined above when a loading block is used. Ball seating is also performed this way when you load a caplock rifle or single-shot pistol.

The gunpowder granulation in the main charge depends on the caliber of the gun, and most often it is either 3Fg (FFFg) or 2Fg (FFg), while the priming powder is 4Fg (FFFFg) when available, and 3Fg (FFFg) if the finer granulation is not available.

To prevent powder from blowing out the vent hole while seating a tight-fitting ball in the barrel of a flinter, two different schools of thought and practice have developed. Colonel Peter Hawker in 1830 in his "Advice to Young Sportsmen", described both the Joseph Manton and the D. Egg hammer improvements which permitted air passage through the priming hole without loss of powder. He also gave the time-honored advice of placing the rifle on half-cock with the frizzen closed, and seating a ball that way after the piece had been primed. Since half-cock notches, especially on old locks, are not always reliable and accidental dropping of the hammer with subsequent discharge could occur, many of today's flintlock shooters have decided to forego authenticity for safety.

Small feathers, gathered either from sparrows, parakeets or canaries, can be used to plug the touch hole. Only the quill of the feather is used, and in most cases, the tailfeathers have been found the best since their quills are large enough, and these feathers are easy to come by. This method of plugging prevents the powder from being blown out the touch hole as a tight fitting ball is forced down the bore.

Donald King, writing in the "Buckskin Report," states that this system was used by some of the old-time flintlock shooters who had reservations about a closed frizzen. So here then are two approved and historical ways of going about seating the ball in a flinter, with the plugging method being the safer and therefore preferred method.

If your flintlock has never been fired before, run a couple of dry patches down the barrel to be sure that any residual grease is removed. Also be sure that the vent hole is clear of obstructions, and that the frizzen and pan are grease-free. Any shipping grease left in these lock areas will impair or even prevent proper firing of the priming powder charge.

For priming the gun the first time, place the hammer on full cock, and raise the frizzen, if you wish, to allow easier filling of the pan with a small charge of 4Fg or 3Fg powder. Now snap the frizzen over the pan, and your gun is ready to fire. It is usually a good idea to fire at least one or two priming charges with a new flintlock. Of course, in actual shooting, the main charge with ball or bullet is seated first, and the priming charge is applied when you are ready to fire.

While authentic paraphernalia, dress and guns are part and parcel of the black powder game, the use of shooting glasses at all times is recommended, and especially when shooting a flintlock. Although the glasses may mar the authenticity of your appearance, their use in shooting black powder guns is even more important than in any other type of shooting.

In contrast to the percussion lock, the flintlock is clumsy and prone to malfunctions, and loading a flinter is a bit trickier since the priming charge also requires care and forethought. In bad weather, the priming charge can get wet, or a breeze can blow part of it away; too large a priming charge does not necessarily insure certain ignition, and produces only spectacular fireworks. The lock time of flintlocks is notoriously slow, and this means that it is much more difficult to hit a moving target with a flintlock than with a caplock gun. Trapshooting with a flintlock shotgun requires not only the skill of being able to swing with a target, but there is also that long lock time that makes using a flintlock such a challenge.

The chain of mechanical events that takes place when a flintlock is fired is long, and seems much longer if you are waiting for the main charge to ignite while the sights of your gun dance and waver. But there is a romance, as well as a challenge, in shooting a flintlock that has kept this ignition system a favorite with dedicated black powder shooters.

LOADING THE CAPLOCK...

As discussed in Chapter I, the percussion lock has certain advantages. However, men like Colonel Peter Hawker and Ezekiel Baker, a master gunsmith of London, found that the flint gun performed better on game and that recoil was less than with a percussion gun. Both were quick to endorse the percussion system for its certainty in igniting the charge in the barrel, and also acknowledged that the percussion system is easier to care for, even under the most adverse conditions afield. As Hawker wrote in

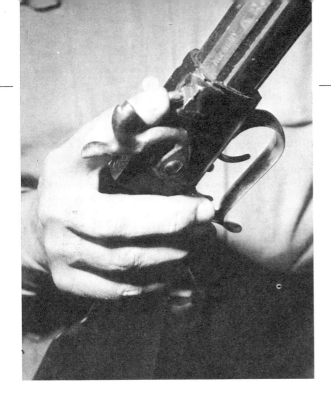

1830: "It seems a paradox that a percussion-gun should fire *quicker*, and yet *not stronger* than a flint-gun; but most assuredly, this is the case."

Seating a patched ball is handled in the same manner as just outlined for the flintlock. Again, if your gun is a new one, wipe the barrel and degrease the nipple. A nipple pick should be used to make certain that the nipple passage is clear. In Chapter V, the various sizes of caps were discussed, and the fact that the cap should fit tightly over the nipple, but without splitting.

Before loading your gun for the first time, fire a cap or two, not only to ascertain that the passage is clear, but also to burn out whatever residue might be left in the nipple passage. When snapping those caps, be sure to point the muzzle of the gun down range, and see to it that no powder containers, flasks or cans are in the way where either the flash from the muzzle or the caps could reach the powder. One trick used by experienced black powder shooters is to fire the caps with the muzzle near a few blades of grass or a leaf or two. When the grass or leaves move after you have touched her off, the nipple and barrel are clear, and after wiping the bore once more, you are ready to commence loading.

The following table, reproduced here with permission of Turner Kirkland from the pages of the Dixie Gun Works, Inc. catalog, shows the relative sizes of percussion caps currently available.

Make	Inside Diameter	Length of Cap
No. 10 Alcan	.167	.178
No. 11 Alcan (Italy)	.168	.153
No. 1075 German	.170	.170
No. F4-12 Eley	.170	—
No. 1055 German	.170	.220
No. 11 Remington	.170	.190
No. 11 Dixie (Italian)	.172	.206
No. F4-21 Eley	.175	—
No. 11 Winchester	.175	.200
No. 12 Alcan	.178	.195
No. 12 Remington	.178	.190

Turner Kirkland was one of the first to prove, via chronographed loads, that the ultimate load performance depends on the potency of the detonating mix in a percussion cap, and shooters often refer to one cap being hotter than that of another make. Hotter caps give better and more complete ignition, and this is reflected in more uniform velocities and ballistic performance.

The larger calibers can be fired with a conical bullet that may either have a solid base or a hollow base, and this is not patched, although here and there a thin paper patch is used by some shotters for special guns. The conical bullet is lubed to give a better gas seal, to keep fouling soft, hence to allow repeated loading and shooting without having to clean the barrel.

The Minie bullet is seated, skirt down in the muzzle, and then pushed down on the charge by means of the ramrod. Remember what has been said about not charging directly from the powder flask.

71

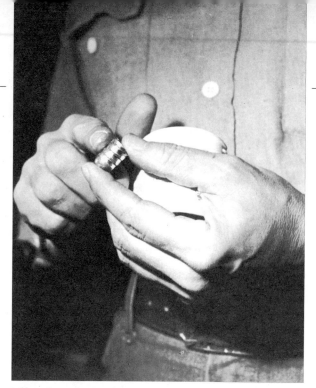

Though perhaps a bit messy, applying lube to Minie bullet is still best done by hand.

In seating the bullet, it is essential to learn to seat the bullet properly since undue force at this point prematurely disfigures the bullet. A smooth stroke of the rod also assures you that the air below the bullet and above the powder is forced out of this space, and that the bullet base is seated directly in contact with the powder charge.

It is best to retain the fired cap on the nipple and to keep the hammer in the down position during the loading of the rifle or musket. Once the loading steps have been completed, be sure to remove the ramrod from the barrel, put the hammer on half-cock, flick off the spent cap and replace it with a fresh one. During the actual seating of the ball or bullet, and while dropping the charge down the barrel, remember, too, to keep your face and hands away from the muzzle and tilt the muzzle away from you, as described earlier.

In applying a lubricant to a Minie bullet, it makes little difference how the lube is applied to the bullet, or what brand of bullet lube is used. Though a bit messy, applying the lube with the fingers is probably the best way to get an even layer of lube into the grooves of the bullet. Most shooters begin with one of the commercial lubes, then experiment with a variety of them until they find one that is to their complete liking – one that gives the best results in their gun, with their load. While an even layer of lube on the outside of the bullet is important, do not neglect to put a dab into the hollow base of each bullet. Once in a while the recommendation is made to apply a dab of lube to every other bullet and into every other bullet base. This is probably the fastest route to poor accuracy that could be devised – try it yourself and you will soon find that there are no shortcuts to accuracy. Just as you maintain a uniformity in your charges and in the way you load your gun, so the lubing your bullets must also be done uniformly.

MORE RIFLE LOADING TIPS...

When seating a patched ball, if you cannot start the ball down the barrel with one smart blow of your hand on the ball starter, your patching material is probably too thick. Once the patched ball has been pushed down with the longer ball starter, seating the ball on the charge with the ramrod must be done with a smooth pushing motion rather than with repeated pounding of the ramrod. Remember that the ball is made from soft lead, and each time you pound on it, a deformation of the projectile occurs. Deformed projectiles are not worth wasting powder on, and since variation in the seating force results in varying degrees of messing up the ball, you won't be able to squeeze the accuracy from your rifle that the gun is capable of delivering.

When seating lubed bullets, be especially careful with starting the bullet down the barrel. The skirts of many bullet designs are quite fragile, and when deformed, accuracy will be lacking.

Some powder measures come with a small funnel. If your measure has such a funnel, use it. Should your measure lack this feature, a small plastic funnel, obtainable from any hardware store or camera shop handling darkroom supplies, can be used. If the powder charge is dumped into the barrel so that some powder granules adhere to the inside of the barrel near the muzzle, neither a patched ball nor a lubed bullet can be started evenly down the bore. The axis of the bullet or ball must be parallel to the axis of the bore for best performance, and even one or two grains of gunpowder adhering to a land will permit tipping the projectile in the bore while seating it.

It has happened – and will continue to happen – to all black powder shooters, no matter how experienced – the rifle is loaded, you've aligned the sights and then pull the trigger – oops, the ramrod disappears down range in a very satisfactory cloud of blue smoke. Many rods, after a light wiping to remove powder fouling, can be put back into use; others are shattered beyond hope of repair. Sometimes the brass furniture on a wrecked rod can be salvaged, and then a new ramrod of suitable length and caliber must be bought. Dixie Gun Works and some other suppliers stock a variety of rods, from good copies of original hickory rods to plastic and nylon replacements.

Since shooting out a rod or breaking one can occur any time, many savvy black powder shooters keep a spare rod or two at home or in their car. Fishing rod carrying tubes, either of fixed length or the telescoping kind, provide good storage for spare rods, and one of these tubes can hold several ramrods without danger of breaking them – a more satisfactory arrangement than having them bounce around in the back of the car.

BALL WITHOUT POWDER...

On a par with shooting out a ramrod is the almost inevitable precision seating of a patched ball or lubed bullet into a barrel without a powder charge.

Basically, there are two ways to remove such a ball, and while both of them work, shooting the ball out, though a bit more tedious, is the preferred method. In trying to pull a stuck ball or bullet, a worm is used. This corkscrew-like gadget must be sunk into the soft lead of the projectile in a straight line to assure that the ball won't work loose from the worm a few inches below the muzzle.

In recent years, special stuck ball removers have become popular, and basically, these consist of a long, self-threading sheet metal screw. The B-Square device, called a Black Powder Termite, is available for .45 and .50 caliber and is threaded for an 8–32 female ferrule on a rod. Other worms are available, with most of them following the traditional style, from such suppliers as Dixie Gun Works, Navy Arms and others.

The trick to starting one of these screws into a stuck projectile is to create a small hole in the top of the projectile so that the screw tip will get an adequate bite into the lead to begin the threading. If the rod with this self-threading tip bounces several times off the top of the ball and the threaded portion of the screw makes forceful contact with the lands, it is a fairly easy matter to ruin the lands.

73

Barrel of Thompson/Center Hawken rifle has been removed from action and stock, is locked into the padded jaws of bench vise. The special T/C breech plug wrench is slipped over the breech plug, and pipe wrench is used to turn out breech plug. This job may be essential if a stuck ball cannot be removed any other way, or if a complete take-down for major cleaning is called for.

In shooting the ball out, work some fine grain powder into the flash channel. This requires the removal of the nipple on a caplock gun, and here the nipple wrench in the shooting kit can save the day. Once the small charge has been worked into the chamber, the nipple is replaced and capped, and the gun is fired down range. If that doesn't work, add more powder to the chamber through the flash channel, seat the ball atop the small charge, cap and shoot. In most cases, this will do the trick.

Should the stuck ball or bullet fail to budge, you have to strip the gun, remove the breech plug with a breech plug wrench, and then try to drive the ball out with a rod. When re-assembling your rifle, be sure that the breech plug is seated properly.

HANGFIRE...

Assuming that you have loaded your gun properly, capped the nipple on a caplock or primed the pan on a flinter, and nothing happens when you pull the trigger, remember that the gun can still go off any second. Therefore, keep the muzzle pointed down range at all times. Let the gun sit for at least one minute, preferably two to be sure. Should the gun still not fire, remove the percussion cap from the nipple and get busy with your nipple pick. Recap with a fresh cap and try again. In a flintlock, be sure that the flint sparks well, and that the vent passage is open. Again, check with a nipple pick to make sure the passage is clear. You may want to add a bit of priming powder to the pan, and then try again.

Chances are that the gun will now fire. If it does not, again wait a few minutes and repeat the checking of passageways and vents. Sometimes removing the nipple and adding a small amount of fine powder, then reseating the nipple and trying it once more with a fresh cap will do the trick. If all else fails, you have to strip the gun, remove the breech plug and drive out the load. Failure of such loads is usually due to moisture or oil in the chamber, the charge being inactivated thanks to whatever residual material was left in the barrel.

LOADING THE SHOTGUN...

Percussion shotguns, both single and double barrel ones, can still be found, and restoring one of these old-timers to a useful life is worthwhile. First, have the gun checked by a competent gunsmith. In all likelihood, the nipples will have to be replaced and you may find, on measuring the inside diameter of

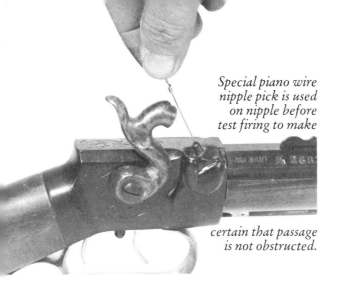

Special piano wire nipple pick is used on nipple before test firing to make certain that passage is not obstructed.

↑
To testfire any old black powder gun, lash the gun to a tire, point muzzle in safe direction, then fire the gun with a long cord tied to the trigger, from a safe distance.

the barrel or barrels, that the gun is some odd-ball gauge. Don't let this deter you, since it only means that you may have to cut your own wads.

Of course, there are a number of very well-made replicas on the market, and after removing the grease and snapping a couple of caps to be sure the vents are clear, you can start loading your black powder scattergun.

Any old shotgun refurbished with new nipples, that has also undergone some minor work and repairs, should be test fired – but not from the shoulder. Place an old tire on the ground and then, after loading and capping the gun, lash it down into the tire so that the heel of the butt rides on the inside of the tire, as shown. Tie a 20-foot length of cord to the trigger, then place the hammer at full cock, step back and pull the long cord to test fire the gun. Repeat the procedure with the other barrel. It is a good idea to fire each barrel at least twice – three times is better – to make sure that the gun will hold up under the load.

You can cut your own cardboard wads with cut-off piece of 12 ga. barrel that has been sharpened. One tap with rawhide mallet cuts a wad with ease, especially when cardboard is backed with a piece of scrap hardwood.

All of the wads used in making up a shot load must fit the barrel tightly, and thus the use of 10 gauge wads in a 12 gauge set of barrels is correct. Once you have determined the gauge, you'll have to look around for suitable wads. Some of the modern wads can be used, but if you cannot find suitable ones, you may have to buy special wads. Dixie Gun Works is a major source for all kinds of wads, and some of them you can cut yourself, either with a store-bought'n cutter or home-made one. For instance, a piece of 12 gauge barrel, sharpened properly, has been used for years to cut wads for an old 12 gauge black powder double.

A milk carton can easily be converted into cup-like wads.

75

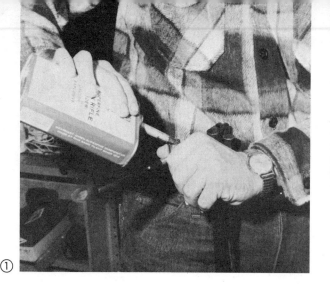

①

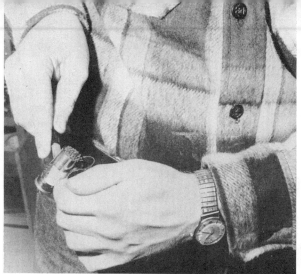

②

In developing loads, remember that you can make them for nearly every purpose, but also remember that these old guns, as well as the replicas, were not designed to be converted to magnums. As a general guideline, you can use the "dram equivalent" found on modern shotshell loads, and use the dram equivalent in black powder – but remember, BLACK POWDER ONLY!

To wring the best performance from your black powder shotgun, you will have to try different loads, wads, charges and powders, as well as shot of different sizes. Patterns for trap shooting should be fired at about 40 yards; for hunting, patterning is best done at a range between 20 and 40 yards, or the distances most frequently encountered under your hunting conditions.

GENERAL RECOMMENDATIONS FOR SHOTGUN LOADS...

In most of the guns patterned, the Gearhart & Owen powders outperformed all other makes, and were only topped when some of the original DuPont powders were used.

Open bored guns, that is cylinder bored guns, usually do better with the larger shot sizes, while choked guns usually perform better with the smaller shot sizes. The 2Fg granulation is the most suitable one for most gauges from 9 ga. on down, while Fg is more suitable for the large gauge guns. Extensive testing has shown that the volume of shot and the volume of powder are usually about the same, and this means that you can use the same dipper for powder and shot while afield.

If the resulting patterns are of the doughnut type or are patchy, try decreasing the powder charge. If that does not help, increase the powder charge a bit. The filler wads must supply the needed cushioning, hence must be selected for their softness. Felt carpet padding is nearly ideal, but other similar materials are also suitable.

Do not attempt to develop your own proofload for an old gun, a double charge of shot and powder may only weaken it. A heavy load reveals inherent weaknesses in the gun, such as a defective soldering joint between barrels or a defective hammer, but it might only wreck a gun that, with sensible loading and care, could have been used for a number of years to come.

Shooting regulation trap and skeet with a black powder shotgun is a real challenge when you use a percussion gun, and calls for a great deal of skill if you use a flintlock. For trap and skeet, when there is not enough time to wipe out the barrel between shots, fouling can be reduced to the irreducible minimum by using damp, or almost wet fiber or fiber filler wads. Soaked in Black Solve or Moose Milk, the wet wads will help to keep the bore relatively clean for hundreds of rounds. However, for hunting, wads should be greased or waxed to prevent rusting.

The plastic wads now used in reloading shotshells do not appear to be very suitable for black powder guns, although some shooters apparently use them without ill effect. Since this has been going on for some time, it would seem that some shooters have better luck with them than others. Some plastic wads appear to have been run through a shredding machine, others form miserable globs of plastic which call for endless cleaning of the barrel.

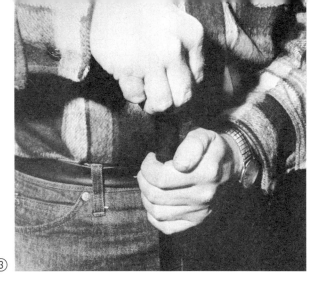

③   ④

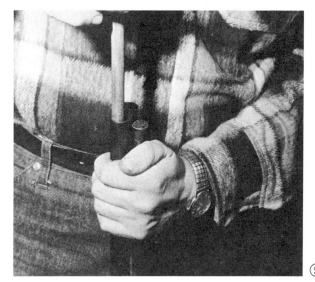

A typical 12 gauge hunting load is assembled in this fashion:

First, snap a cap on each nipple to assure yourself that the nipple passage is clear. Experienced scatter-gunners next fire a half-charge of powder, held in place by a simple card wad, to make sure the gun is ready for loading and firing.

For this 12 gauge replica gun, the charge is 3 1/2 dram equivalent of 2Fg.

Seat a card wad or cup wad, cup down, on the powder charge. Cup wads are most frequently made from milk cartons, can be purchased commercially.

A nitro card wad, either .200" or .125", comes next. As mentioned before, the fit of the wad must be tight, and seating is accomplished by means of the ramrod. Push the wads down with a smooth stroke rather than hammering them down with uneven strokes of the rod.

The wet fiber wad comes next. In the winter, wads are soaked in windshield washing fluid, and moisture is squeezed out of each wad before seating. In summer, a solution of Ivory liquid in water is used for making wet fiber wads. As mentioned before, greased or waxed wads would be substituted in instances where the load might remain in the barrel for a time before firing. Next come two 14 gauge cardboard nitro wads – the thickness of the wads must be determined by trial and error since no two guns behave alike with the same load.

⑤

① *Powder charge for a 12 gauge muzzleloading shotgun is measured with powder measure.*
② *If powder measure is turned smartly on its side, the powder charge will go down the barrel without spillage.*
③ *Card wad is seated in muzzle. Wads must be slightly oversize to give proper closure, but should not be tipped in barrel.*
④ *After card wad has been seated with ramrod, the wet wad is seated in muzzle. Wet wads are not recommended for hunting use since they can induce rusting, but should be used for trap shooting since they effectively reduce fouling and the need for periodic cleaning between shots.*
⑤ *Wet wad is pushed down the barrel with ramrod until it is seated on card wad.*

77

Measure out 1 3/8 oz. of 7 1/2 shot.

Insert a thin over-shot wad, followed by a cardboard wad.

Cap the nipples, and good luck on that next covey!

When it comes time to reload one barrel of a double barreled shotgun, heed this caution: REMOVE THE LIVE CAP FROM THE NIPPLE OF THE UNFIRED BARREL, and lower the hammer until it rests on the nipple. Recap when you are ready to resume hunting.

The wad column for a trap load would include: A cup wad, cup down on the powder, two nitro card wads (.070" and .135", but can even mike .200"), a dry or damp fiber wad, a wet fiber wad, milk carton wad, and the shot charge held in place by an over-shot wad.

Patterning is the only way you can determine how your loads perform, but patterning will not tell you how hard your shot load hits. Turner Kirkland has found that if the individual shot pellets are capable of punching through one side of a tin can, the load has enough oomph to kill small game.

If the shot pattern must be tightened, try decreasing the powder charge; change the shot size to one smaller or larger; increase the shot charge 1/8 ounce. Fair results can also be obtained by using either granulated polyethylene or cornmeal in the shot charge – of course, polyethylene is often used by shotshell reloaders with excellent results.

If you want to open the pattern somewhat, increase the powder charge 1/2 dram; or decrease the shot charge by 1/8 ounce; or divide the shot charge into three equal parts, separating each shot segment from the next one with a thin over-shot B wad, thus in effect, making a spreader load.

In loading any black powder shotgun, remember that the load you place into a barrel undergoes the same stresses as a load contained in a shotshell. Therefore, you keep the powder gases out of the shot charge, you cushion the shot from the effect of the powder burning, you keep the shot as round as possible during its travel the length of the barrel, and you try to keep fouling to a minimum.

The large bore guns, that is 4 and 8 bore, are usually British, and some of them were used for big game hunting. The 10, 12, 16 and 20 gauge are the favorite hunting gauges, with the 12 ga. being by far the most popular. Many old European shotguns from the percussion era have found their way into the hands of American shooters, and the following diagram gives you a quick comparison between our gauge designations and the metric equivalents.

Although it can hardly be classed as muzzleloading, there has been revived interest in shooting black powder shotshells in the past few years. A great many hammer guns with centerfire firing pins have been begging for a home for many years, and collector interest in those guns has been almost nonexistent. Now that 12 gauge black powder shotshells

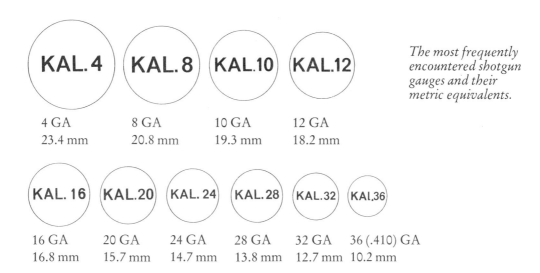

KAL. 4	KAL. 8	KAL. 10	KAL. 12
4 GA	8 GA	10 GA	12 GA
23.4 mm	20.8 mm	19.3 mm	18.2 mm

KAL. 16	KAL. 20	KAL. 24	KAL. 28	KAL. 32	KAL. 36
16 GA	20 GA	24 GA	28 GA	32 GA	36 (.410) GA
16.8 mm	15.7 mm	14.7 mm	13.8 mm	12.7 mm	10.2 mm

The most frequently encountered shotgun gauges and their metric equivalents.

are imported from Germany by Navy Arms, there is a vastly increased interest in these guns.

Shooting these black powder shotshells is mechanically indentical to shooting any modern shotshell, but of course, guns must be cleaned thoroughly thanks to the black powder. Shooting these black powder shells is becoming quite popular, and swing and follow-through on the target are identical to shooting a smokeless powder load. However, the cloud of smoke issuing from the muzzle places this kind of shotgunning in a class by itself.

Spent hulls can be reloaded without the use of a shotshell loader. Decap the spent primer with a home-made punch, seat a fresh primer with the help of a wood block, select a powder and shot charge from the following table, and proceed as follows.

Measure the powder, place in the recapped case, then insert the wads and tamp them down tightly.

Call for the clay pigeon, get a sight picture, and there goes that load of shot, dusting the pigeon in a most satisfactory manner.

79

Old Belgian hammer shotgun was first tested on tire setup for safety, can be fired with these Geman black powder shotshells imported by Navy Arms.

About 1/2-inch of over-powder wadding will do the trick. Measure out the shot charge, pour it on top of the wad, seal the shot column with the over-shot wad. Remember that the thin wad goes over the shot charge, the thick one goes over the powder charge. These hulls can be closed manually, but any of the shotshell loaders set up for 12 gauge shells can be used to effect a good closure on the case mouth.

SUGGESTED BLACK POWDER LOADS FOR MUZZLELOADING SHOTGUNS

Gauge	Powder/Grains	Shot/Ounces	Use
4	218-273	3	Medium
10	136.75	13/4	Heavy
10	123.0	11/2	Medium
10	109.0	11/2	Light
12	112.75	13/8	Heavy
12	102.5	11/4	Medium
12	88.75	11/8	Light
16	85.4	11/8	Heavy
16	82.0	1	Medium
16	68.35	1	Light
20	75.2	1	Heavy
20	65.0	1	Medium
20	54.7	3/4	Light
28	54.7	5/8	Medium
32	47.8	1/2	Medium
.410	41.0	1/2	Medium

LOADING THE HANDGUNS

As with the long guns, the ignition systems most often used are the flint and the percussion lock. The single-shot handguns are loaded, primed and fired in very much the same fashion as their longer counterparts, and here you find that the most accurate handgun load is usually one that uses the lightest possible charge without giving the projectile a rainbow-like trajectory.

The first of the replica handguns – as matter of fact, the replicas started with the handguns – was a cap and ball revolver, a Colt. The open frame Colt was occasionally considered to be somewhat weaker than the solid frame guns based on the Remington

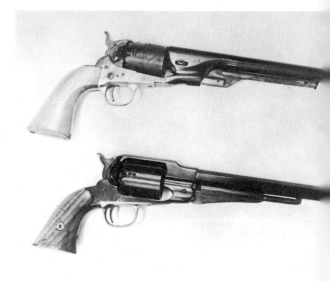

Colt sixgun replica, like all muzzleloading Colts, does not have a top strap in contrast to replica Remington gun shown below.

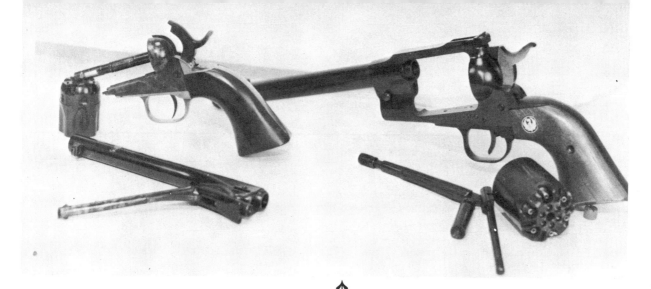

↑

Take-down of both Colt and Remington-type sixguns is simple. In Colt gun at left, not shown is barrel wedge and wedge retaining screw. Ruger version of Remington caplock, at right, can be taken down for cleaning without the use of tools.

design, but it seems that this was more a matter of personal likes and dislikes than of facts based on shooting experience. The Colt design sixgun is perhaps somewhat easier to maintain and clean once the barrel wedge retaining screw has been backed out and the wedge removed.

The oft-repeated tale that hard-pressed horseback riders armed with Colts were able to exchange a fired cylinder for a loaded and capped one, while fleeing across the prairie from a large horde of Indians, seems to have been just that – a tall tale. First of all, some designs have a wedge retaining screw that must be turned out before the wedge can be pounded out, requiring a screwdriver and a drift punch, or at least a small wedge tool. To manipulate all this gear with one hand, while the other hand clutched the gun – all astride a fast moving horse – seems quite unlikely.

Regardless of the design of your sixgun replica, the loading and firing steps are the same. After you have ascertained the correct size ball to use in your gun, completely degrease the gun, running patches into the chambers of the cylinder until the patches come out as clean as they went into the chamber. Be sure that the nipples are not only clear and degreased, but that they are also properly turned in – check this with a suitable nipple wrench. Residual grease and blocked nipple vents are the chief causes for misfires, so be sure you start with a clean gun and keep it that way!

Next snap a cap or two on each of the nipples, this further ensures that nipple channels are clear and dry. When you snap those caps, hold the muzzle of the gun near some dust or scraps of patching material – when the debris moves as the cap goes

off, there are no obstructions in the chamber just tested.

As a safety precaution, experienced cap and ball sixgunners load only five chambers, leaving the sixth one empty so that the hammer can be lowered on the nipple of that chamber.

Flick off the fired caps, put the hammer on the safety notch, and with the help of a suitable powder flask, carefully pour the correct amount of powder into each of the five chambers. This is best done by holding the gun upright in your left hand and manipulating the powder flask or measure with your right. Next seat a ball, sprue up, atop the powder, and with the loading lever apply uniform pressure to each ball. The cast ball should be slightly oversized for the chamber so that when it is forced down in the chamber, a slight ring of shaved lead appears around the mouth of each chamber.

Some shooters feel that a tight ball is adequate to prevent chain firing, while others prefer to fill the remaining space in the chamber above the ball with a suitable lubricant. Chain firing is the unintentional firing of more than one chamber when a shot is being fired, and though not dangerous providing you wear shooting glasses, it is disconcerting. Even Col. Colt complained about it.

The lubricant not only seals the chamber mouth and thus forestalls chain firing, but it also softens

81

Each chamber that will be fired is charged with powder from flask that delivers a precisely metered charge of black powder. A special flask or calibrated spout is used for each caliber to deliver accurate charge of powder to chamber.

Ball is seated sprue up in chamber, and levered down on top of powder charge by means of rammer. A slight shaving of the ball should occur, and constant pressure on the handle of the rammer should be used.

fouling. Thus, it is the recommended method of closing off the chamber. Lube can either be applied directly from the bottles or tubes in which they are sold – such as Hodgon's and Lyman's special lubes, or you can get a small cake decorator tube, fill it with Crisco, and use this to top off each loaded chamber.

If somewhat over-size balls, or lube ahead of the ball in the chamber do not appeal to you, you can fall back on the lubed felt wads. You can either cut these wads yourself from old felt hats with a com-

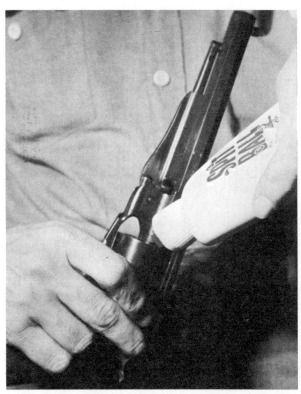

To prevent chain firing, the space left in the chamber after the ball has been seated on the charge is filled with lubricant.

↑Straight line capper is used to fasten caps on nipples of sixgun that has been loaded. Many shooters prefer to use a capper since it makes handling of small caps easier.

←Lee powder scoop is used to measure out quantity of cornmeal that is used to fill chamber of sixgun. Although this is an extra step in loading a cap and ball revolver, the improved accuracy makes it worth the trouble.

mercially available cutter, and then lube them, or you can buy the wads already lubed. If you cut your own, use felt about 1/8" thick and make each wad about 1/16" larger than the largest chamber. These wads are seated flush on the powder charge with the help of the rammer, but care should be taken to avoid tipping a wad in the chamber, since this might prevent proper ball seating.

Now point the muzzle of the loaded gun down range, cap the nipples of the loaded chambers, aim and fire.

Internal chamber dimensions vary from chamber to chamber in nearly all revolvers, not only cap and ball but in centerfire as well as rimfire guns. Target shooters – and a great many serious target shooters participate in cap and ball events annually – have found that any revolver usually has at least one chamber that delivers somewhat superior accuracy. Often, when rules permit it, they will load and fire this one chamber throughout the course of fire, thus squeezing a bit more of a score from their guns.

The most accurate black powder load is seldom, if ever, the hottest or the maximum load. As a matter of fact, a series of tests, conducted by several match shooters and the ballistics staff at Lyman, has shown that the most accurate sixgun load is usually about one-half the standard load of a chamber. Rather than force the ball on top of this half-load, the space between charge and ball is filled with an inert filler, such as cornmeal. Cream of wheat can also be used, but requires rather precise measuring since it cannot be compressed, while cornmeal can be compressed without too much trouble and therefore need not be measured out. The ball, on seating in the chamber, should shave a slight halo of lead, and some sort of lube is used to seal the chambers, at least by the majority of the cap and ball paper punchers.

Capping can be done manually or with the aid of capper – much depends on personal preference and on your adroitness in handling the caps, especially on bitterly cold days. Mention has been made that the caps must fit properly. Not only should the cap fit

These three cylinders, from a Colt, Lyman and Ruger respectively, show the difference in nipple recesses and safety notches between nipples.

tightly, but pinching the skirt of it a bit will help prevent recoil from decapping it.

Some of the cap and ball revolvers come with special notches cut in the rear of the cylinder so that the hammer need not ride on a nipple. This is a nice feature, but the same end result can be achieved by lowering the hammer on an uncapped nipple.

HANGFIRE

Should the charge in a chamber fail to fire even though the cap did go off when it was hit by the hammer, wait a minute or two and keep the muzzle of the gun pointed down range. Next, rotate the cylinder until you can remove the fired cap from the nipple of the hangfire chamber. Using a nipple pick or any similar tool (a pipe cleaner is nearly ideal and of correct diameter) see if you cannot clear the obstruction in the passage. Seat a new cap and try that recalcitrant chamber again. Should the charge again refuse to fire, you may have to turn the nipple out and add some fine grained powder as primer.

BEFORE YOU WORK WITH A LOADED GUN, POINT THE MUZZLE DOWN RANGE AND REMOVE ALL LIVE CAPS FROM THE NIPPLES. If the cylinder must be removed for easier handling, never leave a live cap on a nipple, but then be sure to recap the nipples before shooting. Wear shooting glasses at all times.

Cap and ball revolver projectiles are not patched, but a patch is used in most of the single-shot handguns where a round ball is used.

To assure that nipples are clear, an opened paper clip or a pipe cleaner can be used if you don't have a suitable pick.

Most of the importers/manufacturers specify suggested ball size, and often even give load recommendations. In recent months, some unusual replicas have made their appearance. Among these is a copy of a Duckfoot pistol and of an Ethan Allen Pepperbox, and the guns are advertised under the name of Classic Arms International, Ltd. It is not known if the company furnishes loading data, but the guns appear to be well made.

SUGGESTED REVOLVER LOAD DATA

With the help of the following data, you should be on your way to developing the best possible loads for your cap and ball revolver. Remember to start low and work up, and that the best load is seldom the one that burns the most powder and develops the greatest amount of recoil.

.31 caliber	Ball weight/diameter	50 gr./.319"
	Charge	3Fg/10.0–13.0 gr.
	Cap size	No. 12
	Velocity	600–700 fps
.36 caliber	Ball weight/diameter	81 gr./.375"
	Charge	3Fg/20.0–27.0 gr.
	Cap size	No. 11
	Velocity	980–1080 fps
.44 caliber	Ball weight/diameter	138 gr./.451"
	Charge	3Fg/30.0–36.0 gr.
	Cap size	No. 11
	Velocity	900–1000 fps
.44 caliber	Ball weight/diameter	155 gr./.450"
	Charge	3Fg/22.0–26.0 gr.
	Cap size	No. 11
	Velocity	700–730 fps
.45 caliber	Ball weight/diameter	185 gr./.457"
	Charge	3Fg/31.0–40.0 gr.
	Cap size	No. 10
	Velocity	840–920 fps

Chapter 7
CARE OF BLACK POWDER GUNS

Between relays, this shooter runs a damp patch down the bore to reduce fouling build-up and to facilitate bullet seating.

Taking care of your black powder gun is really quite simple. Too often, would-be newcomers to muzzleloading are scared away from the sport when they hear that it takes hours and hours to take care of the gun to prevent corrosion and rust. To be sure, you do have to clean your gun thoroughly, since black powder fouling tends to corrode metal, and black powder guns are somewhat more prone to rusting than centerfire guns.

Rusting is an oxidation process and is caused by humidity or moisture getting to areas where the black powder fouling has not been removed fully or completely. Thus, get rid of the powder residue, and you won't have any rust problems, unless you live in an area of high humidity. As you can see already, this all boils down to cleaning your muzzleloader immediately after shooting it. Cleaning should be done as soon as possible; most black powder shooters carry a cleaning kit with them at all times. This way, they can tend to their smokepoles and get the first cleaning done while still on the range or in the hunting camp.

GUN CLEANING...

Literally, reams have been written about the subject, and much of this is highly repetitive, with one writer following the example of another. The traditional method goes something like this:

Remove the barrel and prepare lots of hot water, preferably with soap or one of the household detergents. Place the barrel, chamber down and muzzle up, into a bucket of this hot soapy water, then run some tightly fitting patches in and out of the barrel. This pumping motion, so we are told, loosens the fouling and leaves the barrel clean, wet, and hot, thanks to the hot water. The heat in the metal helps to dry out any residual moisture and this, at least according to the "authorities", leaves you with a clean barrel.

At the very most, one bucket of hot soapy water is needed per gun, and nobody has ever explained what is to be done with the rest of the hot water that was collected for this major undertaking of cleaning a gun or two. Maybe it's like in the movies where the imminent arrival of a baby calls for vast amounts of hot water – nobody ever tells you what the water is for.

There are several problems with this bucket-of-hot-water treatment. First of all, where on any range do you find the hot water, even if you bring your

These are the most popular black powder cleaning agents. By using them, you can avoid the messy but traditional hot water treatment of the barrel.

own bucket and soap? Could it be that those recommending the system are trying to tell us something?

Getting fouling and powder residue out of the barrel and other structures connected with the firing system is important, and any method that loosens the fouling will do the job. Ed Trump, riflesmith at the Green River Rifle Works, writing in the March 1975 issue of The Buckskin Report offers this system for caplock rifles with patent breech.

When you get through shooting or when fouling builds up to such an extent that seating a patched ball or bullet becomes too difficult, wipe the bore out with a patch moistened with water. Several such treatments may be required to allow you to continue shooting. Be careful not to get the patch too wet, just get it moist. If the patch is so wet that it leaves moisture in the nipple or the breech, you are inviting misfires and hangfires.

Keep at the moist patch treatment until the patches come out almost clean. Oil another patch very lightly and run it down the bore. This is adequate protection for short-term storage and with this thin oil coating you can continue to load and shoot. If the gun is to be stored for a spell, take the barrel out of the stock. Hooked breech actions, according to Trump, won't be hurt or damaged by this, and he points out that the hook breech was designed for easy take-down.

Often you will read the advice that the nipple and the cleanout screw should be removed before you begin your gun cleaning. If you think about this for a minute, you will see that it is bad advice. Let's say that you shoot your gun once a week, hence clean your gun weekly. That means that you would unscrew the nipple and cleanout screw at least 50 times a year, and this is bound to play hob with the

threads. And loose threads in either the nipple or the cleanout screw mean that, sooner or later, you are converting a safe gun into a dangerous one. As Trump points out in his article, leave the nipple and cleanout screw alone unless it becomes absolutely essential to remove them.

With the barrel dismounted, pour cold water into the muzzle until it comes out the nipple. Now push a patch down the bore and loosen some more of the fouling, then repeat the water treatment. Again, use a tight fitting patch, until the water from the barrel under the pressure of the patch comes squirting out the nipple as clean as when it was poured into the barrel. At this stage of cleaning a muzzleloader, the one single advantage of the hot water treatment becomes apparent: the heat of the water is transferred to the steel of the barrel and hence drying is helped somewhat. However, it must be pointed out that water must be very close to the boiling point to heat a heavy barrel sufficiently for it to retain that heat. In using cold water to clean the barrel as just described, do not attempt to heat the barrel in any way to speed drying, but simply stand the barrel, muzzle down, on some newspaper or paper towels in the corner of a warm room. In the summer when the sun supplies plenty of heat, stand the barrel somewhere out in the sun, but be sure to find a corner where it cannot be knocked over accidentally.

Oiling the innards of the barrel comes next. Time was when a liberal dose of a good quality oil was applied to barrel passage and thus to the inside of the nipple, and this effectively prevented rust. It also meant that the oil had to be removed completely before the next shooting session and getting out all the oil – which on long sitting sometimes congealed and

87

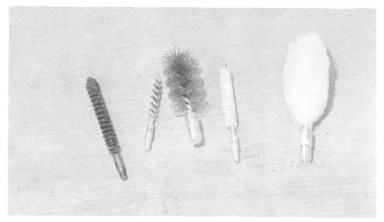

At far left, old-style wire brush that has been used only a dozen times. Compare this with the two brushes in center which have been used for several months. Both mops have seen use for an equal time. The new Hoppe brushes and mops are described in the text, and these shown have been washed repeatedly.

hardened – was as bad as trying to remove long-standing rust, corrosion and fouling. Any residual oil or remains of the chemical agent used to get the oil out of barrel and chamber leads to misfires, hangfires and more cleaning.

A very lightly oiled patch run in and out of the bore two or three times is much better. Use a similar patch on the outside of the barrel, and be sure to remove all fouling from the bolster and outside of the nipple, then apply a very light coating of oil to this area too.

If the gun is to be stored for some time, repeat the oily patch treatment every week or two. If you don't get carried away and use too much oil, the gun can be loaded and fired without wiping out the bore before loading. For prolonged storage, a somewhat heavier coat of oil is recommended, both inside and outside, and this, of course, must be removed before the gun is loaded the next time.

Whether you decide to follow the hot or the cold water treatment, here are a few tips to simplify cleaning. When pouring water down the barrel, you are almost certain to spill some. A bucket or fairly large deep pan in which the chamber rests will catch the spills and whatever surplus water runs down the outside of the barrel. A plastic measuring cup with spout is handy and certainly holds enough water to fill any bore.

A plastic funnel – a glass one is too easily broken – with a rubber or plastic hose attached is also handy. Of course, the hose or tube must be under bore size, and to be sure that the water flushes all accumulated fouling out of the chamber, the tube should be long enough to reach at least 2/3 of the way down the barrel .

While most ramrods can be equipped with a patch-holding jag, the new plastic-coated one piece rifle cleaning rods are better since the plastic protects the bore. The only problem with long barrels is that long cleaning rods of this type have not yet been marketed. Hoppe, a division of Penguin Industries, recently introduced new bore brushes and mops which should be a real boon to the muzzleloader if they become available in black powder sizes as scheduled. The traditional wire brushes mat down and wear after a time and become practically unseless. These are being replaced with a tough plastic which does not mat down or break, and the brushes can be washed in warm soapy water, looking and feeling like brand new after their bath.

The new bore mops are also plastic. These mops were made of cotton waste at one time, and they too matted down badly. Moreover, once one of these mops got really dirty with powder fouling and solvent, ist was questionable whether the mop was really doing the job or whether it was simply introducing more dirt into the bore. These new Penguin plastic mops feel like cotton and do as good a job as the cotton ones, with the added advantage that they, too, can be washed in hot soapy water and are like new once they have been rinsed and dried. Repeated washings do not harm the new mops, and lightly oiled, one of these mops will do a fine job of coating the bore of a muzzle-loader with a thin film of oil to prevent rust.

FOULING AND MODERN CHEMISTRY...

Realizing that the traditional hot soapy water bath for barrels is not to everyone's liking, custom gun-

After bore has been wiped out with solvent, it is dried with clean patches until a patch coming out of the bore is as clean as it was when it was pushed down the bore. Patch shown has been in and out of the barrel twice.

smiths specializing in black powder guns began to experiment with chemical cleaning agents. Some of these products worked very well, but others proved to be no better than the hot water treatment since they contained chemicals which attacked not only the fouling but the metal of the barrel as well. The better products survived for a while and then faded from the scene because the inventors and purveyors of the stuff were not set up for mass mail order sales.

With the increased interest in black powder shooting, a number of the larger chemical houses catering to shooters and gunsmiths began to experiment with black powder solvents. Hoppe's, long recognized as the leader in gun care and cleaning products, twisted some molecules around in their Hoppe's No. 9 and the result is Hoppe's 9 Plus. Birchwood-Casey developed a compound sold under the name No. 77, and other manufacturers followed suit.

While the traditionalists among the black powder fraternity may frown on cleaning a muzzleloader with chemicals only, the fact is that these new chemi-

cal agents do the job quickly and easily, without having to mess around with water and then trying to dry the bore in one way or another.

This does not mean that you can postpone your gun cleaning session indefinitely. The compounds mentioned, as well as others on the market, are good, but rust and corrosion will still make their unwelcome appearance if the fouling is not removed soon after shooting. To be sure, getting rid of fouling and rust is made somewhat easier when using a chemical treatment, but the chemical agent that will prevent fouling and subsequent rusting after the gun has been fired has not yet been invented. As a matter of fact, there is little chance that such a preventive chemical will make its appearance.

The chemical compounds used to soften and remove black powder fouling are best used in the following manner. Moisten a cleaning patch thoroughly with the preparation of your choice. Be sure that the patch size is such that it will fit the bore of your gun tightly enough so that moving the cleaning rod up and down, even in a clean barrel, requires some effort. If you use a slotted jag, be sure that the slot is big enough to accept the patch, and if you use the pointed jag type with the patch wrapped around it, make sure that you cannot lose the patch halfway down the barrel.

To save some money as well as to avoid frustration, do not buy your patches in the small blister packs. There are not enough of them in such a pack to clean a couple of guns thoroughly and the packs are much more expensive that way than when you buy them in large quantities from such suppliers as Brownell's.

89

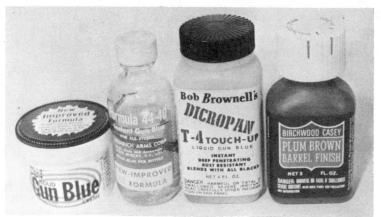

These four products will do a nice job of touching up bluing and can also be used to blue or brown, as the case may be, a whole gun. In any bluing, be sure to follow instructions.

First run a patch well-soaked with the solvent down the bore and back up again. Discard the patch and use a fresh one, this too fairly wet with the black powder solvent of your choice. Repeat this procedure until patches come out of the gun without too much fouling on them. Then run a couple of dry patches up and down the bore and see if there is much fouling left. If there is, repeat the treatment with solvent-moistened patches until the patches come out of the bore almost clean, then repeat the dry patches several times.

Once the dry patches come out of the barrel clean, lightly oil a patch and run it up and down the bore several times. Be sure that the cleaning rod does not rub against the muzzle, thus damaging the lands or grooves, and make certain that the rod with patch bottoms out at the breech. A patch moistened with solvent is then used on frizzen and pan, or the bolster and nipple. Wipe with a dry patch until you don't pick up any more powder fouling on the patch. Use a nipple pick to make sure that the passage is clear, use a lightly oiled patch on the lock system and the rest of the barrel, and that's it.

The same method of cleaning is used on handguns if they cannot be readily taken down. The Colt and Remington-type replicas are best taken down, and of course, the barrel, cylinder and frame are treated with the solvent-soaked patches first, and these are followed with dry ones until they come out clean. Smoothbored guns can be cleaned with patches or with a bore mop, preferably one of the new synthetic ones that are washable.

GUN STORAGE...

A light oiling of the inside and outside of the barrel will be adequate for short term storage. If it will be several months before the gun will be used again, use a bit more oil on the patches, especially in the bore, but don't just pour oil down the bore. If it gums – and all oils do this eventually, at least to some degree – you will have your work cut out for yourself trying to get the gunk out of the chamber and bore. Avoid getting oil on the stock or furniture. If you cannot find a stock wax, a light application of a fine furniture wax on stock and brass will do the trick.

If guns are not kept in a gun cabinet that can be closed, dust is almost certain to settle on the guns. If they are stored upright in a gun rack, protect the bores from dust. Small paper cups, placed upside down over the muzzle of long guns, will do the job, and have the advantage that they also cover the front sights. Plastic barrel plugs are very suitable for protecting shotguns from dust accumulation, but sometimes they are hard to find.

When storing guns, do not leave the hammer in the cocked position, but lower it carefully. Avoid keeping springs under tension, particularly those on older guns since they may break due to metal stress and fatigue. Never store a gun with caps on the nipples, and never leave a charge in a gun. Before putting the gun away, pull out the ramrod and run a lightly oiled patch over the wood and the brass fitting at the end of the rod, then replace the ramrod on the gun.

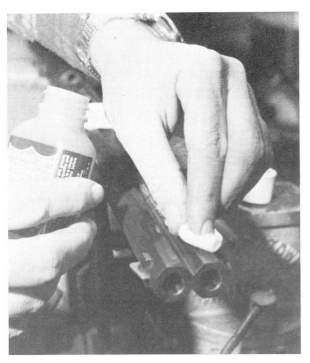

Rusted barrel was treated first with steel wool and oil, is now being cleaned and degreased with Birchwood-Casey Cleaner and Degreaser prior to bluing.

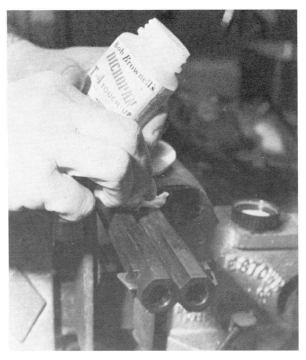

Brownell's Dicropan does the touch-up bluing quickly and without fuss. Wipe on, wipe off and then use a light coat of oil, and that's all there is to that job.

If during storage, the brass parts of the gun have lost some of their eye appeal, you can restore that pristine beauty easily. Most jewellers and stores where silverware is sold have polishing cloths impregnated with jeweller's rouge. Polishing brass with such a cloth will restore brass to its shining beauty. No matter how dull lackluster the brass appears, never use any of the copper and brass cleaners designed for use on kitchen utensils and other household items. Most of them contain fairly strong chemicals which can wreck the finish on a gun faster than anything else. Moreover, most of these brass and cooper cleaners require thorough rinsing with water, certain to be injurious to stock finish and to other parts of the gun.

Powder horns should be emptied before storage, and rubbing the horn with a few drops of fine oil will enhance the appearance and prolong its usefulness. Metal flasks should also be emptied. Although most of these flasks are lacquered at the factory to give them the desired luster, a light coat of wax once in a while will work wonders. All areas where wax is applied should be polished with a soft cloth, pre-ferably flannel. Most fabrics are too harsh and will leave scratches, and while wool is usually soft enough, the wool fibers tend to catch on any surface not perfectly smooth and flat. Round head brass nails protruding from furniture, inlays and the like are almost certain to catch wool fibers, and these are most troublesome.

MINOR REPAIRS...

Surface rust can appear on any gun, whether standing in an open rack or tucked away in a drawer, and you need not live in an excessivly humid climate to encounter light surface rusting on guns. While much of this rust can be removed simply by rubbing the spot with your fingers, there is a better way of getting it all off, even the last stubborn vestiges of it. Take some very fine steel wool, make a little pad of it and moisten it well with a fine grade oil, the same oil you use in your gun cleaning will be suitable. Rub the rusted area vigorously with the oily steel wool – go ahead and rub, and don't worry about wrecking the bluing or browning job. This method will remove the rust and rust marks but won't touch the bluing unless done to excess.

Should rust be deeper than skin-deep, you can resort to Birchwood-Casey's Blue and Rust Remover. This preparation has the advantage that it protects all bare metals for two to four weeks, so if you don't get around to retouching the bluing immediately, you need not worry. Rust removers found in hardware stores are usually too harsh to be used on blued areas of guns, and some of them require washing to neutralize their chemical action.

If the bluing has to be restored, be sure to degrease the area that needs rebluing and here again Birchwood-Casey sells a cleaner and degreaser that will do the job very well. Let the degreased area dry completely, then use one af the many touch-up bluing preparations on the market. Be sure to read the directions on the label of the touch-up bluing. Some of them require rinsing in water to stop the action of the compound, others are simply wiped off with a clean dry patch.

When the touch-up bluing has dried, look at the area under a good light. You may want to repeat the bluing so that the entire area looks evenly blued, and when the last coat of bluing has dried, a drop or two of fine oil applied to the reblued area and rubbed slightly will often produce amazing results.

Very much like touching up bluing or browning damages, the minor stock repairs you are likely to encounter should not throw you for a loss. Dents in wood can be raised, and such repairs sometimes don't even require refinishing the stock.

It is best if the barrel is removed and perhaps also the lock, although it is not essential. Apply a piece of cotton bedsheet that has been soaked in water and wrung out, fold it so that there are at least two to four layers covering the dent in the stock. With either a steam iron or a regular dry iron, apply heat to the dented area, putting the iron right on the wet cotton material. Shallow dents usually come right up with one or two applications of heat. Be sure that the cloth covering the dent is wet – you are, in essence, steaming the wood, hence must have moisture to raise the grain. On larger jobs you may have to repeat this treatment several times. The end result may show some fuzziness since the wood grain was raised considerably.

With very fine sandpaper dress down the area, then refinish with the same stain, if possible. If that is not possible, you may have to sand the stock down to the bare wood, then refinish the entire stock.

If a small piece of wood should break out in the inletted area around the tang or alongside the barrel, it can be glued back into place, sanded and the finish touched up. White glue has long been favored for this sort of repair, and if some of it oozes out, it can be sanded off smoothly without trouble. Small glue jobs must be clamped just like larger jobs, but with some minor repairs, it is often not possible to apply adequate clamp pressure. A wide and fairly large rubberband can be used in lieu of a clamp and the slack can be taken up either with clothespins, clamps or even friction tape – anything that will keep tension on the rubberband.

Kentucky stocks, because of their length, are especially prone to cracks in the forearms, and the slender wrists on some stocks also suffer from the same weakness. Before you begin to hunt for a new

Poorly inletted patch box is being re-inletted so that all parts of the brass box are on the same level of the stock.

stock or try to run a stove bolt through the cracked parts, try to repair the crack with epoxy glue. Take the barrel and lock out of the stock and remove any brass or other trim that might interfere with working on the damaged part. Gently twist the crack to see which way the split runs in the wood. Lock the larger part of the stock into the well padded jaws of your bench vise and make up the epoxy glue. Take a toothpick or two and shave each end down so that it can be inserted into the split. With the glue properly mixed and ready to be applied, twist the free end of the stock so that the crack opens up, and apply the epoxy with a shaved toothpick. Flow as much of the epoxy glue into the crack as you can, then release the twisting pressure and apply clamps. Be sure, however, to pad the pressure points where the clamps make contact with the wood. If clamping is not possible, use either a wide rubberband or a padded canvas strap – anything that will hold the pieces together under good tension. If the crack repair is in the forearm, be sure to support that end of the stock so there is no pull on the repaired area. It is best to permit such epoxy jobs to set for at least 48 hours before you remove the clamps and check the repair. If some epoxy oozed out of the crack, you'll have to sand the area and refinish. Since the advent of epoxy glues, more stocks have been saved this way than by any other means.

If you enjoy shooting muzzleloaders and don't feel any compunction about not sticking to historically accurate guns, you may want to add a better rear sight. You may simply want to replace the one now riding on the barrel of your gun with one that gives you a better sight picture. If you are lucky, the new sight can simply be drifted into the old dovetail slot. If the new base is bigger than the existing slot, you simply have to open up the slot with a file and then use your touch-up blue.

If the base of the new sight is smaller, you have two options – either shim the base into place in the old slot, silver solder and dress down with a file before you blue the job, or you may have to cut a new dovetail slot. A slot blank for the old slot can be bought from the local gunshop, and once in place, it too is dressed down with a file and the area is reblued with one of the cold blues or a touch-up blue.

Thompson/Center, Navy Arms, Dixie Gun Works and others offer the muzzleloader a variety of target sights. Most of them are peep sights that are installed on the tang or right behind it. It is best to move the sight behind the tang, since installation on the tang means that the sight has to come off every time you take the barrel out of the stock. If the sight is mounted on the stock, be sure that the folded sight won't poke you in the face during recoil, and then use wood screws which are long enough to hold the sight base safely. Pre-drill any holes you make into wood to avoid splitting when the wood screws are turned in. Whether you mount the sight on the wood or on the tang, be certain to scribe a centerline first, then position the sight base and align it with the centerline. Next use a very sharp scribe to make a

93

Installation of sling swivels on black powder hunting rifle is easy, requires little skill and gives gun greater versatility.

witness mark on both parts so that you can be certain of realigning everything quickly, should something slip, without having to resort to squares and other tools.

If you feel the need for a scope on your muzzle-loading rifle, or even on your handgun, go ahead and install one. Of course, if you shoot with the purists, you will come in for some razzing and some unkind words, but the poor eyesight that requires a scope should atone for the sin of installing a modern contraption on a replica. However, putting a scope on an original Hawken is like using a Colt Dragoon to drive nails into the barn door – it jest ain't bein' done!

If you take a scope job to your local gunsmith, take the entire gun along so that he can see precisely how you mount the rifle and thus allow for eye relief and recoil. If you decide to do the job yourself, and it is not difficult (but does require care) tape the scope, complete with mounts, on the barrel where you think you want it. Take into consideration recoil and eye relief, and adjust your temporary scope hold-down until it satisfies you. Mark the location with a plain pencil, just a line fore and one aft where the blocks make contact with the barrel. Since most scope bases are curved and your barrel may be octagonal, your first job is to file the bases flat until they sit level on the upper flat of the barrel.

Locate the screw holes for the barrel by means of the blocks, and ascertain what size screws came with the mounts. Use a centerpunch before starting to drill, and be sure to use the proper size drill. If you don't have a drill press or access to one, you can use your electric hand drill, but be sure to hold the drill perfectly vertical to the work. You will have to take the barrel out of the stock and level the barrel in your vise before drilling.

Measure how far the base screws protrude from the bottom of the base, and check the thickness of the barrel. Don't drill more than two-thirds of the way through. An extra thousandth or so is permissible, but be careful that the drill does not bottom out. Neither should the holes be too shallow, since the screwheads will then protrude from the top surface of the blocks. Use cutting oil when drilling and also when threading the holes. Suitable drills and taps can be bought from a number of suppliers, such as Brownell's, Dixie Gun Works, B-Square and others. Most of the screws are 6-48s and you may even find the suitable drill and tap in your local hardware shop.

Mount your bases, but don't tighten the screws fully, install the scope and tighten the rings or screws that hold the rings together. Check once more to be sure the location of the scope is right for you. You can still move the scope back and forth in the rings in case the eye relief is not great enough. Then take the scope off again, put a drop of Loc-Tite on each of the base screws, cinch each one tight, then give the screwdriver a whack with a hammer or mallet while the blade is still in the slot of the screwhead, then complete tightening the screw. Follow the same procedure with the remaining screws, then use Loc-Tite on the screws that hold the rings together. Should the time come when you must remove the scope and bases, start by putting the blade of the screwdriver into the slot of the seated screw and whack the screwdriver hard with a mallet. This will break the Loc-Tite seal and the screws will then turn out without trouble.

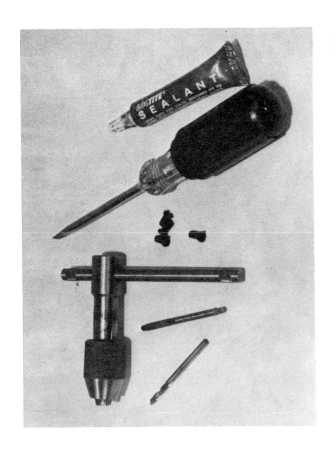

Patch boxes are handy to carry caps, patched balls and other small items, and you may want to install one on your rifle. A number of different patch boxes are offered by Dixie Gun Works, and all you need to do is mark the precise location of the box, then chisel away the wood, and presto, you have inletted a patch box.

If you are artistically inclined, you can get German silver from Dixie and, at your leisure, you can replace all of the brass fittings with fittings you have made yourself from German silver.

Once you learn to take care of your black powder rifle and begin to dig into the lore of the frontloaders, you will find a number of things that you can do to enhance the value of your black powder guns and to set you and your guns apart from others. Most of these jobs are simple and require a minimum of tooling. Not only will you have the satisfaction of having done the job yourself, but you will also have saved some money by not taking the job down to your gunsmith.

Aside from a few military rifles and muskets, few black powder guns were equipped with sling swivels. Since interest in hunting with muzzleloaders has taken such an upswing in recent years, more and more hunters have wanted to put sling swivels on their charcoal-burners. As a result, Lyman and Uncle Mike's now offer do-it-yourself sling swivel kits designed especially for black powder guns. Lyman offers such kits for Lyman guns only, while Uncle Mike's two styles of QD sling swivels fit either the T/C Hawken and similar guns or the H&R Huntsman and several others.

The rear QD swivel base is set into the butt stock, while the forward one comes with a replacment ferrule for the ramrod, the ferrule now also holding the swivel stud. Installation of these swivels is quite simple and this is another job that you can do, thus improving the versatility of your muzzleloading rifle.

A number of the currently available frontloading replicas do not have patch boxes. This may be a matter of economics, or perhaps the original did not have a patch box and hence it was left off the replica.

Chapter 8 BLACK POWDER HUNTING

Shooting the Muzzleloaders

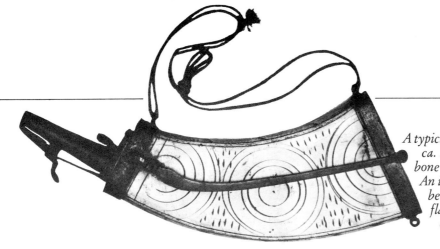

A typical German powderflask ca. 1740–1760, made from bone with iron mountings. An interesting feature is the belt hook so the powderflask can be carried either on the belt or in the normal way with thongs.

Thanks to television and popular ballads, the exploits of the early mountain men, scouts and settlers in the hunting fields have become legend. Who has not heard about the slaughter of the buffalo by hide hunters, or who does not know that Dan'l Boone killed a bear with his muzzleloading rifle?

The hunting feats of a number of the early settlers are well documented, but some of the reports tax the credulity of the reader. Thus, stories about deer kills at well over 100 yards may make one wonder about the veracity of the early reporters or their sources for such tales. On the other hand, literally every sort of big game in the United States and Canada has fallen to replica black powder rifles, and even some of the bigger caliber handguns have been used on medium-size game.

Considering our black powder heritage and the greater availability of muzzleloading guns today, it was only a question of time before hunters began taking to the woods with muskets and rifles. Unfortunately, the reports about successful hunts of our pioneer forefathers were none too specific when it came to telling about the caliber of gun used, the weight of the ball, or other such information. Reasoning that the early settlers lived by their rifles and depended on them for winter meat for their bellies, with the hides and furs for their clothing, all too many of the modern-day Dan'l Boones selected either the wrong caliber or the wrong projectile for their first hunts, often with disappointing or even disastrous results.

← *Toby Bridges took this white fallow buck in the Smoky Mountain region of Tennessee with a .50 caliber Mowrey Allen and Thurber reproduction muzzleloader.*

Shooting the Muzzleloaders

The picture was taken at the Bisley-Range, England.

Perhaps the major reason for these early failures of muzzleloading guns to bag the winter meat was correctly placed on the ballistics of the black powder projectile and on misjudging distances. An analysis of these early failures often showed that the hunter, in his eagerness to prove that he and his gun were up to the job, fired at distances where the hunter with a centerfire rifle would have had to depend more on luck than on skill.

The other reason these early black powder hunters failed to bring home the venison was traced to the use of too small a caliber or a projectile of the wrong design. A .36 caliber caplock rifle, fired with round balls at 50 yards from a rest, can deliver absolutely amazing accuracy, and the neat round holes in the paper seem to bespeak the effectiveness of the projectile. Nothing could be further from the truth. For target shooting – that is, punching tidy holes into paper or tin cans – this is a fine caliber and the projectile is just right. But for hunting, at the very best, the round ball should not be used on any game much bigger than a ground hog or a fox, and even then the wisdom of such a choice can be open to discussion.

The ballistic efficiency of black powder guns depends on the same factors as it does in centerfire rifles. It depends on the charge or the amount of powder, the burning rate of the propellant and the granulation of the powder particles. The size, shape and weight of the projectile plays an equally important role, and the depth of the rifling, the rate

← *Turn-barrel .45 caliber caplock rifle was used by Les Morrow, noted Canadian outdoor writer, to drop this good-size black bear, but it required only one shot to bring down the bear.*

of the twist, and of course the barrel length also affect the ultimate performance of the projectile.

Val forgett, head of Navy Arms and the man who helped instigate the replica craze back in the late 50s, feels that the round ball, while excellent for target shooting, should not be used on any game larger than a rabbit. For barking squirrels, the ball is almost traditional and Val agrees with this choice, although somewhat hesitantly.

The term knock-down power has been defined in various ways, but essentially we are talking about the energy of a projectile at the given distance where it makes contact with its target. Mathematically, energy, expressed in foot/pounds (ft/lbs), is a function of the weight of the bullet and its velocity in feet-per-second (fps). The large and heavy bullets are driven at slower speeds than the smaller and lighter ones, and the heavier bullets, because of their greater weight, do not retain velocity as well at the longer ranges. Hence, the long-standing argument of the heavy-bullet-at-slow-speed group versus the clan favoring the light-bullet-at-higher-speed may seem academic to many shooters.

In black powder guns, the projectile configuration – that is, round ball versus conical bullet – plays an important role. The flight characteristics of the conical or Minie bullet are far superior to those of the round ball, no matter how large the diameter of the ball. A number of black powder shooters, who are also hunters, have tackled the problem of the most suitable caliber and projectile shape by conducting range as well as field tests. Although there are some slight differences of opinion, most of the test results agree with Val Forgett's conclusions

Val Forgett with the Navy Arms Hawken Hunter rifle he used on his African safari.

which are based on range tests as well as considerable hunting experience.

For big game, and that includes elk, moose and similar domestic big game, the .58 caliber guns are more than adequate, while the .50 caliber guns are marginal for the large mammals but have proved more than adequate for such game as whitetail deer, black bear, mule deer. Forgett, and a year later, Turner Kirkland of Dixie Gun Works, took several black powder rifles to Africa on safari to confirm their ideas that, properly loaded, a black powder rifle will take the world's biggest and toughest game.

LOAD CONSIDERATIONS...

Here is a summary of Forgett's finding regarding the selection of bullets, powder, and percussion caps.

When it comes to selecting a bullet for a big game muzzleloading hunt, Val leans to the Minie bullet, and here he prefers a hollow base design. In selecting the proper diameter for the bullet, he slugs or mikes each barrel, then uses a mold casting a bullet that, after being passed through the Shiloh sizer, fits the barrel tightly. A well-lubed bullet that fits the bore tightly gives a better gas seal, hence increases the gas pressure behind the bullet, and this translates into higher velocities.

Val also favors the use of the heaviest possible bullet, especially when hunting big game such as elephant. While some may argue that not every black powder big game hunter goes after elephant, Val and others who have hunted moose and other such game with the large caliber rifles are quick to point out that a clean kill is essential, and that it is far better

to err on the side of the large and heavy bullet than on a light one that does not do the job quickly and efficiently.

In working out the suitable powder charge, that amount of powder which burns completely without residue is the best. To reduce the amount of fouling, the bullet must be well lubed – a fact that was stressed repeatedly by experienced hunters. While the larger calibers are usually loaded with the coarser granulated powders such as 2Fg (FFg), a number of shooters interested in black powder burning rate compared with bullet performance have found that a finer grained powder, such as 3Fg (FFFg), burns cleaner and more completely than the coarser powder.

Chronograph tests have confirmed this, and extensive shooting tests under controlled conditions also confirmed this. These tests were conducted with a thoroughly cleaned barrel which was first fired with the coarse powder charge. Then the barrel was taken out of the rifle, the breech plug removed and the bore inspected with a bore scope. The patches used in cleaning were saved, the gun was reassembled and fired with the finer powder. Again, the gun was taken down, the bore inspected and the patches used in cleaning were saved and then examined microscopically to check the amount of unburned or partly burned powder granules. The tests were repeated with three brands of powder, with a total of four different rifles being used.

Judging from the results of these tests, there can be little doubt that in most of the guns the finer grained powder burns more completely, leaves less unburned and burned powder or powder traces. Since burning was more complete, velocities were more uniform.

Close-up of Forgett's .58 Caliber Hawken rifle which proved to be more than adequate for even the biggest game.

For these tests, each charge was weighed and each bullet was miked and weighed before being lubed. After each bullet was lubed by hand, it was weighed again to make certain that an equal amount of lube had been applied. The loading was done by one experienced shooter and was observed by another one to make certain that no variations in loading procedures were inadvertently introduced into these tests.

In anticipation of hunting dangerous game – that is, African elephant and Cape buffalo – Forgett also checked the performance of percussion caps. As was pointed out earlier, the cap must fit the nipple properly and tightly. Val found that the German and British caps are just about equal in quality, while the Italian caps were somewhat lower in brisancy and therefore did not deliver the consistent velocities and pressures the German and British caps delivered with identical charges. Forgett found that the German RWS pistol caps gave the most reliable ignition and also delivered the most uniform velocities.

In working up hunting loads for any black powder rifle, it is important to use consistent powder charges, and bullets should be weighed to ascertain weight uniformity. Minor variations in charge weight or bullet weight will affect the accuracy of the load. In casting bullets, develop a casting system that will avoid prolonged and tiring sessions at the casting bench, and be sure that only soft, pure lead is used. Such bullets upset well in game, and expansion is considerably more uniform and better than that obtained from bullets cast from the same mold but from a somewhat harder alloy mix. The hollow base Minie bullets were the better choice, when it came to testing and comparing their performance with that

Forgett dropped this Tanzania tusker with the Hawken rifle, and recovered bullets showed a minimum weight loss.

of conical bullets with solid bases. A special bullet expansion medium was used which closely resembles animal tissures.

FORGETT'S SAFARI...

For his Africa hunting trip, Forgett selected two .58 caliber rifles from his line of black powder guns. One was a Hawken Hunter which approaches in performance the .458 Winchester Magnum when a 610 grain hollow base Minie bullet is backed up by

101

Val dropped this good water-buck at 80 yards with his .58 caliber Buffalo Hunter muzzleloading rifle with a 610 grain Minie bullet.

These two pure lead Minie bullets were recovered from African game animals. Note how well bullets upset, and how they accepted the rifling which is clearly visible.

175 grains of 3Fg powder. The other gun was the Navy Arms Buffalo Hunter which also was used with the 610 grain bullet backed by 125 grains of 3Fg powder. The mold selected by Val is the one made and sold by Shiloh, and bullets were sized in a Shiloh sizer.

With the Hawken Hunter rifle, Forgett shot an elephant, Cape buffalo, a good sable and a hippo. The Buffalo Hunter was used to collect a good lion. The Shiloh bullet went through both shoulders, breaking the heavy shoulder bones, and the lion dropped in his tracks. The Cape buffalo bled to death internally, thanks to the 610 grain bullet driven at a muzzle velocity of 1600 fps. The Hawken Hunter rifle also dropped an excellent impala and a wildebeest that made the Roland Ward record book.

Both these rifles with the above loads have a rainbow-like trajectory, and the rather hefty muzzle velocity delivers adequate energy at the close ranges.

However, at 100 yards, the velocity drops considerably, hence even the heavy bullet will fail to deliver the desired knock-down punch at this distance. These guns were sighted in at 50 yards to print dead-on and then targets were fired at 100 yards to determine the exact amount of bullet drop. If desired, a 75 yard target can be used to determine the amount of drop between 50 and 100 yards with greater certainty, and this will also allow the hunter to take a shot at ranges between 50 and 100 yards with some assurance of placing the shot correctly, since the drop figure for this intermediate range is then known. In the hands of an expert rifleman, the big .58 caliber guns have proved more than adequate for big and medium game up to 100 yards, although most hunters prefer to shorten the shooting distance to 75 or 80 yards.

In selecting a big bore muzzleloading rifle for hunting, the question of sights must be considered. Nearly all of the available big bore muzzleloading rifles have a rear sight that is set into the dovetail cut into the barrel. This allows a small amount of windage adjustment with the help of a brass drift and small hammer. If this sight arrangement is not to your liking, it is a relatively simple matter to install a peep sight or a fully adjustable rear sight. Some hunters have even installed low power scopes on their black powder hunting rifles, and although the purists frown on this, a scope makes a lot of sense, especially when there is a sight impairment. Drilling and tapping barrels is not difficult, especially since the large caliber guns have thick-walled barrels, and the scope base installation becomes even easier if the barrel is octagonal and the barrel flats are wide.

①

②

③

KIRKLAND'S SAFARI...

Turner, instead of using his own rifles on this safari, fell back on a 100-year old W. G. Rawbone 4 gauge double rifle. Each of these damascus twist barrels was loaded with a 1030 grain lead ball backed by 300 grains of 2Fg (FFg) powder. With this rifle Turner downed an elephant with two shots, although a third shot was needed to anchor the tusker permanently. The two recovered balls had flattened to a diameter of 13/4", and internal destruction of tissue was enough to stop the elephant in his tracks. Turner also used a .45 caliber Dixie Kentucky rifle to collect impala, lechewe, wildebeest and a tsessabe, second cousin of the hartebeest.

The .45 caliber frontloaders used by Turner, Ernest Tidwell and outdoor writer Jim Carmichel accounted for kudu, sable, and warthog. Both Ernie and Jim also collected a Cape buffalo each, using muzzleloading double rifles.

The .45 caliber Kentucky rifles were loaded with 70 to 90 grains of 3Fg (FFFg) behind a patched .440" ball. Most of the shots taken with these Dixie guns were between 70 and 100 yards. "We had no trouble hitting our targets once the guns were sighted in properly for these longish ranges," according to Kirkland. Carmichel killed a big lechewe at a measured 110 yards. The soft lead ball went clear through the rib cage of the 200-pound antelope.

Carmichel also used, as mentioned, an old 6 gauge double rifle. This antique was loaded with a 730 grain patched round ball which was backed up with 175 grains of 2Fg (FFg) powder. When Jim hit a wildebeest with one of these balls, the animal was completely knocked off its feet.

① *Jim Carmichel, shooting editor of* Outdoor Life, *used an antique six gauge double to take this large wildebeest, using a 730 grain patched ball which dropped the animal in his tracks.*
② *Turner Kirkland used a century-old W.G. Rawbone four bore muzzleloader for his elephant hunting on the same safari. Estimated weight of the elephant was six tons.*
③ *Ernie Tidwell, veep of Dixie Gun Works, needed only one shot from his .45 caliber Dixie Pennsylvania rifle for this big lechewe ram. Hunt took place in Botswana.*

Goose hunting is a special challenge with a muzzleloading shotgun. Since ranges may be a bit on the long side, be sure that the gun will withstand the heavy loads needed for geese, especially if the gun is an old one.

A Dixie lightweight 12 gauge muzzleloading scattergun was used by Toby Bridges to collect this limit of squirrel. Load was 60 grains of 2Fg behind 1 1/4 ounces of //5s.

AND THEN THERE ARE SQUIRRELS...

Not every hunter has the time and the needed money to go on a leisurely black powder safari in Africa. In many states and in most of the provinces in Canada, hunting with a muzzleloading gun, rifle or smoothbore, is legal. A number of states have even set aside special areas, usually reserved for hunters using primitive weapons, a misnomer if ever there was one.

But since the days of the pioneers and the mountain men, hunters have gone afield with black powder guns. Hunting ducks, pheasants, quail, rabbits and squirrels with a frontloading shotgun, most often a percussion piece is a challenge, but don't believe for a minute that hunting this way is merely an exercise in futility!

If you can hit a moving target with a load of shot, swing with the target, and know how to load and care for a muzzleloading gun, you too can limit out with any type of upland game. Ducks call for a bit more swing, and geese can be taken with a black powder shotgun if they are coming in to a well set out batch of decoys. Experience has shown that spreads containing a number of over-size blocks help quite a bit in bringing the honkers, and for black powder hunting, the more such big decoys can be added to the spread, the more efficient the spread becomes.

Aside from potting rabbits, the most widespread upland game hunted with a muzzleloading shotgun must be the squirrel. According to Toby Bridges, who nearly always gets his limits of bushytails, he loads his 12 gauge Dixie lightweight duble with 60 grains of 2Fg (FFg) behind 1 1/4 ounces of No. 5's.

A single-barrelled percussion rifle made by the British gunsmith D. Mortimer, London, circa 1840.

To speed up reloading, Toby favors the Remington 1 1/4 ounce plastic shot wad, but others prefer to follow the loading methods outlined in Chapter VI.

Between the squirrel and the elephant, there are a number of species which are hunted annually with muzzleloading guns. Elk, moose and black bear are taken quite regularly with black powder rifles. Deer of all types, javelina, wild boar and feral goats are the most frequent targets for the muzzleloading hunter.

A number of the big game preserves, where exotic as well as domestic game can be hunted for a fee, welcome hunters using muzzleloaders. This is not really too surprising since experienced guides and hunters know that the man using a black powder gun must execute his stalk with greater care than the hunter shooting a centerfire rifle at the longer and often more uncertain ranges. The vast majority of those hunters who now take to the woods with a muzzleloader know the limitations of their gun and the projectiles it delivers to the target.

For the man using a .45 caliber caplock rifle, the Thompson/Center Maxi-Ball, ahead of about 90 grains of 2Fg (FFg) powder, is potent medicine for deer-sized game. It makes little difference if you try for your venison with a .45 or a .50 caliber gun, but you should remember that the slightly increased caliber does not necessarily allow you to attempt accurate shot placement at much greater ranges.

Although not as popular as hunting with a caplock rifle, hunting with a black powder handgun is becoming more widespread. Revolvers are most frequently used since they allow a quick second and third shot, and the .44s are the most popular ones. The smaller calibers are not suitable for hunting since they are too small to be effective on game, and the

A .45 caliber New Yorkshire muzzleloading rifle, sold by Dixie Gun Works, dropped this Tennessee boar. Toby Bridges used the Thompson/Center Maxi-Ball ahead of 90 grains of 2Fg powder.

sight radius on handguns is too short for accurate aiming.

Whatever sixgun is selected, it should be chosen not only for caliber, but also for the choice of available rear sights. Ruger's Old Army, which is not really a replica, but a somewhat restyled Super Blackhawk with cap and ball features, and Navy Arms Remington style Target Model are offered with fully adjustable rear sights, thus making these .44's a good choice either as a sidearm or as a primary handgun to take afield.

Chances of getting a picture-book shot like this at your winter meat are slim, but a skilled woodsman can easily get within muzzle-loading range of even a wary buck.

A skilled amateur or a gunsmith can easily install a scope on most of the black powder handguns which are suitable for hunting. As in the case of the caplock rifle, such a bastardized gun may not find widespread approval, but as long as it has not been outlawed in the game regulations and you feel more comfortable with a scoped cap and ball gun, by all means, scope it.

Guns such as the two .44s mentioned above can fire round balls as well as conical bullets, and there is considerable merit in loading alternate chambers with balls and bullets. However, you should remember that ball and bullet will not shoot to the same point of aim, and that they will require different loads. Hence, an extra powder measure or flask must be included in your hunting bag.

The 1855 Dragoon pistol is a single-shot .58 caliber percussion gun that, when equipped with a fitted shoulder stock, offers the hunter not only a rock-steady way of aiming a handgun, but also a caliber

↑ Here are a few reasons why the muzzleloading hunter must make his first shot count. If you place your shot badly, you may suddenly find yourself in urgent need of a climbable tree.

← Display of old hunting items in the manor-house of the Counts of Erbach near Heidelberg.

↑
Somewhere under this cloud of black powder smoke is an evil-tempered wild boar. This photo, by Toby Bridges, shows why proper shot placement is important when hunting with a muzzleloader.

that is big enough to take most game. Of course, reloading is a bit slow, thus a back-up gun or another Dragoon pistol should be carried, especially when the game can be dangerous, or is hardy and tough. Navy Arms offers this 1855 Dragoon, as well as the Colt Third Model Dragoon .44 caliber sixgun that can also be equipped with an excellent replica shoulder stock.

HUNTING TIPS...

The huge cloud of white smoke that issues from your black powder rifle or shotgun is dramatic, a pretty sight, but it can also get you into trouble, especially when facing dangerous game.

Every year, incidents occur where a buck charges a hunter or an innocent bystander, instances where a moose in rut becomes even more ornery, and where already short-tempered game has been made even more aggressive by a badly placed ball or bullet – these are legion. Some of the wild boars – not only the Russians, but also the feral hogs inhabiting the

Tennessee hills – turn nasty when their retreat is cut off. They get even nastier when hit by a badly placed bullet or ball.

The cloud of white smoke can conceal such an animal and then the unlucky hunter can get into serious trouble. It is for this reason that hunters who have only recently taken to the field with muzzleloading guns are always cautioned by their more experienced brethren: Shoot only when a perfect shot presents itself, especially when hunting dangerous game at close ranges.

That cloud of white smoke will dissipate fairly rapidly if there is a breeze blowing, but lacking this, you might as well stand in a fog bank. Your field of vision is not going to improve very much, and then it becomes a matter of trying to walk away from the smoke without giving your location away by the racket your movements are making, and without losing sight of the downed game through a change in

107

position. Of course, not every buck or feral hog mounts a charge, but those who have been chased by an irate javelina through prickly pear cactus maintain that this might be a laughing matter for their cronies, but definitely was injurious to their dignity!

Although the single-shot rifle has made a comeback in recent years, it has been and will remain the rifle of the expert marksman and hunter. Similarly, most of the muzzleloading hunting rifles are single-shots, and since reloading such a rifle takes longer than slipping a new cartridge into the chamber of a centerfire rifle, the black powder huntsman owes it to himself and the game to learn how to reload his gun quickly and safely. More than one eager hunter has tried to shoot his quarry with a ramrod, and more balls and bullets have been seated hastily in a chamber that lacked a powder charge.

There is only one way to learn to reload quickly – practice, and then practice some more. Of course, once the rifle is ready for firing, you might as well try your marksmanship at a 50 or 75 yard target, shooting off-hand, of course, to duplicate hunting conditions.

Recoil, though very real, is largely a matter of personal habit, gun mounting, and to a large extent, also of experience. If you have started with a small caliber black powder rifle, and then decide to go hunting with a larger caliber rifle, be ready to absorb more recoil. The .58 caliber caplock rifles, when loaded as described by Val Forgett, are in effect very similar to the .458 Winchester Magnum as far as performance goes. And this also includes recoil. Test your loads for accuracy from the bench, but do not attempt to shoot such a rifle from the prone position without at least a shoulder pad. If recoil seems un-

bearable, get a bag of shot and place it between your shoulder and the butt of the rifle while shooting from the bench.

In Chapter VI, some hints were given on how to load your rifle. The hunting paraphernalia is best carried in a leather bag slung over the shoulder, while the powder flask or horn, loading block and ball starter are hung around the neck. Loading your cap-lock rifle on the range can be done with the help of a powder measure or scoop, but for hunting it is best

← Even a small moose can become cantakerous when in rut, and may start a charge without being shot at.

↑ A flock of wild turkeys can be encountered by the woods-wise muzzleloading hunter. Don't get too anxious, but pick your bird and wait until he gets into range and into a position that will allow you to fire the shot that will mean turkey dinner.

to pre-measure your charges. These charges can be carried in plastic pill bottles, and the trick of gluing two such bottles together, bottom to bottom, has a great deal of merit. If you are using a rifle with Minie bullets, you can carry a lubed bullet in one bottle, while the other bottle contains the measured or weighed powder charge. If you use a ball, a loading block with the already lubed and patched ball is ready to be set over the muzzle, and you need only dump the measured charge down the barrel.

If you carry unlubed bullets into camp, be sure that you wrap each bullet in a piece of facial tissue to prevent damage to the bullet, and pack the bullets so that they cannot rattle around in their container. Some foolhardy souls carry their lubed bullets in a small deerskin pouch; this is not only messy, but cam also lead to damaged bullet skirts. Often such bullets cannot be seated in the barrel without further damaging the bullet.

It is not necessary to carry a whole box or tin of percussion caps with you. A day's supply can be carried in a home-made leather capper as shown in Chapter V, or you can fill your store-bought'n capper with enough caps to last you for the day. Just

The .54 caliber, breechloading Gallager percussion rifle, complete with rear adjustable sight, is an excellent gun.

be sure you can operate the capper swiftly and surely when the time comes.

Include in your hunting pouch or "possibles bag" some clean patches, a small plastic bottle or a metal oiler with your favorite black powder solvent in case the barrel needs cleaning. Also include in your gear a worm and hope that you won't need it – but if you should have to use it, and yours is at home or back in camp, you will be one very unhappy fellow.

After years of hunting with a black powder rifle, the following hunting routine was worked out and has proven itself under all hunting conditions. Before you leave camp in the morning, charge your rifle with powder and bullet, then lower the hammer on the nipple. Do not place a percussion cap on the nipple yet. If you were to cap nipple at this time and then set the hammer at half-cock, the cap could get knocked off while working through brush. Sometimes you will hear that the hammer can be lowered on the capped nipple, and that this is a safe way to go a-hunting. The slightest jar can start the fireworks when the hammer is lowered on the cap this way, thus endangering yourself or your hunting partner. And starting the fireworks accidentally could also scare the very buck you are stalking.

When you get close to your target or are starting a carefully planned stalk, place a percussion cap on the nipple and be certain that the cap is well seated, then place the hammer on half-cock. Cock the hammer only when you are ready to shoot. However, do cock the hammer before you align your sights, since the cocking action and force needed to bring the hammer to full cock tends to move the gun just enough to spoil your sight picture.

If you fire and see that buck go down, reload and cap the rifle with hammer on half-cock, before you inspect your downed trophy. It happens every year – the game was only stunned, and as the hunter approaches, the buck jumps up, bowls over the hunter, and takes off totally unscathed. This sort of happening is not limited to black powder hunters, and more than one hapless hunter has leaned his rifle against a tree to take a picture, only to have his intended photograph take off in high gear.

If you hunt all day without firing your gun, cap the nipple when you get back to camp and fire the gun. Dew, rain, snow or condensation in tent or hunting shack can introduce moisture into the charge, and this usually results in a misfire. After firing, clean your rifle, make certain the nipple passage is not obstructed, then pass a lightly oiled patch in and out of the bore. Some hunters like to use the same patch to go over the outside of their gun, but be careful not to get any traces of oil on the nipple. If there is some residual oil on the nipple, remove it completely the next morning before leaving camp.

Next morning, run a dry patch through the bore, check to see that the nipple passage is clear, then charge your gun again, following the routine of the previous day. If you fire your gun during the day and reload, be sure to replenish your hunting bag's supply of caps, bullets and powder charges that evening in camp.

The old-timers developed a neat trick which is worthwhile remembering. Knowing the frequent need for a fast second shot and realizing that seating a patched ball in a fouled bore can try the patience of a saint, the savvy woodsman carried two different

Shooting the Muzzleloaders

size balls for his rifle. The smaller one was loaded with the conventional lubed patch, but the large one was just a bit large and was seated without patch. If the unpatched ball could be seated in a somewhat fouled barrel with one stroke of the ramrod, the chosen size was just right. Thus, re-charging was simplified and speeded up since it required but three operations – pour the measured charge of powder into the barrel, ram the some-what over-size ball down the bore until it made contact with the charge, cap the nipple, then fire that second shot. A third and even a fourth shot could be loaded and fired just as quickly if the need arose.

In some double guns, rifles as well as shotguns, the repeated firing and then reloading of one barrel has been known to jar loose the load in the other hitherto unfired barrel. If this load is permitted to keep moving forward in the barrel or chamber, thanks to recoil, and is subsequently fired, it is possible to ring or even burst that barrel. To prevent this, simply run the ramrod down the unfired barrel after you load the other one – make this a habit when you shoot a muzzleloading double of any kind, and you won't have to worry about a ringed barrel.

RANDOM NOTES ON HUNTING GUNS...

With the increased interest in black powder guns and hunting with such guns, state game depart-ments have, in most cases, established certain minimum caliber limitations. Some of the regulations

Although the new replica does not use a foil cartridge, the brass container holding the powder charge and lightly seated bullet makes this gun ineligible for some primitive weapons hunting areas.

are quite explicit, specifying not only caliber, but in some instances also diameter and weight of projectile and the powder charge and granulation.

Some of the regulations were dreamed up by someone who never saw a black powder rifle, others make a lot of sense since too small a caliber or too light a projectile can often wound game which be-comes easy prey for predators.

In recent years, some of the caliber restrictions have been extended to cover specific guns as well since it was felt that the use of certain rifles would give the hunters using them a greater edge than they would have using a conventional muzzle-loader. This tightening of rifle regulations for black powder hunters was due, at least in part, to the efforts of many dyed-in-the-wool black powder buffs.

For many years, all the organized black powder shooters were represented by the National Muzzle Loading Rifle Association, and matches are still held under the auspices of this organization. The monthly publication of the N.M.L.R.A. is *Muzzle Blasts*. The organization welcomes all black powder shoot-ers and it does not make any difference whether you shoot an original or a replica, excepting that

111

A painting by Frederic Remington showing a trapper in the Canadian North woods. The French called these types „Coureurs du Bois" – Rangers of the Forest.

The H & R Huntsman is offered in .45 and .58 caliber as well as in 12 gauge. This top-break gun strongly resembles H & R's Topper. Hammer has only full cock, and upright bar in action, when depressed, opens the action.

some of the Friendship matches are restricted to original guns.

From this group sprang the National Association of Primitive Riflemen, and the monthly publication of this group is *The Buckskin Report*. This publication and the organization it represents is "dedicated to the preservation of the authenticity of muzzle loading firearms and the activities associated with those same firearms."

The original Gallager, also spelled Gallagher, was a breechloading percussion gun utilizing the Poultney foil cartridge. The replica gun, made by Erma Werke in Germany and imported by Jana of Denver, is a .54 breechloading percussion carbine that uses a spun brass container that just barely resembles the original foil cartridge. Since it is a breechloading rifle, reloading the gun is speedier, and thanks to the brass container that holds bullet and power charge, the load is protected from inclement weather. Thus, the Gallager replicas should make good hunting rifles – adequate caliber and easy reloading, while still meeting the criteria of black powder shooting. Unfortunately, the Gallager, though not outlawed by name, is not welcome in some of the primitive weapons hunting areas.

A black powder gun of current production and not really a copy or replica of an earlier design is the Harrington & Richardson Huntsman single-shot percussion gun. It is available in .45 and .58 caliber as well as in 12 gauge shotgun configuration. Based on the H & R Topper action, this topbreak gun is loaded from the muzzle, and when the gun is broken, the percussion nipple becomes accessible for capping. Once capped, the action is locked, and now the firing system of the gun is fully protected from

←←Once broken, the percussion nipple of the Huntsman rifle or shotgun becomes accessible. Barrels on these guns are not interchangeable as in the Topper model.
← Twin tubes of the turn-barrel .45 carry individual sights and percussion nipples. The barrels are simply rotated for that fast second shot – a very real advantage in case of bad shot placement. Yet the gun is outlawed in some states and areas because of its second-shot capability.

weather and from accidental loss of the cap. The hammer is independent of the opening mechanism and does not have a half-cock, hence the gun can be carried with the hammer in the lowered position without the likelihood of setting off the cap inadvertently or prematurely. The Huntsman also has been excluded from a number of the primitive-weapons-only hunting areas.

Interchangeability of barrels and hence calibers has been a topic of interest to hunters and shooters for many, many years. Since there is no headspacing and only a few critical dimensions and mating of parts are essential, it is surprising that so little has been done with interchangeable barrels. This would be a definite boon to the hunter on a limited budget but with a variety of game to hunt.

J. Hall Sharon, owner of the Sharon Rifle Barrel Co. (Box 106, Kalispell, MT 59901), has done something about the situation. He is offering interchangeable barrels for the Thompson/Center Hawken rifle, and will probably add other barrels for other replicas to his line of quality tubes in short order. It is only necessary to unhitch the barrel, complete with breech plug, from the rest of the gun, then take the Sharon barrel drop it into the stock, join everything back together and presto, you have a smaller caliber rifle or a 12 gauge shotgun, depending on what barrel you select. The Sharon barrels come with their own nipples installed and match the barrel dimensional specs of the T/C rifles, with only minor fitting possibly being needed. The interchange of barrels requires no skill and no workshop facilities, and it takes less than two minutes to make the switch.

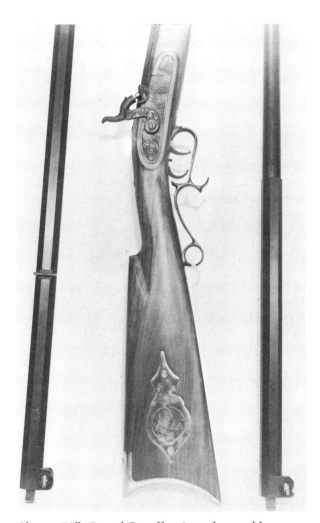

Sharon Rifle Barrel Co. offers interchangeable barrels for the .45 and the .50 caliber T/C Hawken. Offered are .45 caliber rifles and 20 gauge barrel, shown right and left of .50 caliber T/C Hawken gun. Also available are a .50 and .36 caliber rifled barrel, as well as a wide selection of other black powder custom barrels.

113

STATE REGULATIONS...

Here are the latest available black powder regulations as of the time of writing. While some states specify caliber and weight of projectile, other game departments make no mention of black powder hunting. If the state you want to hunt in has not listed specific rules and regulations, write to the state fish and game department for information. Remember that you can be in violation of the game laws if you don't know or understand the prevailing regulations.

ALABAMA: No restriction or limitation published. Black powder hunting is not specifically mentioned in the latest available rules. Write to: Department of Conversation and Natural Resources
Game and Fish Division
64 N. Union Street
Montgomery, AL 36104 (Telephone: 205–269–6701)

ALASKA: No projectiles are listed. In good hunting territory, the muzzleloading hunter with an accurate rifle can take good trophies. Non-resident hunters must employ a guide. Write to:
Alaska Department of Fish and Game
Subport Building
Juneau, AK 99801 (Telephone: 907–586–3392)

ARIZONA: Muzzleloading rifles are permitted for big game, but no restrictions as to caliber or weight of projectile are listed. Write to:
Arizona Game and Fish Department
2222 W. Greenway Road
Phoenix, AZ 85023 (Telephone: 602–942–3000)

ARKANSAS: Permits the use of a flintlock or percussion gun of at least .40 caliber, firing a single ball or slug only. Write to:
Arkansas Game and Fish Commission
2 Capitol Mall
Little Rock, AR 72201 (Telephone: 501–371–1025)

CALIFORNIA: Muzzleloading rifles are legal for big game, and no restrictions as to caliber are mentioned in the current regulations. Write to:
California Fish and Game Commission
1416 Ninth Street
Sacramento, CA 95814 (Telephone: 916–445–5656)

COLORADO: For the deer hunter, the muzzleloading rifle must be at least .40 caliber, and for elk the minimum caliber is .50. Write to:
Colorado Division of Wildlife
6060 North Broadway
Denver, CO 80216 (Telephone: 303–825–1192)

CONNECTICUT: Black powder hunting is not mentioned in the most recent hunting regulations for this state. Write to:
Connecticut Department of Environmental Protection
State Office Building
165 Capitol Avenue
Hartford, CT 06115 (Telephone: 203–566–3356)

DELAWARE: Hunting with muzzleloaders is not mentioned in the regulations.
Write to:
Department of Natural Resources and Environmental Control

Division of Fish and Wildlife
D Street
Dover, DE 19901 (Telephone: 302–678–4431)

FLORIDA: No mention is made in the regulations about black powder guns. A number of successful black powder hunts have taken place in this state, although quite a few of them have been on game preserves. Write to:
Florida Game and Fresh Water Fish Commission
620 S. Meridian
Tallahassee, FL 32304 (Telephone: 904–224–0115)

GEORGIA: For deer, the minimum caliber is .40, and muzzleloading guns are also legal for small game, although no caliber limitations are specified.
Write to:
Georgia Department of Natural Resources
Trinity-Washington Building
270 Washington Street, S.W.
Atlanta, GA 30334 (Telephone: 404–656–3500)

HAWAII: Some years ago, Hawaii was an excellent hunting area for the black powder aficionado. No restrictions are listed in the most recent game rules, but neither are muzzleloaders mentioned. Write to:
Hawaiian Division of Fish and Game
1179 Punchbowl Street
Honolulu, Hawaii 96813 (Telephone: 808–548–5917)

IDAHO: No mention is made of muzzleloaders in the most recent hunting regulations, but black powder hunts have taken place in this state in the past. Write to:
Idaho Fish and Game Department
600 S. Walnut, Box 25
Boise, ID 83707 (Telephone: 208–384–3700)

ILLINOIS: Single-shot muzzleloading rifles are legal for deer, and there are no caliber restrictions.
Write to:
Illinois Department of Conservation
605 State Office Building
Springfield, IL 61706 (Telephone: 271–525–6302)

INDIANA: During the deer gun season, flintlock or caplock single-shot rifles are permitted, the minimum caliber is .44, and the hunter can use either a ball or a bullet. Write to:
Indiana Division of Fish and Wildlife
607 State Office Building
Indianapolis, IN 46204 (Telephone: 317–633–5658)

IOWA: Flintlock or percussion muzzleloaders and muzzleloading muskets with rifled barrel are legal if the caliber is at least .45, but not larger than .775, and a cloth-patched ball must be used. Write to:
Iowa Conservation Commission
Information and Education
300 Fourth Street
Des Moines, IA 50319 (Telephone: 515–281–5971)

115

KANSAS: For deer hunters, muzzleloaders of .40 caliber or larger are legal. Write to:
Kansas Forestry, Fish and Game Commission
Box 1028
Pratt, KS 67124 (Telephone: 316–672–6473)

KENTUCKY: Muzzleloading rifles of .38 caliber or larger are legal for deer. All muzzleloaders are legal for squirrel, but must be of the type fired from the shoulder which theoretically would make a sixgun with shoulder stock also legal. Muzzleloaders may also be used for turkey. Write to:
Kentucky Department of Fish and Wildlife
Resources
Capitol Plaza
Frankfort, KY 40601 (Telephone: 502–564–3400)

LOUISIANA: No mention is made of black powder hunting in the current game regulations. Write to:
Louisiana Wildlife and Fisheries Commission
400 Royal Street
New Orleans, LA 70130 (Telephone: 504–527–5126)

MAINE: Although muzzleloaders are not mentioned in the hunting regulations, some excellent hunting has been reported from this state by black powder hunters. Write to:
Maine Department of Inland Fisheries and Game
State Office Building
Augusta, ME 04330 (Telephone: 207–289–3371)

MARYLAND: Legal for deer are muzzleloaders of not less than .40 caliber and using not less than 60 grains of black powder. Write to:
Maryland Department of Natural Resources
Natural Resources Building
Rowe Blvd. and Taylor Ave.
Annapolis, MD 21401 (Telephone: 301–267–5186)

MASSACHUSETTS: The use of muzzleloaders is not mentioned in the current hunting regulations for this state. Write to:
Massachusetts Division of Fisheries and Game
State Office Building, Government Center
100 Cambridge Street
Boston, MA 02202 (Telephone: 617–727–3151)

MICHIGAN: Muzzleloaders with a minimum of .44 caliber may be used by deer hunters. Write to:
Michigan Department of Natural Resources
Mason Building
Lansing, MI 48926 (Telephone: 517–373–1230)

MINNESOTA: Smoothbore and muzzleloading muskets of not less than .45 caliber and rifled muzzleloading muskets of not less than .40 caliber which cannot be breechloaded may be used in those areas where taking a deer a with shotgun using a single slug is legal. Write to:
Minnesota Division of Game and Fish
390 Centennial Building
658 Cedar Street
St. Paul, MN 55155 (Telephone: 612–296–2894)

MISSISSIPPI: Hunting with black powder guns is not mentioned in the latest hunting regulations, but in past years a number of black powder hunters reported excellent hunting. Write to:
Mississippi Game and Fish Commission
Box 451
Jackson, MS 39205 (Telephone: 601–354–7333)

Loading shot into the muzzle of a flintlock shotgun.

MISSOURI: Muzzleloading rifles must have a caliber of at least .357 for deer. Write to:
Missouri Department of Conservation
North Ten Mile Drive
Jefferson City, MO 65101
(Telephone: 314–751–4115)

MONTANA: There is no mention of muzzleloading hunting in the most recent hunting regulations, but in the past, good hunting luck has been reported by those using muzzleloaders. Write to:
Montana Department of Fish and Game
Helena, MT 59601 (Telephone: 406–449–2535)

NEBRASKA: Muzzleloading rifles of caliber .40 or larger are legal for big game animals. Write to:
Nebraska Game and Parks Commission
P.O. Box 30370
Lincoln, NB 68503 (Telephone: 402–434–0641)

NEVADA: No mention is made of hunting with a black powder gun in the latest hunting rules. Write to:
Nevada Department of Fish and Game
Box 10678
Reno, NV 89510 (Telephone: 702–784–6214)

NEW HAMPSHIRE: This state offers black powder hunters a special license ($ 15.50 for a non-resident in 1974) and for deer, the minimum caliber is .40. Write to:
New Hampshire Fish and Game Department
34 Bridge Street
Concord, NH 03301 (Telephone: 603–271–3421)

NEW JERSEY: There is no mention of hunting with muzzleloaders in the most recent regulations. Since the use of a rifle is not permitted, except for woodchuck with a special permit, the use of a black powder gun may also be prohibited. Write to:
New Jersey Division of Fish, Game and Shellfisheries
P.O. Box 1809
Trenton, NJ 08625 (Telephone: 609–292–2965)

NEW MEXICO: For deer, cougar, bear and pronghorn antelope, the muzzleloading rifle must have a caliber of not less than .36; elk and mountain sheep may be hunted with a muzzleloading rifle of at least .40 caliber. Write to:
New Mexico Department of Game and Fish
State Capitol
Santa Fe, NM 87801 (Telephone: 505–827–2651)

NEW YORK: Muzzleloading rifles are prohibited in those areas of the state where other rifles are also prohibited. No other restrictions are listed. Write to:
New York Department of Environmental Conservation
Division of Fish and Wildlife
50 Wolf Road
Albany, NY 12201 (Telephone: 518–457–5690)

NORTH CAROLINA: No mention is made of hunting with muzzleloading guns in the latest state regulations. Write to:
North Carolina Wildlife Resources Commission
Albemarle Building
325 N. Salisbury Street
Raleigh, NC 27611 (Telephone: 919–829–3391)

NORTH DAKOTA: Muzzleloading rifles must be at least .36 caliber and minimum barrel length is 16 inches for deer hunting. No other limitations mentioned in the latest rules. Write to:
North Dakota State Game and Fish Department
2121 Lovett Avenue
Bismark, ND 58501 (Telephone: 701–224–2180)

OHIO: Deer may be hunted with a single-shot muzzleloading rifle having a caliber of at least .38. Write to:
Ohio Division of Wildlife
Department of Natural Resources
1500 Dublin Road
Columbus, OH 43212 (Telephone: 614–469–4603)

OKLAHOMA: Although there is no mention of minimum caliber for muzzleloaders, nor is there any mention of minimum powder charge or any other restrictions, this state in 1974 offered a special black powder deer season which lasted nine days. Write to:
Oklahoma Department of Wildlife Conservation
1801 North Lincoln, Box 53465
Oklahoma, OK 73105 (Telephone: 405–521–3851)

OREGON: The State Game Commission in past years arranged for a special muzzleloading hunt for deer, but the most recent hunting regulations do not indicate that there are any special restrictions regarding the gun used. Write to:
Oregon State Game Commission
1634 S.W. Alder Street, P.O. Box 3503
Portland, OR 97208 (Telephone: 503–229–5551)

PENNSYLVANIA: No mention is made of black powder hunting in the latest available hunting regulations for this state. However, in past years, this state has been an excellent bet for the muzzleloading hunter. Write to:
Pennsylvania Game Commission
P.O. Box 1567
Harrisburg, PA 17120 (Telephone: 717–787–3633)

RHODE ISLAND: Although the state has a very long deer season for the bow and arrow hunter, there is no mention of muzzleloaders in the latest game re-

Shooting the Flintlock-Pistol. The shooter with the top-hat is never seen in a competition without his chimney-pot.

gulations. Write to:
Rhode Island Department of Natural Resources
Veterans' Memorial Building
Providence, RI 02903 (Telephone: 401–277–2285)

SOUTH CAROLINA: This is another game-rich state where muzzleloading hunters have reported a high success ratio, but the latest available hunting regulations make no mention of black powder hunting or caliber restrictions. Write to:
South Carolina Wildlife and Marine Resources Department, Division of Game
1015 Main Street, P.O. Box 167
Columbia, SC 29202 (Telephone: 803–758–2561)

SOUTH DAKOTA: Muzzleloading rifles firing a projectile of less than .42 caliber are not permitted for taking big game, which in this case means whitetail deer, since the antelope season in this state is restricted to resident hunters. Write to:
South Dakota Department of Game, Fish and Parks

State Office Building
Pierre, SD 57501 (Telephone: 605–224–3485)

TENNESSEE: Legal are flintlock and caplock rifles with a single barrel, having a caliber no less than .40 and no larger than .58". Write to:
Tennessee Game and Fish Commission
P.O. Box 40747
Ellington Agricultural Center
Nashville, TN 37220 (Telephone: 615–741–1421)

TEXAS: No mention is made of muzzleloaders in the most recent game regulations, and no special seasons were set aside for the black powder hunter in this state. Write to:
Texas Parks and Wildlife Commission
John H. Reagan Building
Austin, TX 78701 (Telephone: 512–475–2087)

UTAH: Muzzleloaders with a minimum caliber of .430 are legal for big game. Note that the restrictions do not specify rifle, but for the sake of accuracy and ballistic performance, only rifled guns should be used. Write to:
Utah Division of Wildlife Resources
1596 W.N. Temple
Salt Lake City, UT 84116
(Telephone: 801–328–5081)

VERMONT: One of the best states for whitetail deer and black bear, but no mention is made of muzzleloading regulations or special seasons in the latest game regulations. Write to:
Vermont Fish and Game Department
Montpelier, VT 05602 (Telephone: 802–828–3371)

119

Shooting the Muzzleloaders

VIRGINIA: No specific mention is made of muzzle-loaders in the latest hunting regulations, and since there are a great many restrictions concerning center-fire calibers, it is best to check with the state agency for specific areas and caliber limitations. Write to:
Virginia Commission of Game and Inland Fisheries
P.O. Box 11104
Richmond, VA 23230 (Telephone: 703–770–4974)

WASHINGTON: Muzzleloading rifles must be of at least .40 caliber, have a barrel of at least 20 inches, and fire a single ball or bullet with black powder. Write to:
Washington Game Department
600 N. Capital Way
Olympia, WA 98501 (Telephone: 206–753–5700)

WEST VIRGINIA: Muzzleloading rifles are permitted for deer, but there is no mention of any caliber restrictions in the latest game regulations. Write to:
West Virginia Department of Natural Resources
1800 Washington Street
East Charleston, WV 25305
(Telephone: 304–348–2754)

WISCONSIN: Regulations specify rifled muskets of at least .40 caliber as legal for big game. Under shotgun restrictions, the regulations state that smoothbore muskets of at least .45 caliber and rifled muskets of at least .40 caliber are legal, and though it is not specified, it is assumed that this refers to big game such as whitetail deer and black bear. Write to:
Wisconsin Department of Natural Resources
Division of Fish and Game

Box 450
Madison, WI 43701 (Telephone: 608–266–1877)

WYOMING: Muzzleloading rifles of at least .40 caliber and using a powder charge of at least 50 grains are legal for big game in this state. Prospective hunters should ask for season dates and other regulations at the beginning of May, and they will be kept informed as hunting dates are firmed up. Write to:
Wyoming Game and Fish Commission
Box 1589
Cheyenne, WY 82001 (Telephone: 307–777–7461)

CANADA

Not too many years ago, the Canadian provinces were heaven for the muzzleloading hunter. You cannot, of course, bring your own black powder along on a plane and importation of it by car may be difficult. Although no black powder gun restrictions have been enforced, severe limitations of another nature have been placed on non-resident hunters. This move originated with clubs and organizations on the local and province level, until in some areas the visiting hunter is no longer made welcome. Shortened seasons, restricted bag limits and excessively high license costs are among the means used to discourage American sportsmen from visiting Canada. This trend is continuing, and what the future will hold for the visiting hunter is uncertain, at best.

Canada-bound muzzleloading hunters are therefore urged to contact not only the nearest Canadian Government Travel Bureau, but also the fish and

AN INTERNATIONAL COMPETITION

*Claybird shooting with a double
barrel flintlock shotgun made
in 1792: charge with powder, load wads
and shot, place the top wad, pack the
charge and fill the flashpan.*

 Ready?

 *Lower the striker, cock the hammer,
take aim and call for your bird.
Did you check the flint? ...will you get
enough spark? Too late, the bird's
away! You start your swing, tracking
the target as you pull the trigger.*

 Whack! ...pfffttt...BANG!

 "AWwS———!"

*R*iflemen (top left) are members of the French team competing with flintlock rifles from Napoleon's time.

Shooter (lower left) wears ear protectors and shooting glasses as he fires his percussion rifle from the prone position.

Handgunner, above, is practicing for the percussion pistol event.

A flintlock pistol generates considerable smoke (lower left).

Even the ladies compete with heavy handguns, unafraid of blackened fingers, and they often shoot as well as the men!

This young lady measures her charge and checks her target ("just one more time") before settling down to the serious business

The battery of a fine flintlock rifle dating from 1780. The flint is wedged in a sturdy leather wrapper between the lips of the

cock. Never handle a ramrod in this manner! An accidental discharge could cause serious injury. Hold it between the thumb and forefinger with your hand positioned off to the side. Load the flashpan with the hammer at half-cock and care-fully lower the striker.

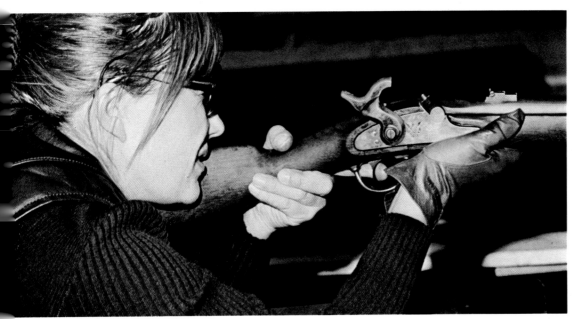

f the next shot!

Safety regulations prohibited a cannon competition but undaunted black powder artillerymen obtained permission to stage blank load demonstrations. Thereafter, cannoneers "saluted" the various events.

The ancient 16th Century fieldpiece, above, had to undergo a Proof House examination before officials would permit it on the "firing line". Note that it is fired by means of an authentic matchpike.

The smaller cannon replica, in the three photos at left, was constructed by a black powder enthusiast from drawings made from a museum piece.

*T*he opening and closing ceremonies of this annual international competition, preceded by parades of the colorful participants, were staged in the Schwaebisch Hall Town Square.

The Church of St. Michael (in the background at left) was originally built in 1141 and is a popular tourist attraction.

Members of the British contingent (below) strike the pose favored by 19th century photographers.

A nostalgic good time was had by all.

*I*nternational muzzle-loading contests are the most colorful of shooting events because competitors frequently dress in the fashions of the muzzle-loading era. Thus, on any international firing line you're apt to see a blend of British landlords, palace guards, western deputies and Civil War cavalrymen.

A member of the German "Home Guard" (at left) holds a modern replica of a traditional muzzle-loading target. (If you look closely, you can even see the bullet holes!)

A picture gallery from
the assorted European
black powder competitions
that preceded the main
event.

Ladies competed shoul-
der-to-shoulder with
"mountain men," "buffalo
hunters," and "western
deputies."

The two grizzled
competitors, at the extreme
lower left, appear to be
settling an issue by peaceful
means.

In competition, shooters generally use only modern replicas of ancient firearms but antiques are fired on occasion for demonstration purposes. Here, Mr. Horlacher prepares to touch off a percussion curiosa having fifteen barrels. Only one percussion cap is used because chambers are connected by a labyrinth of ignition tunnels; the first shot ignites the second, and so on. Circa 1850, this "machine rifle" pre-dates Gatling's gun.

At right, a cased pair of pocket pistols from the same period.

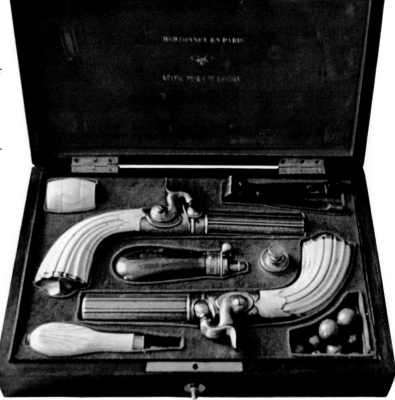

In past centuries, European matches were conducted with picturesque targets donated by the sponsors of the competitions. Elaborately painted by well known artists, these were subsequently awarded to the winners...the "Schutzen-konigs." Scenes ranged from historical events to everyday peasant life. This one illustrates a hunting scene toward the end of the 18th Century. It was won by „Schutzenkonig" Sitzler, a forestry superintendent.

Here we have a target dated 1790 honoring Emperor Leopold II, son of Franz I and Maria-Theresa of Austria. Leopold was an outstanding political negotiator at the 1790 Reichenbach Convention which marked the end of the war between the Austrians and the Turks.

This target is dated August 19th 1793 and portrays a returning sovereign who had abandoned his country and people for eight months. The artist tactfully neglected to mention his name and, since there were many small monarchies (and many such sovereigns) at the time, his name is forever lost to history. (We wonder what "her" name was!)

This is a painting of Johannes Fridericus Haspel... a Physicus Ordinarius which, translated, means "general practitioner". Painted in 1792, the picture shows the good doctor as he is receiving a patient. The doctor's library, gracing the far wall, was designed to impress upon his clients the fact that he studied much.

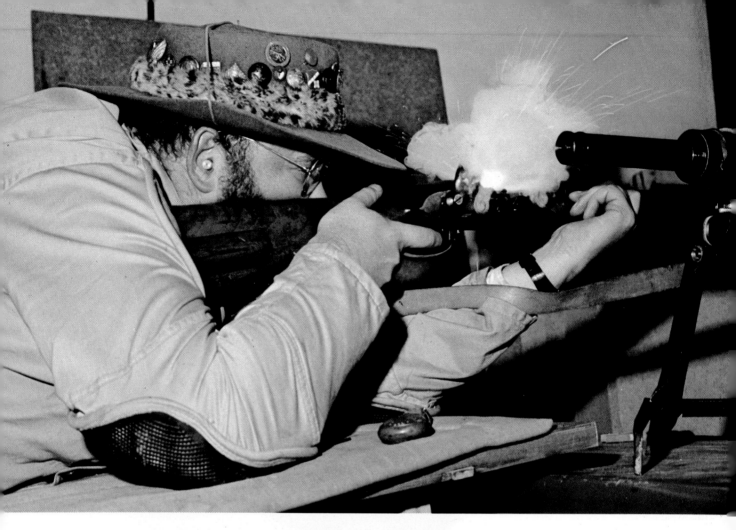

*I*mpressions from the last international competition held at Schwaebisch Hall, West Germany.

(Top) A British rifleman firing his flint-lock rifle; photographed at the moment of ignition.

(Left) The German team at the winner's ceremony. Muzzleloading competitors are rarely teamed except for ceremonial purposes. Once the shooting starts, it's "every man for himself."

(Below) The winners gain medals, plaques, bowls and goblets.
(The latter, of course, are filled with appropriate festive spirits when celebrating a victory.) The trophy shown here was the award for the Championship in Percussion-claybirding.

game department of the province he wants to hunt in. When working up suitable loads, it should be done with the Canadian C-I-L powder since this is the black powder you are most likely to be able to buy in Canada. There are no restrictions in bringing along your own muzzleloading rifles and shotguns, but handguns of any kind are best left at home. Bring with you, or ship ahead, whatever balls or bullets you want along, and since percussion caps of the same make as sold domestically are not always available in the more remote spots, you had best bring these along too.

For detailed hunting information, write to the conservation departments listed here.

BRITISH COLUMBIA:
British Columbia Fish and Wildlife Branch
Department of Recreation and Conservation
Parliament Buildings
Victoria, B.C. (Telephone: 604–382–6111)

MANITOBA:
Tourist Branch, Department of Tourism
Recreation and Cultural Affairs
408 Norquay Building
Winnipeg, Manitoba (Telephone: 204–946–7533)

NEW BRUNSWICK:
New Brunswick Department of Natural Resources
Fish and Wildlife Branch
Centennial Building
Fredericton, New Brunswick
(Telephone: 506–453–2433)

NEWFOUNDLAND & LABRADOR:
Newfoundland Wildlife Department
Department of Tourism
Confederation Building
St. John's, Newfoundland
(Telephone: 709–722–0711)

NORTHWEST TERRITORIES:
Superintendent of Game
Government of the Northwest Territories
Yellowknife, NWT

PRINCE EDWARD ISLAND:
Fish and Wildlife Division
Environmental Control Commission
Charlottetown, Prince Edward Island

ALBERTA:
Department of Lands and Forests
Natural Resource Building
109th Street and 99th Avenue
Edmonton 6, Alberta (Telephone: 403–229–4461)

137

NOVA SCOTIA:
Nova Scotia Division of Wildlife Conservation
Box 516
Kentville, Nova Scotia (Telephone: 902–678–4198)

ONTARIO:
Ministry of Natural Resources
Parliament Buildings
Toronto, Ontario (Telephone: 416–365–4251)

QUEBEC:
Quebec Department of Tourism, Fish and Game
Parliament Buildings
Quebec City, Quebec (Telephone: 418–693–2220)

SASKATCHEWAN:
Saskatchewan Wildlife Branch
Department of Natural Resources
Government Administration Building
Regina, Saskatchewan (Telephone: 306–522–1691)

YUKON TERRITORY:
Department of Travel and Information
Box 2703
Whitehorse, Yukon Territory
(Telephone: 403–667–5228)

It is important to note that some of the hunting regulations specify that the muzzleloading rifle be a single-shot, capable of firing a single projectile. Thus, the over/under or turn-barrel .45 caliber cap-lock, sold under the Hopkins & Allen name as well as under the Esopus Gun Works name, may well be outlawed in such a state.

While a game warden may be willing to give the hunter with such a rifle the benefit of the doubt if the hunter claims that one barrel is not loaded, it is doubtful that this claim would stand up under the strictest interpretation of the regulations. The turn-barrel gun has the distinct advantage that, by simply rotating the barrel, the second already loaded and capped barrel is brought into line with the hammer, thus enabling the hunter with such a rifle to fire an almost instantaneous second shot.

Shooting the Muzzleloaders

139

Chapter 9 BUILD YOUR OWN!

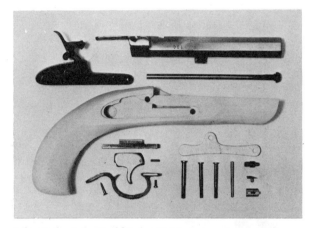

The Colonial pistol kit by C. V. A. is a simple one, and even the rank amateur can build himself a black powder pistol in an evening or two.

Dremel Moto-Tool is handy when it comes to removing a fair bit of wood in inletting barrel into stock. Thanks to the built-in speed control, the Moto-Tool can be used for a wide variety of jobs.

The idea that anyone can now build his own black powder gun has caught on. Not only is there the intense satisfaction of having created your own smokepole, but also in the fact that you have saved some money in doing so – money that can be spent for accessories or for more powder and caps, without making any further dent in the budget.

Today, you can buy kits for making flint or percussion handguns of the single-shot variety, as well as kits for cap and ball revolvers. There are also rifle kits, and Dixie Gun Works even offers a kit that will make up into a good double barrel shotgun.

Just how complex are these kits, and how much work do you have to put into making your own black powder gun? The great majority of these kits are delivered with about 90 per cent of the work already done for you. All of the kits examined came with good to excellent instructions on how to go about assembling your own muzzleloader, and on the whole, the instructions also had adequate illustrations to show the step-by-step assembling details.

The companies offering these build-your-own kits long ago realized that not every potential kit buyer is a skilled gunsmith, tool and die maker, or a whizbang gun tinkerer. Therefore, some of the kits reach you with all parts almost finished, and include all the material needed to do your own bluing, stock finishing and staining. In many of the kits, the lock is completely assembled and ready for use. The majority of these locks could stand some tuning, but this can be done later, after the gun has been assembled and fired for a while. Unfortunately, lock tuning instructions are sadly lacking in any but the most advanced kits.

Although not advertised as such, there are three basic types of kits: Beginner, Intermediate and Ad-

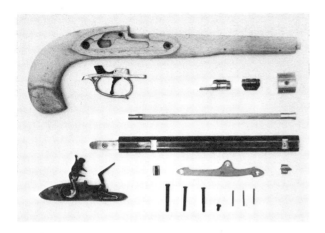

The Kentucky flintlock pistol kit from The Armoury calls for some light metal polishing, such as on the trigger guard, inletting, bluing the barrel and finishing the stock.

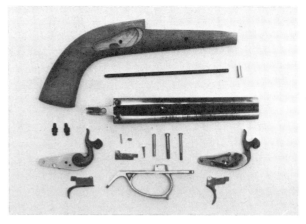

Double barrel Corsair pistol in either .36 or .44 caliber is just as easy to make as a single barrel pistol from Armoury kit.

vanced — these terms being applicable to the skill of the fellow tackling the project. Even if you have had considerable experience as a home handyman, it's a good idea to start with a simple kit. There is a lot of difference between building a bookshelf and inletting a stock so that the end result does not look like it was done by a hungry beaver. Similarly, the pre-bluing draw filing and buffing requires some skill and a light touch, since haste or inattention can quickly ruin what could have been a near-perfect polishing or buffing job.

In selecting a starter kit, it seems best to begin with a kit that will enable you to make some sort of single-shot handgun, preferably with a percussion lock. Such locks are somewhat easier to tune, should the lock require it. Inletting a short stock and properly bedding the barrel of a handgun is considerably simpler than trying to bed a long barrel in the long stock of a Kentucky rifle, for instance.

A few of the kit instructions listed the precise tools required for the job, while others included in the kit some minor items, such as sandpaper, which were barely adequate for the job. If you have, for example, never done any stock work, even such a minor job as relieving a pressure point between wood and steel, don't attempt to use whatever scraper you have on hand. Most of the paint and wood scrapers are much too coarse and too big to allow entry into the barrel channel, and are usually ground the wrong way. It is therefore best to invest a few dollars in suitable tools.

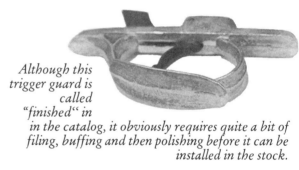

Although this trigger guard is called "finished" in in the catalog, it obviously requires quite a bit of filing, buffing and then polishing before it can be installed in the stock.

Laying out the hole for the front sight requires a small square. Layout blue is not essential, but helps you to see your marks. Be sure to use center punch before starting to drill.

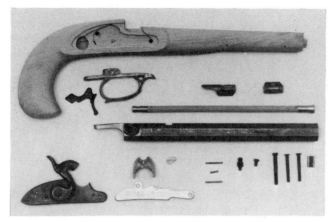

Even if you are not skilled and have to work very slowly, you can make this Kentucky pistol from the Armoury kit in three evenings at most, not counting drying time of stock finish.

TOOLS, NEEDED AND USEFUL...

You will need barrel channel inletting scrapers, probably two or three of them. A small-bladed pocket knife with a sturdy blade sharpened to perfection can be used for some of the smaller spots where a bit of wood has to be removed. Therefore, a large square and a large round inletting blade should do for a starter. A small ballpeen hammer or, better yet, a brass mallet and a few drift punches round out the hand tool requirements.

A Dremel Moto-Tool is handy, not only for making your black powder gun, but also for many other jobs around the house. A center punch, a few sharp drills suitable for drilling holes into metal, and two or three files should do it. Not essential, but very helpful, is a set of Swiss needle files and a small pair of needle-nosed pliers.

For finishing the stock, a Birchwood-Casey black powder gun finishing kit is suggested. This contains wood stain and finishing materials, plus more than enough material to blue or to brown the barrel – you select the metal finish that is most appropriate for the gun you are building. A package of the finest grade steel wool and some extra fine sandpaper should also be on hand.

If you decide to forego the use of the Birchwood-Casey finishing kit, you will need some stain. Water-soluble stain is probably the better choice since it is a bit easier to work with than the alcohol-soluble stains, especially when it comes to the last stages of finishing the stock.

You can buy either cold bluing or cold browning solutions, but the stuff sold by Birchwood-Casey is your best bet. Not only does each bottle come with complete instructions, but the products have been thoroughly tested and work well if you do your share. In any bluing or browning, it is essential to have the surface that is being treated completely free of grease, and that includes fingerprints. Even the slightest trace of residual grease will spoil your best efforts to blue or brown evenly and perfectly.

GUNSMITHING TRICKS TO REMEMBER...

If the barrel of the gun you are making is not crowned and you will be shooting patched balls, take the barrel to your local gunsmith and have him crown it. An uncrowned barrel will cut the patch as the ball is being seated, thus largely defeating the purpose of the tight patch. If you have access to a lathe and know how to operate it, you can of course crown the barrel yourself. Some hardy souls do a creditable job of crowning a barrel with a brace and suitable bit, but be forewarned that if the bit is not seated dead plumb in the muzzle, you will ruin the muzzle.

Dressing down slightly over-size steel ramrod from a pistol kit. If lathe is not available, the job can also be done on a drill press. As a last resort, lock the rod into your bench vise and use emery cloth, rotating the rod every so often and miking the rod frequently to be sure that too much metal is not being removed.

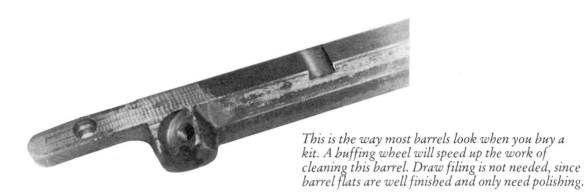

This is the way most barrels look when you buy a kit. A buffing wheel will speed up the work of cleaning this barrel. Draw filing is not needed, since barrel flats are well finished and only need polishing.

If your gunsmith does not want to tackle the crowning job, you can try this professional gunsmithing trick. Obtain a number of large, round-headed brass wood screws. The heads must be as large as, or preferably a bit bigger than the inside bore diameter. Chuck the threaded part of the screw into a hand drill, apply some fine valve grinding compound to the rounded part of the screw head, align the head of the screw with the muzzle and operate the drill slowly. Be sure that you stay plumb with the muzzle, and in a few minutes, you will have crowned your first barrel.

A drill press is handy, but not essential. If you have an electric drill, you can buy a stand that converts the drill into a small drill press.

You may already have a small electric bench grinder. Many of the screws found in these kits have narrow screw head slots and standard screwdriver blades don't fit these heads too well. Check your screwdriver, then grind down the blade so that you have a snug fit of blade into slot. In this way you will avoid having the screwdriver slip out, marring the screw head. Should this happen, dress the head of the damaged screw with a fine Swiss file, polish with

steel wool, degrease, and apply touch-up bluing. Then only you will know that the screwhead is not perfect, unless someone uses a magnifying glass to inspect your handiwork.

Sight dovetails are usually pre-cut, but most of them require some dressing so that the base of the dovetail will fit. Brownell's dovetail or sight base file is probably the best tool for this purpose.

Depending on the kit, the barrel may or may not need polishing. If polishing is needed, a large bench grinder can probably be converted into a buffer, and the necessary wheels and buffing compound are best bought from a gunsmithing supply house such as Brownell's. Bob Brownell's Polish-O-Ray, used according to instructions, is the best polishing product for buffing prior to bluing.

Birchwood-Casey has a degreasing compound that removes all traces of grease and skin oil from metal prior to bluing. If you cannot get that locally, use acetone. Never use lighter fluid, since some brands contain an additive that will not allow the bluing to take on the metal.

When using metal files, either a draw file or a large mill bastard, run a piece of chalk over the teeth be-

Brazed or soldered tenon of this barrel from a rifle kit is not set properly. You must either make tenon cut in stock at the same angle, or remove tenon and braze it back in place at the correct angle. Surplus metal from brazing must be dressed off to assure good fit in stock.

143

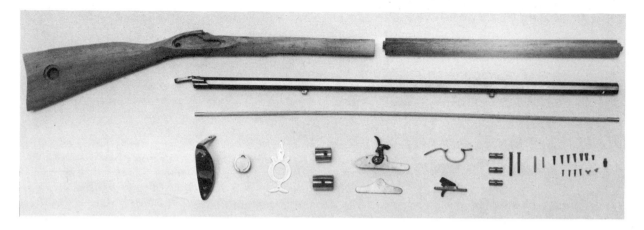

Kentucky rifle kit from Armoury is available either 90 per cent finished or semi-finished. In the former, the patchbox area is inletted, but in the semi-finished model, you have to do this. This has the advantage that you can select a patchbox that appeals to you more than the one furnished with the kit.

fore you start. This effectively prevents clogging of the teeth with metal filings. Trigger guards in most of the replica kits are castings, and some of them require quite a bit of filing and polishing. If you don't have the needed files and lack the buffing wheel, the Dremel abrasive rods and points chucked into the Moto-Tool will do the job quickly. However, work slowly and support the hand holding the power tool so that the polishing head does not "walk" off the work.

When locking metal parts, or even the stock, into your bench vise, be sure to pad the jaws of the vise so that the parts won't be marked. While inletting the stock, or completing the job that was done at the factory, pad the jaws of the vise and tighten the vise just enough to hold the work without slippage. If you tighten the vise too much, inletted, and therefore thinner, areas of the stock can crack. When holding soft brass parts, the same rule applies. It is much better to have to tighten the vise a bit while working than to clamp down so hard that you damage the stock or furniture.

In some of the kits examined, the ramrod was over-size for the ferrules or pipes. To cure this, chuck the rod either in a drill press or the headstock

of a lathe and center the other end in the tailstock of the lathe. If using a drill press, make a wooden jig to hold the bottom of the rod: Take a piece of board and drill a hole into it that is just a bit larger than the diameter of the rod, but do not let the drill bottom out when drilling the hole. Clamp the board on the drill press table, insert the bottom of the rod into the hole in the block, and chuck the other end into the drill press. Don't tighten it too much or you might damage the rod.

Run either tool at medium speed and use a strip of fine sandpaper to remove excess wood. Use your micrometer frequently to check the diameter of your work. You will have to refinish the rod, of course, and you can use the same finishing materials you use on the stock of the gun.

In some kits, the screws in the locks, as well as some screws that hold the trigger guard and other parts, are a bit on the long side. Cut the excess off with a fine hacksaw, running the saw blade between the threads. Be careful not to ruin the thread, but if threads should be damaged, measure the thread and re-cut it. Remember that some of the kits come from Europe and therefore the threads may be metric.

If you should remove a bit too much wood while inletting a stock, here is one way to repair the damage easily. Using some of the fine sawdust from your work, mix it with white glue, and patch up the damaged area. If you use the sawdust from the wood you

Intermediate stage of buffing trigger guard. It is better to use buffer than a file, since too enthusiastic use of a file can remove too much brass very easily.

Lyman Pennsylvania pistol kit is a good choice for the man who has gone beyond the rank amateur status. Metal parts are nearly finished, but ramrod has to be equipped with brass tips. On most of the barrels with dovetail slots, some filing is needed to permit insertion of rear sight. Be sure that fit between base and dovetail cut is snug enough that the sight must be drifted in. That way, it will remain in the slot when shooting.

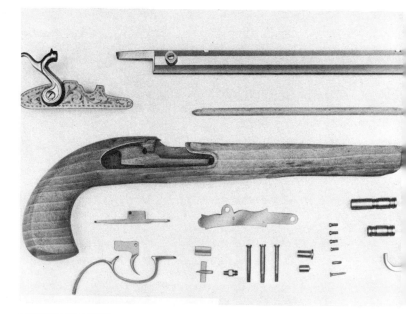

are working with, and if the repair is done with care, you may not be able to see the repair once the stock is finished. If you don't have any sawdust, you can use pastic wood, but without the glue, of course. Permit the repair to set at least 24 hours, 48 hours would be preferable, then sand with fine sandpaper, raise the grain, and sand again. Whenever you do have to make such a repair, use a somewhat darker finish on the wood.

If you have to cut a dovetail for the rear sight and there is enough metal in the barrel, you can cut a dovetail without the benefit of a milling machine or drill press. A compound vise on the table of your drill press converts the tool into a small milling machine with the milling cutter running vertically. Lacking a drill press, you can use a fine-toothed hacksaw. Since the barrel will still be in the white – that is, unblued – use some machinist's layout blue to mark the precise location and depth of the dovetail you want to cut. Scribe your lines cleanly with a thin scribe, measure the distances between the lines and compare them with the measurements of the sight base. Be sure that you don't remove too much metal when you use the hacksaw on the two sloping cuts. Then make a number of vertical cuts to the base line. Remove the metal waste and file the three sides of the dovetail flat with the sight base file from Brownell.

If you work with care and measure every cut you make in metal, and check drill sizes before using them, you won't run into trouble. But an oversize dovetail or oversize hole for the front sight does not necessarily mean a wrecked barrel. If the front sight hole is just a thousandth or two oversize, you can use some fine steel wool and a couple of drops of

Classic Arms offers a variety of kits, all of them fairly easy to assemble. Stock needs sanding and finishing, but metal parts are pre-finished and assembled.

145

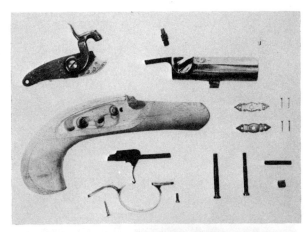

This Armoury Derringer kit only looks more complex since there are more parts than in some of the other kits from this firm.

C. V. A. Derringer kit makes up into fully shootable gun and is another good choice for a first attempt at building a muzzleloader.

Adjustable stand with padded crossbar is helpful when working on a long stock that is locked into the padded jaws of the bench vise.

Loc-Tite to keep the sight in place. If the hole is bigger than that, you can resort to silver soldering.

Should the dovetail be oversize, lock the barrel into the vise and level it in all directions. Insert fitting pieces of thin shim stock until the sight, drifted into place with a brass drift punch, won't move even when finger pressure is exerted. If much shim stock had to be used, again resort to silver solder to give the job a neat appearance and to assure that the sight will stay put. If necessary, dress the area with a file and then polish. The sight is usually blued at the factory, and if the original bluing has been damaged during this process, use a touch-up bluer to restore it.

When inletting a barrel into the stock and checking fit between wood and metal, you will appreciate a means of telling precisely where there is too much wood left or where there is contact between wood and metal. The professionals use a special inletting blue, and a small bottle of this stuff will last for a long time. To use inletting blue, obtainable from such firms as Brownell's, apply a very thin coat of it on the part of the barrel that will fit into the stock. Fastidious souls can use a Q-tip and thus keep fingers clean, or you can apply it with a finger tip. When press-contact is made between wood and metal, a little bit of the dark blue-black will be transferred to the wood, and that's the piece of wood that you want to remove. Most of the dye will stay on the steel, and the next time you drop the barrel into the stock, the dye on the wood will again indicate where wood has to be removed. When the inletting has been finished, just wipe the inletting blue off the barrel with a shop rag.

Kentucky rifle kit, from C. V. A., is offered in percussion as well as in flintlock configuration. This is a kit suitable for the more advanced craftsman who has somewhat more than the basic skill and tools.

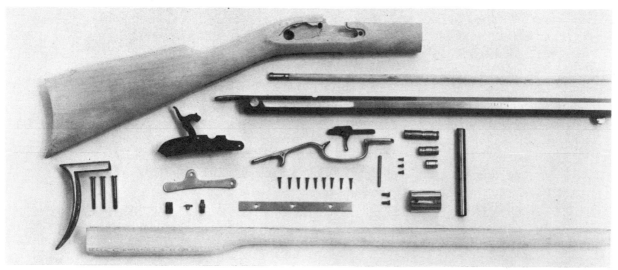

When inletting a long rifle stock, on a Kentucky rifle for instance, lock the area of the action into the padded jaws of your bench vise. This will leave a couple of feet of stock hanging in the air, and working on the forward end of the stock would be difficult since you cannot exert the necessary pressure to scrape wood from the barrel channel. This is a simple matter to overcome. If your vise is one that swivels, clear the top of your bench and gently clamp the forend of the stock into the vise, leaving the butt extending over your bench. Now support the butt end — sandbags from the range are just right and usually handy. Support as much of the butt stock as possible in this way. Before you apply the first

Dixie Gun Works is one of the sources where the advanced gun tinkerer can buy a variety of locks, both domestic and imported. Dixie also features some gunsmithing tools, supplies and accessories for muzzleloaders.

147

For the advanced black powder gun tinkerer, here is a wide selection of locks to choose from for your next project. External and internal views of six different locks, both percussion and flint, being offered by The Armoury for the do-it-yourselfer.

Numrich's Hopkins & Allen over/under or turnbarrel .45 caliber rifle was made from kit sold by Numrich. Where a two-shot rifle is legal and game sought is not too large, this rifle is a good choice for the muzzleloading hunter.

scraper, make sure the stock is level in all directions. If this is not feasible, make a stand with a padded crossbar on top, and have the stand adjustable for height. Slip the padded crossbar under the forend, adjust the stand for height, level off the stock in both directions, and you have the perfect setup for inletting even the longest stock.

Some rifle stocks have very slender forends, and frequent setting of the barrel into the barrel channel and then removing it can exert torque on the wood. Should it be warped, have the grain running the wrong way, or should the barrel hang up as you try to remove it, splitting can occur in the forend. Use a long ramrod to help lift the barrel out of the barrel channel.

Bluing and browning are, chemically speaking, rusting or oxidizing processes. Modern bluing is done by what is known as the "hot" method and this requires a complete setup in a separate room, since the fumes from the hot bluing will tend to rust everything in sight or within reach of the fumes. The cold bluing methods available to the amateur gun tinkerer are easier and much safer to use and do not present the rusting problem that goes hand in hand with the hot method. Moreover, the cold bluing is a lot easier and less expensive to use, at least as far as equipment is concerned.

Complete and thorough degreasing is essential, as mentioned earlier. In cold bluing, you must differentiate between those products that require water rinsing after bluing and those which are simply permitted to air dry. There is little difference in the end result, and your choice between the two depends

This .44 caliber Remington revolver kit from Armoury primarily requires finishing the metal parts by buffing. By following directions on the bottle of cold bluing agent, you can do a lasting bluing job even without the benefit of hot bluing.

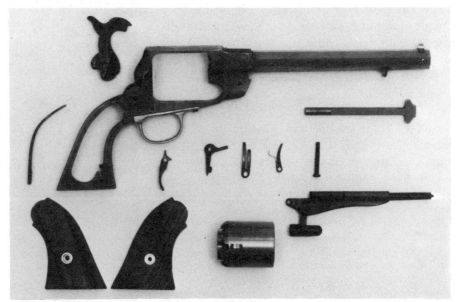

Shooting the Muzzleloaders

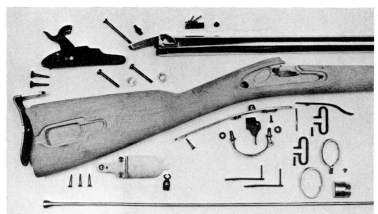

C. V. A.'s *Zouave rifle kit calls for some skill and care on the part of the hobby gunsmith. Most of the inletting needs additional whittling, metal parts need buffing, some need filing and then buffing and finishing. If no buffing wheel is available, use carbon waterproof abrasive paper, sold under the name Watersand, and specify No. 9–3010.*

on your shop layout and whether or not you have ready access to running water.

The deep lustrous blue seen on commercial guns is the result of hot bluing and the cold blue products, good as they may be, seldom, if ever, produce that same kind of deep blue. However, some of the cold blue products can produce a bluing job that is nearly as good. Read the instructions that come with the bottle of bluing solution – some of them can take a second coat of bluing, thus deepening the color effect. A patch lightly oiled and passed over all newly blued parts after they have dried will further enhance your home bluing job.

This is one for the advanced gun tinkerer and stock maker. If you find an old gun in someone's collection that is especially pleasing to you, ask if you may take a tracing of it. This calls for removal of the barrel and lock, and common courtesy dictates that you have the owner do this take-down job. Take a large sheet of light weight white paper, although brown wrapping paper will do in a pinch. Carefully trace the complete outline of the stock, being careful to hold your pencil perfectly perpendicular to the paper. If possible, trace both sides of the stock and note all of the width measurements.

Then, when you find a suitable stock blank, fasten your tracing on the blank, and with the help of a dressmaker's pattern wheel, transfer your tracing to the stock. If you can take photos of the stock – even Polaroids from all four sides will do – keep them with the pattern, and don't be too hasty in destroying the pattern after you've completed the job. The pattern can be re-used, and advanced black powder gun tinkerers are often happy to be able to borrow such a tracing for a stock of their own.

MORE ABOUT KITS...

The kits offered by C. V. A., The Armoury, Lyman and others are designed for the man who has little or no experience in putting together a black powder gun. Most of the kits come with 80 to 90 per cent of the hard work done for you. Aside from inletting the lock, trigger guard and barrel, there is little precision work required. Other kits, including some from Dixie Gun Works, are more complex, and assembling such guns calls for a fair amount of skill and know-how. Skill and dexterity come with experience, and Turner Kirkland's estimate that the average tinkerer should assemble four or five simple kits to gain such experience is not far off the mark, at least in the author's opinion. If you follow this suggestion and eventually come to the point where you make comparisons between the first and the fourth or fifth black powder gun you have put together, you will readily see what Turner is talking about.

Don't begrudge the time, effort and costs that went into the first guns – you have the basic metal work on hand, that is barrel and lock, and you can eventually make your own stock for that lock and barrel if your original handiwork no longer pleases you. You can even add your own brass furniture and fittings.

This brings us to the second class of kits. These are about 40 to 60 per cent finished, and they include the semi-inletted stock as well as a great deal of the metal work such as lock, fittings and all other hardware.

Dixie Gun Works, without a doubt, is the largest supplier of gun parts for the muzzleloading gun tinkerer. The catalog issued by this company fea-

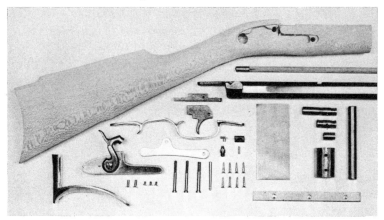

The percussion rifle kit also calls for more skill, and the ultimate touch to the finished gun is carving a game scene on the right side of the butt stock. The original rifles of this type did not have checkering on the straight grips, so do not go overboard on wood decoration.

tures many items for the do-it-yourselfer, from ramrods and sights to stock blanks, new and rebuilt locks and brass stock to make your own fittings.

This brings us to the third type of kit which is recommended only for the very experienced man who has a lathe, drill press, and possibly even access to a milling machine. Frequently, such "kits" are an assembly of necessary parts in a paper bag, plus a rough shaped stock, with few, if any, instructions. Some parts may require hardening before the gun is completed. In essence, the home gunsmith begins with a design idea, then buys the needed parts and combines these to make his own gun. This may also include rifling the barrel or fitting a breech plug to a home-made barrel. Most of these men buy commercial locks, and custom lock makers advertise regularly in *Muzzle Blasts* and often sell their wares at the Friendship shoots.

For instance, a hobby black powder gunsmith known to the author buys up every used and shot-out black powder rifle barrel he can find. Sometimes he re-cuts a barrel that appeals to him and builds a

rifle with it. In other instances, he cleans the barrel, then cuts it off to desired length and makes a single-shot handgun of his own design, buying only the locks and a few hunks of wood for the stocks.

Such gun-building projects are only limited by the ability and skill of the man, and more than one avid muzzleloading hobby gunsmith has built his own rifling machine, collects the wood for his stocks and saws it or has it sawn, under his close supervision into suitable blanks. Of course, with experience, you soon learn how to make a muzzleloader that appears to be an original. Old barrels are frequently pitted on the outside, and a couple of good coats of bluing or browning, suitably aged, will make such a rejuvenated barrel look like it came from one of the old pioneer gunshops before the turn of the century.

When it comes to making a stock look old, even though the wood is relatively new – if you consider a couple of years of drying – the "antique" furniture maker can teach us a few things. After sanding the wood smooth and raising the grain and resanding, let the inletted stock bang around for a while. Just

For the advanced gun tinkerer, Numrich Arms, as well as others, offers unfinished barrels. Most of these barrels are finished inside, but are left heavy on the outside and without thread for a breech plug so that the home gunsmith can make his own.

151

Putting together this Colt Baby Dragoon from the Dixie Gun Works' kit calls for skilled hands and a thorough working knowledge of Colt revolvers.

Better than 80 per cent of the metal work has been done on this .44 Remington brass frame revolver kit from Dixie. Barrel catch and sight have to be soldered, and the kit comes without instructions – the final test of your skill will be to convert all of the parts into a shooting cap and ball revolver!

don't make it too obvious. A dent here, and a few nicks there are all you need. Then make up your own stain, or get some antique furniture stain. One coat usually does it, but be sure that the stain has soaked into the wood well. If it has not, give the wood another coat, and don't try to make it a light one. Then let the wood dry for at least four days.

A carefully done handrubbed oil finish is unbeatable for a home-made replica. If an oil finish is not to your liking, try one of the good paste furniture waxes, and use three or four coats of the wax, buffing by hand enthusiastically between wax applications.

Don't forget that many of the old black powder guns which have been junked because of broken locks, stocks or wrecked barrels, have salvagable pieces of wood in the stock, as well as re-usable metal parts such as patch boxes, ferrules and the like.

When you reach that stage of gun tinkering, you won't need to have plans or kits. Maybe you'll be making kits and selling them to the newcomers to the black powder field.

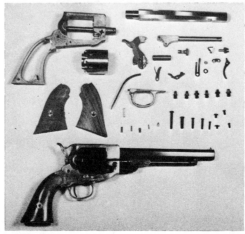

The Spiller & Burr kit, also from Dixie, can challenge even the most skilled man. Considerable metal working knowledge is needed, and knowing how to index gun properly is essential if you want to shoot the revolver.

Chapter 10
BLACK POWDER BALLISTICS

External ballistics is the science of a projectile in flight. This includes gravitational pull exerted on the projectile; velocity and hence energy; trajectory; the rotational spin of the projectile if fired from a rifled barrel, plus a few other physical factors such as barometric pressure, temperature, air density, humidity and so on.

Internal ballisitics is the glib phrase that is applied to all the goings-on that occur in the chamber, from the moment the cap or primer is struck and the propellant charge goes off. The ultimate performance of the projectile, that is the external ballistics, depend entirely on what happens in the chamber of the gun.

The granulation of the powder, its temperature and its temperature of ignition, the way the propellant is packed, how close or far away the source of ignition is (cap or primer), and how hot the flash is from cap or primer. Oil or dampness, which can either be rain or humidity, affect the burning rate of the propellant. The internal finish of the chamber and how the projectile is seated both affect the performance of the powder, and its burning rate, and hence also the behavior of the projectile.

Patch thickness, amount and type of lube, evenness of seating and the cast projectile itself also influence the performance of the gun and the projectile. Depth of groove, twist, barrel length, and barrel temperature as well as chamber temperature, all of these play considerable roles in internal ballistics.

The pressure created by the gases which result from the burning of the powder is the force that starts the projectile moving up the barrel – and the projectile can be a round ball, a Minie bullet, or a load of shot. The weight of the wads, or even the weight of the patch, must be added to the weight of the shot or ball to get the true total weight of the projectile when doing ballistic calculations.

In contrast to the smokeless powders, black powder – and this includes all makes and types of granulation – is a relatively forgiving propellant, a fact that has been mentioned before. While an overcharge of a grain or two of smokeless powder can destroy or damage a centerfire gun, black powder loads are not nearly as critical. But this does not mean that you can pour black powder into the chamber by the by-guess-or-by-gosh method.

The standard of comparison in all ballistics work is pressure, that is chamber pressure, and velocity. The velocity is determined by means of a chronograph, and pressure with the help of a crusher gage in most cases, although other systems, such as the strain gage, have been used with considerable success.

Because of the number of variables that affect each single shot fired, it must be understood that one or even six identical velocity and pressure readings do not necessarily mean that the load will always give the same performance. As far as the ballistician is concerned, he simply happens to get six more or less identical readings, which may or may not be significant. For instance, the range temperature or the temperature of the barrel and chamber or the powder can upset that delicately balanced apple cart.

PRESSURE GUNS...

Pressure guns for smokeless powder cartridges have been around for many years, but it was only in the last few years that pressure guns for black

153

Custom-made breech plug that was designed for determining chamber pressures in Thompson/Center Hawken barrels. Compression of crusher is measured with a micrometer, then psi are read from tarage table.

powder were being put to use. Thompson/Center designed and constructed such a muzzleloading pressure gun, following basically the design used for centerfire guns.

A special Hawken breech plug was ported into the rear of the chamber of the barrel. Into this was inserted a steel piston that transfers chamber pressures to a lead crusher of a known and accurately measured length. At the other end, a clamp was installed to serve as an anvil and to prevent the lead crusher from moving rearward.

When the gun is fired, gas pressure is transferred onto the piston and hence onto the lead crusher. Since the crusher cannot move to the rear, the gas pressure is actually exerted on the lead crusher, compressing it. The crusher is then removed from the pressure sleeve and measured. By means of carefully calculated tarage tables the pressure exerted on the crusher can then be determined.

In themselves, none of the pressure readings compiled for a series of shots are absolutes. When identical projectiles are chronographed and fired for accuracy, and all three of these tests remain more or less identical for a string of shots, then the ballisticians have a workable load for that specific barrel. However, a production gun with a simliar barrel and the same load will probably not give the same test results as the laboratory barrel which is locked into the pressure system and shot from a machine rest.

Obviously then, loading tables and data given anywhere are not only open to criticism, but must be used with some care, since the load that performs satisfactorily in one gun may be either too hot for another or, perhaps, even a dud. If the data you decide to start with are near the permissible maximum, reduce the starting charge at least 10 per cent, and in some cases the reduction should be 15 per cent of the original load. If the load is known to be conservative, start a few grains below the load given and work up.

Since you probably won't have ready access to an indoor range with photoelectric screens and a chronograph, as well as pressure equipment, your only

criteria for load performance will be your targets. If a load repeatedly delivers identical groups – and the smaller the groups are, the closer you are to the ideal load – the better your loading technique and the load itself.

Earlier in this book, it was stressed that load uniformity is essential. This means not only the type of patching used, the brand and size of the cap, and consistently uniform seating of the ball, but also precise measuring of the powder charge. Last, but not least, is the way you handle the ramrod, the amount of force you use in seating the ball or bullet on the charge, and of course, how well the projectile fits the

Standard pressure gun and receiver in which center-fire rifle and handgun ammo can be tested for pressure. Fired bullet also records velocity as it passes through hole in wall and goes through distant screens which are not visible.

barrel. Now the reason for the repeated caution about doing your loading uniformly becomes apparent.

Remember what has been said about powder granulation. Extending this a bit more and borrowing from the field of smokeless powder ballistics, it now becomes clear that each make and granulation of powder operates best under a given set of circumstances. The primary one here is the pressure range at which the powder burns evenly or uniformly so that the gases are formed in a progressive and consistent manner. If there are pressure peaks and these peaks are far apart on the time/pressure curve, resulting chamber pressures will be erratic, and then the average pressure can well be on the high or excessive side.

Experimental work conducted by T/C, Lyman and the author has shown that:

1) As the powder charge is increased, so the pressure levels increase, while accuracy tends to fall off, and velocity may increase or could even decrease. With some excessive loads fired under controlled conditions, recorded velocities were markedly reduced although it was not possible to establish a mathematical relationship between pressure, velocity, and accuracy.

2) It has long been assumed that an excessive load of black powder won't burn completely, and that excessive loads are in themselves harmless in contrast to smokeless powder loads. Microscopic examination of test barrels showed that most of the powder did actually burn, regardless of load density or the amount of powder in relation to bore size and projectile weight. Thus, a

155

SAECO lead hardness tester helps to determine if your casting mix is of identical composition. Although of course not as accurate as a complete metallurgical analysis, the degree of hardness is a good indicator of purity of lead.

load that contained 20 grains of powder in excess of the standard load a .58 caliber rifle showed only traces of unburned powder and a slight increase in barrel fouling, but photographically measured recoil increased more than 20 per cent. These excessive powder charges also produced high pressures. Thus, while black powder is more forgiving than the smokeless propellants, you cannot over-charge your muzzleloading gun forever – something is going to give under excess pressure.

3) While excessive powder charges increase pressure, any increase in velocity is not in a predictable ratio with pressure levels. As pressure increased, recorded velocities increased little, and sometimes were even lower than anticipated. There is also a very definite relationship between velocity and barrel length. The Kentucky and Plains rifles, originals and replicas alike, have long barrels and it had been thought that a long barrel would give a patched ball greater velocity. As with centerfire guns, there is a barrel length maximum, and once this is reached, the greater barrel length is not reflected in higher velocities, or recorded velocities may not be consistent.

Some of the tests that were conducted with patching materials, lubes, over- and under-sized balls and bullets, and variations in loading techniques cannot be considered scientifically valid since the number of tests conducted were either inadequate, or did not include all of the possible or known variants. As far as it is known, the hardness of the metal used in casting balls and bullets does have an effect on the ballistic properties of the projectile, but little or no conclusive work has yet been done along those lines.

BULLET PERFORMANCE...

For instance, a brief chemical analysis of three lots of allegedly pure lead revealed that none of the three lots were pure lead, and hardness tests conducted on a Rockwell hardness tester showed that all three lots had greatly divergent hardness ratings. Although the black powder shooter can avail himself of a lead tester such as sold by SAECO, metallurgists are quick to point out that hardness itself is but the measurement of one physical property and does not indicate the purity of the lead or the alloy.

The weight of the projectile governs, to some extent, the powder charge required, and a charge de-

signed for a heavy bullet will not burn completely if the heavy bullet has been replaced with a lighter one.

The depth of the rifling also affects projectile performance. The ballistic behavior of a skirted bullet vs. that of a solid conical or even a patched round ball varies greatly. The skirt, under the pressure of the powder gases, flares out, thus creating a seal between bullet and rifling. The conical, solid base bullets have a slightly over-size ring near the shoulder, and when the push of the gases begins, the bullet is actually somewhat shortened to effect a seal. For this reason, this type of bullet must be at least of bore size when loaded, and it is best when slight engraving marks are made as the bullet is seated.

As already mentioned, the depth of rifling also affects the performance of the projectile. Very shallow rifling is best suited for conical bullets, while slightly deeper rifling is more suitable for patched balls. Some barrels, designed specifically for the conical bullets, have fewer lands and grooves than a barrel made primarily for patched round balls. Muskets, such as the Zouave and the Enfield, have therefore sometimes only three groove barrels, in contrast to the four to eight grooves of Kentucky guns designed for ball loads.

The rate of twist not only plays an important role in the flight of the projectile, but it was also found that the faster the twist, the greater the amount of fouling. Conical bullets, with or without hollow bases, do better with a fast twist. Obviously, the conical bullet requires a fast twist to stabilize, and Ramage and associates at Lyman recently demonstrated this by showing that skirt deformation was not the cause of accuracy loss – the bullets had not stabilized in the slower twist barrels.

The Civil War Army charge for the Zouave was 60 grains of 2Fg (FFg) powder, and this load is still popular today. It is an accurate load, but match shooters and skirmishers, who try to wring that little bit of extra accuracy from their guns and loads, reduce that load, sometimes to as little as 40 grains. Increase the Army load, and besides a larger cloud of smoke and somewhat increased recoil, little or nothing is gained in accuracy, and only pressure and velocity increase.

Thanks to some extensive work along those lines at the Lyman lab, excessive fouling is now better understood than it was five or 10 years ago. Excessive fouling makes loading difficult, and forcing any projectile down a fouled barrel can deform it; such a ball or bullet will not deliver the usually accurate performance.

According to Lyman, excessive fouling also prevents a bullet, skirted or solid, from expanding properly in the barrel. As a matter of fact, excessive fouling ahead of the bullet can lead to deformation of the projectile, and hence to poor ballistic performance.

The relatively thin skirt of the Minie bullet can be deformed in handling or carrying in the hunting pouch without protection. Careless seating, or perhaps tipping the bullet while pushing it down on top of the charge, also tends to damage or deform the bullet. Since they are loaded so that they will just slide down the bore – that is, they are not engraved as are the solid conicals – the Minie can be seated in a barrel that is fouled to the extent that a solid or even a patched ball could not be made to load.

157

A good and reliable chronograph for the amateur ballistician is the B-Square Model 75 which uses printed screens, hence is less costly than the units using photoelectric screens.

OTHER FACTORS...

The long vs. the short barrel clan have loaded, fired, chronographed, and then cut another inch off roughly a dozen replica barrels. From a 39-inch barrel to a 30-inch barrel, under controlled lab conditions, the average velocity loss per inch of barrel was 9.6295 fps. When the barrel was cut off even more, one inch per 10-shot string, the velocity loss per inch of barrel became variable. With the hotter loads, the average velocity loss per inch was 21.9246 fps, while the velocity loss with somewhat lighter loads averaged 10.1966 fps.

When some of these loads were fired in sawed-off barrels, shooting from the shoulder rather than in the machine rest, muzzle blast became unpleasant and a plastic face guard was added to the shooting glasses and ear protectors. Even with the best loads – that is, the most accurate and with the most uniform velocities – increased muzzle blast was noted in every caliber gun with the exception of one .36 caliber muzzleloading rifle.

One .45 caliber barrel was fired on the indoor range, under controlled temperature and humidity conditions, with a variety of loads, and a performance comparison was made of the various powders used. Every brand of powder fouled the barrel. However, in two different .45 caliber rifles, fired with identical loads which included weighed charges, there was a noticeable difference in the fouling, although there was no accurate way of determining the precise amount. The conclusion that one barrel was fouled to a greater degree than the other would, of course, have been subjective.

Identical loads of the different powders, all fired from the same test gun, showed a wide variation in velocities. Since mechanical malfunction of the photoelectric screens or of the chronograph itself was ruled out by test rounds fired at periodic intervals, these velocities must be taken as relatively accurate. As in all chronographing, there often was a considerable spread in the velocity data which cannot be explained readily.

In testing a number of small-bore muzzleloading rifles with patched balls, the following general observations were made repeatedly. Although it is accepted procedure to seat the ball always with the sprue up, seating the ball with sprue down in a test string did not affect accuracy. However, when balls were seated any old way, accuracy quickly fell off. There was also a very noticeable difference in groups when the barrel was wiped out between shots, in contrast to groups fired where the barrel was not wiped between shots.

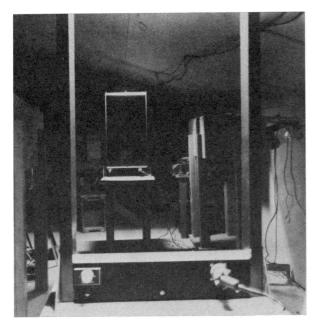

View of indoor range with photoelectric screens ready to record the velocity of bullet or ball. Such a chronograph setup allows running a greater number of tests in a minimum of time. Indoor range has the advantage that tester is not dependent on weather, time of day, supply of printed screens.

Regular spit ball, that is the patch moistened with saliva, leaves a lot to be desired in a number of respects, hence the use of a commercial lube is suggested. Among the major faults of the traditional spit patch: increased fouling; inadequate moistening of patch, hence difficult seating of the patched ball; patch cutting; erratic velocities in some instances. The old rule of thumb that a patched ball should be bore diameter and that the patch should be thick enough to require between 18–20 pounds of pressure may be the answer to the question of how thick the patch should be and what the diameter of the ball should be. But there is no known method of determining that pressure accurately without expensive lab equipment, and the by-guess-and-by-gosh method appears to work just as well.

In swabbing the bore, as in seating a ball or bullet, uniformity of the rod strokes and tightly fitted patches are the answer to better performance and improved accuracy.

The amount of cap fouling and debris appears to vary with the make of the cap. As was noted in several other sections, ignition of the caps varies a great deal, and proper ignition, to some extent, also depends on the shape of the nipple and the diameter of the nipple passage. Fouling, residual oil, or moisture from wet-cleaning the barrel or from powder solvents definitively affects the performance of the cap, and apparently does so in a very unpredictable way.

Centerfire riflemen and shotgunners have long known that each gun is a law unto itself. The same can be said about muzzleloading guns, and that includes handguns. For instance, the chambers of four cylinders were measured, all cylinders being of the

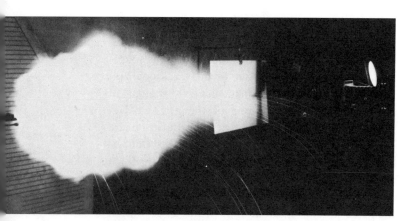

High speed photo setup used by Lyman to produce bullet-in-flight pictures which allow study of ballistic behavior of the projectile and which also indicate certain characteristics of the load used.

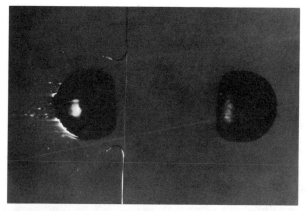

This double round ball .560" projectile was pushed along by 120 grains of 2Fg, is the same one being fired in preceeding picture. Photos: Courtesy of Lyman Products for Shooters.

same make and caliber, of course. Rough chambers were found in three cylinders, but not all the chambers exhibited the same degree of roughness. In only one cylinder did four of the six chambers show the same precise inside dimensions, and inside dimensions varied less than .003".

Obviously, trying to squeeze maximum accuracy from of these cylinders would be nearly impossible, unless the shooter went to the trouble of making up special balls for each chamber, and marked each chamber so that he could reload quickly and efficiently. One cylinder was removed after firing the gun, it was thoroughly cleaned and dried, and then each chamber was polished by hand until the inside micrometer indicated that all chamber dimensions were identical. The gun was then loaded with balls of the suitable size, using the same powder charges and brand of caps as before – the change in accuracy, as well as in more consistent velocity readings,

was most gratifying. Obviously, the handgunner should take the time and trouble to check the chambers of his sixgun, and if there are variations in chamber dimensions, the chambers should be polished with care.

A WORD OF CAUTION...

Foreign-made muzzleloading rifles, shotgun and handguns must undergo proof tests by law in the country of origin. In most cases, these laws are concerned with barrel strength and safety, and if the proof pressures are published, they are usually given in the metric system.

Since pressure equipment for black powder guns is not readily available and must be custom-made, do not try to duplicate these proof tests. Remember that increasing the powder charge may not improve

velocity, and that it is possible to create excessive pressure levels, even in muzzleloaders! It is far better to strive for improved accuracy, and usually, the most accurate load is also the most ballistically correct one.

Although domestically made muzzleloading guns do not have to undergo proof tests, our manufacturers are just as concerned with gun safety as the manufacturers abroad.

You may gain something by polishing out the chambers of your black powder revolver, but beyond that, reasonable loads that group tightly are the only worthwhile consideration. Some tuning of rifles and handguns is possible, such as glassbedding or adding somewhat better sights, or more accurate ones.

Above all, remember that black powder is not quite as tolerant as it is often thought to be.

BLACK POWDER LOAD DATA FOR RIFLED LONG GUNS [1,2]

CALIBER	PROJECTILE ⌀ in./gr.	POWDER	CHARGE gr.	CAP	FPS (Vo) average	FT/LB (Eo) average
.36	RB[3] .350–.360/71 gr.	3Fg	35–50	11	1762	458
.40	RB .395/92 gr.	3Fg	50–75	11	1952	785
.44	RB .437/127 gr.	3Fg	60–80	11	1543	673
	#445599 .445/250 gr.	3Fg	30–70	11	1120	736
	#445369 .445/291 gr.	3Fg	50–65	11	1283	1071
	RB .445/140 gr.	3Fg	50–65	11	1422	742
.45	RB .440–.445/140 gr.	3Fg	50–70	11	1810	967
	#454616 .455/230 gr.	3Fg	50–75	11	1522	1195
	#454613 .454/265 gr.	3Fg	50–65	11	1344	1073
	#454612 .454/300 gr.	3Fg	45–65	11	1321	1174
	.45 T/C Maxi-Ball/220 gr.	2Fg	80–100	11	1653	1340
.50	RB .498/180 gr.	3Fg	100–150	11	1072	1717
	#504617 .503/370 gr.	3Fg	60–85	11	1331	1462
.50 T/C Hawken	T/C Maxi-Ball/370 gr.	2Fg	80–100	11	1653	1340
	RB .490/165 gr.	2Fg	70–110	11	1889	1499
50 Custom	RB .500/170 gr.	3Fg	120–160	11	2073	1620
.50 Issue Maynard [5]	.517	3Fg	50			

BLACK POWDER LOAD DATA FOR HANDGUNS[1,2]

CALIBER	PROJECTILE ⌀ in./gr.	POWDER	CHARGE gr.	CAP	FPS (Vo) average	FT/LB (Eo) average
.31 Baby Dragoon Replica	RB[4] .319/50 gr.	3Fg	10–13	12	647	47
		4Fg	10–13	12	744	61
.31 Original Cap & Ball Revolvers[5]	RB .321	3Fg	15			
.36 Replicas	RB .375/81 gr.	3Fg	20–26	11	1023	188
		4Fg	20–26	11	1019	187
	#37583 .375/150 gr.	3Fg	9–13	11	530	95
		4Fg	9–13	11	620	129
.36 Original Cap & Ball Revolvers[5]	.376	3Fg	22			
.40 Replicas[5]	.395	3Fg	25			
.41 Derringer[5]	.395	3Fg	10			
.44 Replica Army	RB .451/138 gr.	3Fg	25–31	11	869	232
		4Fg	25–34	11	910	254
	#450229 .450/155 gr	3Fg	19–25	11	793	219
		4Fg	19–25	11	797	219
.44 Dragoon[5]	.453	3Fg	40			
.44 Original Colt & Remington Army[5]	.453	3Fg	28			
.44 Dragoon Replica	RB .451/136 gr.	3Fg	38	11	990	298
.45 T/C Patriot	RB .440/128 gr.	3Fg	25–32	11	820	194
.45 Ruger	RB .457/185 gr.	3Fg	20–40	10	887	322
		4Fg	20–40	10	1000	410
	#45468 .454/185 gr.	3Fg	26–34	10	765	240
	#45467 .454/190 gr.	3Fg	26–33	10	757	240
		4Fg	26–34	10	856	319
.54 U.S. Pistols Models 1819–42[5]	.535	2Fg	35			
.58 U.S. Springfield Model 1855[5]	.570–.575	2Fg	40			
.67 Tower Flint Pistol[5]	.650	3Fg	35			

Footnotes:

1 Lyman Black Powder Handbook
2 Hodgdon's Black Powder Data Manual #1
3 Gearhart-Qwen powder was used for all tests
4 Round balls were not patched for sixguns, single-shot handgun balls were loaded patched as in rifles.
5 Data from Dixie Gun Works

BLACK POWDER LOAD DATA FOR RIFLED LONG GUNS [1,2]

CALIBER	PROJECTILE Ø in./gr.	POWDER	CHARGE gr.	CAP	FPS (Vo) average	FT/LB (Eo) average
.50 Smith Carbine [5]	.515	3Fg	50			
.52 Sharps [5]	.535–.555	3Fg	60			
.54 Gallager original [5]	.535	3Fg	55			
.54 Burnside [5]	.558	3Fg	60			
.54 Greene Carbine [5]	.565–.569	3Fg	68			
.54 U.S. Miss. rifle [5] & Models '04, '04, 1875 [5]	.535	3Fg	75			
.54	RB .535/220 gr.	3Fg	90–130	Musket	1752	1510
	#533476 .533/410 gr.	3Fg	80–110	Musket	1421	1849
.54 Hall Carbine [5]	.535	2Fg	85			
.54 .54 Hall Rifle [5]	.535	3Fg	100			
.58	RB .560/260 gr	2Fg	110–160	Musket	1410	1158
	#57730 .577/570 gr.	2Fg	75–100	Musket	971	1203
	#577611 .577/539 gr.	2Fg	120–170	Musket	1159	1587
	#575213 .575/505 gr.	2Fg	110–140	Musket	1194	1602
.58 Zouave [5]	.570–.575	2Fg	60			
Confederate muskets and U.S. Models 1855, '61, '63: Same data as .58 Zouave [5].						
.58	#575494 .575/315 gr.	2Fg	100–140	Musket	1278	1158
	#575602 .575/400 gr.	2Fg	100–140	Musket	1141	1163
.577 Enfield Rifle Original [5]	.570–.575	2Fg	60			
.577 Replica Enfield Musketoon from Jana, made by Parker-Hale	#575213 .575/500 ge.	2Fg	70	Musket	1045	1220
.69 U.S. Muskets 1808–1842 Models [5]	.680	2Fg	80			
.69 Whitneyville Plymouth Navy Rifle [5]	.680	2Fg	70			
.75 Brown Bess smoothbore	RB .715/545 gr.	2Fg	70–120	4FG	953	1118
				Priming Charge-Flintlock		

Footnotes:

1 Lyman Black Powder Handbook

2 Hodgdon's Black Powder Data Manual #1

3 Gearhart-Owen powders used primarily in these tests. Curtis & Harvey powders consistently gave lower velocities with the same charges, and accuracy with C & H powder was not as good and consistent as with G-O powders

4 All round balls were patched and lubed with Hodgdon's Spit Patch

5 Data from Dixie Gun Works

BLACK POWDER MATH...

Ballistic calculations are based on some of the known data about the projectile: its velocity, or perhaps even the energy from which the velocity can be readily calculated. Why mold makers indicate the weight of bullets on the mold boxes, but never the weight of a round ball, is one of the minor mysteries of the bullet casting field. Of course, you can always weigh 10 or 20 balls and get the mean, or average, weight of them, but this takes time and also requires that you have a scale handy.

There is an easy way to calculate the weight of a round ball. If:

W = is the weight in grains
c = is the caliber of the round ball,

Then:

$$W = 1500 \, (c)^3$$

Thus, the weight of a .45 caliber round lead ball is calculated this way:

$$W = 1500 \, (.45)^3$$
$$W = 136.6875 \text{ grains}$$

If, on the other hand, the weight of a big Minie bullet is given in ounces, multiply the ounce figure by 437.5 to obtain the weight of the bullet in grains.

Energy, and this means energy at all ranges, is a mathematical function of the projectile weight and velocity, expressed in feet-per-second, or fps. Sometimes, the bullet energy is also called kinetic energy, and the formula for this is:

$$E = \frac{WV^2}{450,240}$$

Where:

V = is the velocity in fps
W = is the weight of the projectile in grains

and:

E = is the kinetic energy expressed in foot/pounds

Chronographing projectiles from black powder guns is not very much different from running chronograph tests with centerfire or rimfire ammunition, except of course that the clouds of smoke can make shooting a bit difficult. When photoelectric screens are used, with the start screen within five feet of the gun muzzle, the billowing clouds of black powder smoke can totally obscure the light source in the screen, thus stopping any further chronographing until the air is cleared.

If shooting indoors, it is essential to have the exhaust fan of the range working at maximum capacity. Indoors, the start screen should be set up between 10–20 feet from the gun muzzle to avoid interference of the powder smoke with the functioning of the photoelectric screen. Since the effective range of black powder guns is somewhat limited, the desire of some black powder shooters to perform velocity tests at 100 yards, and sometimes even at longer ranges, seems somewhat useless.

On the whole, chronographing with black powder guns is best done on an outdoor range, although it must be understood that conditions at such a facility will almost certainly introduce some variable artifacts, such as temperature, humidity, wind, mirage

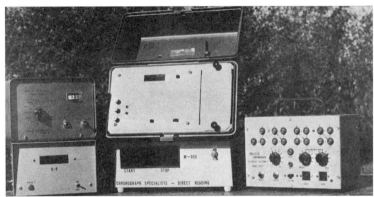

A few of the chronographs which were tested with black powder projectiles. Chronographs using printed screens are somewhat more tedious to use than photoelectric screens, but have the advantage of lower cost. Moreover, they are not affected by clouds of powder smoke.

and others. A simple chronograph is more than adequate for all black powder ballistics, since extending calculations to long ranges poses a mass of hypothetical questions and eventually becomes an exercise in futility.

A battery operated chronograph, either dry cell or wet cell from your car, will do nicely. The newer chronographs with ambient light screens, while great for measuring the speed of a bullet fired from a centerfire gun, apparently are affected by the powder gases, often giving false readings, since the smoke "breaks" the light screen. Thus, the ambient light screen records, in effect, the speed of the powder smoke. For this reason, the printed circuit screens have worked out better, at least they did when 15 chronographs were tested for performance with black powder guns.

To obtain ballistic information about your projectiles, you need to have the ballistic coefficient of the projectile and a set of Ingalls Tables, which can be found in such texts as *Hatcher's Notebook,* and in computerized form in Lowry's *Exterior Ballistics of Small Arms Projectiles.*

The ballistic coefficient is the ratio of the sectional density of the projectile to its coefficient of form. The sectional density is the ratio of a projectile expressed in pounds to the square of its diameter expressed in inches. The coefficient of form is a mathematical index that describes the shape of the projectile point or the ogive of the projectile.

To calculate the ballistic coefficient – and this figure is needed for both the Ingalls and the Lowry tables – use the following formula:

$$C = \frac{w}{id^2}$$

where:

C = ballistic coefficient
w = weight of projectile in lbs.
d = diameter of the projectile in inches
i = form factor

In the case of a round ball, the form factor is in direct relationship with the velocity of the ball. If the velocity exceeds 1300 fps, the form factor is 1.40; if the velocity is between 1000 and 1300 fps, the value of i is 1.70; if the velocity falls below 1000 fps, then the i value is 2.00.

Thanks to the relatively poor ballistic configuration of the round ball and its limited range, the form factor of 1.70 can be used for all round ball ballistic calculations. Interpolating the form factor and other data, the ballistic coefficient for round balls is:

Caliber	Ballistic Coefficient
.31–.32	.040
.36	.045
.40–.41	.050
.44–.45	.057
.50	.071
.54	.068
.58	.071

If you are using the Lowry tables, this is all of the information you need to carry out the ballistic calculations both for round balls and conical bullets — you can determine the ballistic coefficient of the bullet by means of the Bugless and Coxe DuPont tables which can be found in *Hatcher's Notebook* as well as in others, such as Whelen's *Small Arms Design and Ballistics*.

In practice, there is relatively little difference in the results obtained with the Ingalls tables and with those obtained when the Hodsock tables are used. Since Ingalls tables are somewhat more readily available, the following formula is used:

$$C = \frac{X}{S9\,(v) - s\,(V)}$$

and S(v) and S(V) are the space functions for velocities v and v

Here,
C = ballistic coefficient
X = range in feet
V = initial velocity or MV

v = velocity at distance X
S(v) = velocity function from Ingalls tables S(u)
S(V) = velocity function from Ingalls tables S(u)

If you have the muzzle velocity, the ballistic coefficient and the distance, you can readily calculate the speed of the projectile at any range.

$$\text{Here, } S\,(v) = S\,(V) + \frac{X}{C}$$

where

V = is muzzle velocity
X = is the range
C = is the ballistic coefficient

Although it is best to determine the mid-range trajectory by actual shooting tests, it is possible to calculate this as well as time of flight, which then allows you to determine the maximum ordinate which is almost identical to the mid-range trajectory.

To determine MRT (mid-range trajectory), this equation is used:

$$H \text{ (in inches)} = 48\,T\,2$$

and if the maximum ordinate is known and time of flight must be calculated, then:

$$T_F = \frac{1}{4}\,\frac{H}{3}$$

and H will be in inches.

With this handful of formulae, a chronograph and the Ingalls tables, you can perform all of the needed ballistics calculations for black powder projectiles as well as for any other bullet or missile. But remember that actual shooting tests will tell you at least as much as all the formulae, and it's lot more fun to shoot than to dope out ballistics tables.

Early powder flasks, left: wood with bone inlay, right: bone with silver fittings.

Shooting the Muzzleloaders

Chapter 11
BLACK POWDER GUN CATALOG

Because of the fluctuating value of the American dollar abroad and increased production costs, the prices given here are, at best, approximations. However, they were correct at the time this listing was compiled.

Relatively few of the currently available replicas are made in the United States, and in some cases, one foreign gun maker produces identical guns for several importers, marking the guns with each importer's name. With but few exceptions, foreign-made guns must undergo the prescribed proof testing of the country of origin so that they can be sold locally or exported. A proof mark indicates that the barrel and, in some cases, the firing mechanism function safely and in a satisfactory manner. However, a proof mark does not guarantee the quality of the finish, stockwork, bluing or inletting. Because of conditions beyond their control, many importers encounter problems in getting products of consistent quality from their foreign suppliers.

Many of the replica guns now offered are relatively true copies of the originals, but equally as many of these guns bear little or no resemblance to any early black powder gun. While black powder purists may frown on shooting a "replica" which is really not one, there are just as many avid and devoted black powder shooters who do enjoy these guns. Very often, a gun tinkerer will modify, change, alter and rebuild such a gun, ending up with a specimen that may resemble an original made by one of the early makers. When each gun was totally hand-made by such a craftsman, resemblance between guns was often almost totally lacking. Many gun tinkerers

install modern sights or copies of original sights, stone hammers, install special triggers, add brass furniture, or even completely restock their modern black powder guns.

Many dealers handle the products of several importers as well as domestic makers, but you can often buy guns directly from the importer or maker since black powder guns do not fall under the Gun Control Act of 1968.

For your convenience, the following listing is grouped first by ignition system, then by type of gun. Thus, the single-shot flintlock handguns are first, then follow the single-shot percussion handguns. These are followed by the percussion revolver and other multi-shot handguns.

Next come the rifles and muskets, again with the flintlock guns leading off the listings, followed by the percussion long guns, with multi-shot rifled long guns closing this section of the catalog.

The last group includes the single and double barrel shotguns — again, the flinters are listed first, with percussion models following.

Because quality varies quite a bit from shipment to shipment, no attempt has been made to comment on the individual guns. The prospective buyer is urged to examine the gun or guns of his choice personally.

SINGLE-SHOT HANDGUNS-FLINTLOCKS

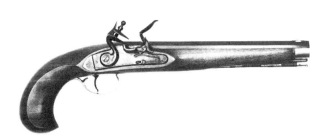

KENTUCKY PISTOL 1830, MODEL P 127
Caliber .45, length 15 1/2 inches, weight 35 ounces.
Gooseneck hammer, casehardened flintlock,
polished walnut stock.
Rifled octagonal barrel, dovetail rear and front blade
sight,
brass-tipped ramrod.

PRICE: $ 63.65 / FROM: The Armoury, Inc.

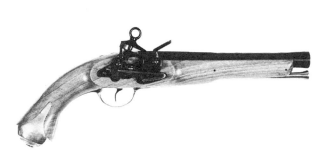

RIPOLL BELT PISTOL, MODEL FP 306
Miquelet-type flintlock
Caliber .61, barrel length 8 3/4 inches,
overall length 15 inches, weight 40 ounces.
Cold-forged, rifled barrel is half-round,
half-octagonal and is slightly flared at muzzle, blued,
brass furniture, polished walnut stock.
Gun has hook for belt carry, ramrod is solid brass.
Made in Spain and carries proofmarks.

PRICE: $ 84.95 /
FROM: Connecticut Valley Arms (C. V. A.)

RIPOLL BOOT PISTOL, MODEL FP 307
A somewhat smaller and more graceful version of the
above model, complete with belt or boot hook.
Caliber .45, barrel length 4 inches, overall length
8 1/4 inches, weight 17 ounces.
Scroll engraving along entire barrel which is octagonal for 2/3 of its length with rounded muzzle, barrel
is cold-forged, rifled, blued.
Brass furniture, polished walnut stock.

PRICE: $ 79.95 / FROM: C. V. A.

169

ENGLISH BELT PISTOL, MODEL FP 302

Good shooter with rifled, fully octagonal barrel. Caliber .45 (.451 bore), barrel length 7 inches, overall length 12 inches, weight 30 ounces.

Blued barrel, casehardened lock that is brass mounted.

Dovetail rear and bead front sight, walnut stock, steel ramrod.

Also available in percussion system, complete with steel nipple wrench.

PRICE: $ 40.95 / FROM: C. V. A.

TOWER PISTOL, MODEL FP 301

Based on English horse pistol, but caliber has been reduced to more manageable .45 (.451 bore).

Barrel length 7 inches, overall length 11 1/2 inches, weight 27 ounces.

Octagonal barrel, blued, brass fittings, casehardened lock, high polish walnut stock, steel ramrod.

Also available in percussion system, complete with steel nipple wrench.

PRICE: $ 57.95 / FROM: C. V. A.

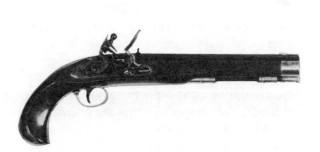

KENTUCKY PISTOL

Caliber .45 (.451 bore), barrel length 10 1/2 inches, overall length 15 1/4 inches, weight 40 ounces.

Octagonal rifled barrel, 7/8 inch across flats, color casehardened lock, hardened frizzen, lock is polished for certain sparking.

Brass Kentucky blade type front sight and dovetail open rear sight.

Brass furniture, hardwood ramrod with brass-tipped concave end.

PRICE: $ 59.95 / FROM: C. V. A.

170

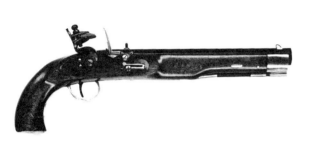

DIXIE KENTUCKY-STYLE PISTOL, MODEL DFP - 41

Caliber .45 (.445 ball), barrel length 9 inches, overall length 15 1/2 inches, weight 33 ounces.
Kentucky-type rifling, barrel measures 13/16 inches across flats,
Kentucky-style sights, brass furniture and brass barrel wedge.
Maple stock finished to resemble cherry wood.

PRICE: $ 89.95 / FROM: Dixie Gun Works

DIXIE TOWER PISTOL, MODEL DFP - 39

Caliber .67 (.670 bore, use .650 mold), 9 1/2 inch steel barrel, overall length 14 inches, weight 40 ounces.
Most of these tower locks are not good sparkers. Dixie will harden frizzen and adjust springs to make lock spark to perfection for $ 4.00 if gun is bought from Dixie, for $ 6.50 if gun is bought elsewhere.

PRICE: $ 36.75 / FROM: Dixie Gun Works

FLORENTINE HOLSTER FLINTLOCK PISTOL, MODEL DFP - 38

Caliber .50, barrel length 13 inches, overall length 21 inches, weight not specified.
Smoothbored barrel, all furniture are ornamental and, with exception of lock, are of antique silver-plate finish.
Walnut stock is handrubbed.

PRICE: $ 209.95 / FROM: Dixie Gun Works

171

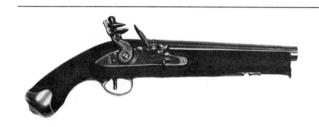

TOWER FLINTLOCK PISTOL, MODEL 1776

Caliber .69, barrel length 9 1/2 inches, overall length 16 inches, weight 3 pounds.
Engraved lock, brass furniture, polished stock.
PRICE: $ 39.95 / FROM: EMF Co., Inc.

KENTUCKY FLINTLOCK PISTOL, MODEL FL 104

Caliber .44, barrel length 10 1/4 inches, overall length 15 1/2 inches, weight not specified.
Lock and side plate casehardened and with light engraving, polished brass furniture, hand finished English walnut stock.
Brass blade front sight, dovetail rear fixed sight, rifled barrel, deep blue finish.
PRICE: $ 49.50 / FROM: EMF Co., Inc.

TOWER FLINTLOCK, MODEL ML 4
(not shown)

Caliber .69, barrel length 9 inches, overall length 15 1/2 inches, weight 3 pounds.
Smoothbored barrel, brass furniture, engraved lock.
Cherry wood stock, ramrod.
PRICE: $ 44.95 /
FROM: Firearms Import and Export Corp.

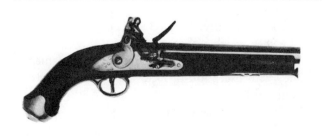

TOWER FLINTLOCK, MODEL 503

Caliber .69, barrel length 8 1/2 inches, overall length 16 inches, weight 3 pounds.
This pistol is sold as a decorator and not as shooter.
Engraved lock plates, brass mountings and furniture, ramrod.
PRICE: $ 39.95 / FROM: Hawes Firearms

KENTUCKIAN FLINTLOCK PISTOL,
IBM: 1811–94

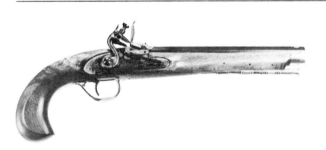

Caliber .44, barrel length 10 1/8 inches, overall length 15 1/2 inches, weight 33 ounces.
Casehardened lock, blued barrel, brass furniture, ramrod, hand polished stock.

PRICE: $ 51.95 / FROM: Liberty Arms Corp.

BROWN BESS FLINTLOCK PISTOL,

IBM: 180599 Standard /
IBM: 180699 Deluxe /
IBM: 181099 Octagonal Barrel /
IBM: 181099 Octagonal Barrel with Stand

Caliber .69, barrel length 8 1/4 inches, overall length 14 inches, weight 40 ounces. Engraved lock, brass fittings, ramrod, well finished stock.

PRICE: $ 32.50 180599 / $ 33.75 180699 /
$ 36.35 181099 / $ 33.75 180899 /
FROM: Liberty Arms Corp.

HARPERS FERRY FLINTLOCK PISTOL,
IBM: 180799 Standard / IBM: 180999 Deluxe

Caliber .54, barrel length 10 inches, overall length 16 inches, weight 40 ounces.
Brass mounted, browned barrel, casehardened lock. Fixed sights, walnut stock.

PRICE: $ 38.95 180799 / $ 40.25 180999 /
FROM: Liberty Arms Corp.

173

ZANOTTI FLINTLOCK PISTOL, IBM: 188 090
Caliber .50, barrel length 12 inches, overall length
19 1/2 inches, weight not specified.
Highly ornate, with good engraving, muzzle is
slightly belled, ramrod.
PRICE: $ 108.00 / FROM: Liberty Arms Corp.

1806 HARPERS FERRY FLINTLOCK PISTOL
Caliber .58, barrel length 10 inches, overall length
16 inches, weight 40 ounces.
Authentic reproduction of the original.
Walnut stock, casehardened lock, brass mounted,
browned barrel, fixed sights.
PRICE: $ 95.00 / FROM: Navy Arms Co., Inc.

REVOLUTIONARY HESSIAN
FLINTLOCK PISTOL
Caliber .69, barrel length 14 inches, overall length
22 inches, weight 2 1/2 pounds.
This classic replica is a true copy.
Brass bound, well finished stock, ramrod, polished
lock.
PRICE: $ 95.00 / FROM: Navy Arms Co., Inc.

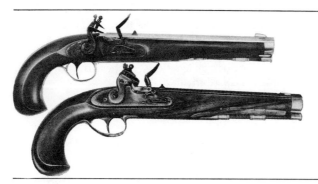

1820 KENTUCKY FLINTLOCK PISTOL
Caliber .44, barrel length 10 1/8 inches, overall
length 15 1/2 inches, weight 32 ounces.
Fixed sights, casehardened lock, polished walnut
stock, brass furniture.
Also offered with brass barrel, and both models a-
vailable also in percussion system.
PRICE: $ 90.00 / $ 95.00 with brass barrel /
FROM: Navy Arms Co., Inc.

PENNSYLVANIA FLINTLOCK PISTOL

Caliber .44, barrel length 10 inches, overall length 15 1/2 inches, weight 32 ounces.
Brass fittings, handrubbed wood, barrel wedge, ramrod.

PRICE: $ 86.00 / FROM: Richland Arms Co.

REVOLUTIONARY WAR HESSIAN FLINTLOCK, MODEL 217

Caliber .69, barrel length 14 inches, overall length 22 inches, weight 2 1/2 pounds.
Brass bound, well executed and finished copy.
Polished stock and polished lock, ramrod. Imported by Navy Arms/Replica Arms.

PRICE: $ 95.00 /
FROM: Smokepole Musket Co., Inc.

KENTUCKY PISTOL, MODEL 219

Caliber .44, barrel length 10 1/8 inches, overall length 15 1/2 inches, weight 32 ounces.
Casehardened lock, polished walnut stock, brass fittings, fixed sights.
Imported by Navy Arms/Replica Arms.

PRICE: $ 90.00 /
FROM: Smokepole Musket Co., Inc.

SINGLE-SHOT HANDGUNS-PERCUSSION

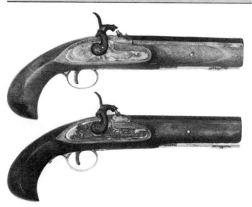

KENTUCKY BELT PISTOL, MODEL PM 25 / MODEL PM 25 D Deluxe

Caliber .45, barrel length 8 inches, overall length 13 inches, weight 30 ounces.
Casehardened lock, full walnut stock, octagonal barrel, brass-tipped ramrod.
Deluxe model has fully engraved lock and barrel.

PRICE: $ 44.45 PM 25 / $ 51.25 PM 25 D
FROM: The Armoury, Inc.

ORIGINAL MODEL 1850 DELUXE KENTUCKY PISTOL, MODEL 125

Caliber .45, barrel length 10 inches, overall length 15 1/2 inches, weight 35 ounces.
Casehardened lock, slim contoured walnut stock, deep rifled octagonal barrel, dovetail rear and brass blade front sight.
Brass-tipped ramrod, nipple in original flash shield bolster.

PRICE: $ 63.65 / FROM: The Armoury, Inc.

PHILADELPHIA TYPE DERRINGER, MODEL DM 1

Caliber .41, barrel length 3 1/8 inches, overall length 8 1/4 inches, weight 17 ounces.
Walnut stock with checkering, engraved back action lock, barrel also engraved, steel ramrod.

PRICE: $ 33.25 / FROM: The Armoury, Inc.

NEW ORLEANS ACE,
MODEL B 10 BP with bayonet /
B 10 RP with ramrod / B 1 RP with rifled barrel /
E 10 P extra smoothbore barrel /
E 1 RP extra rifled barrel
Caliber .44, barrel length 4 1/2 inches, overall length 9 1/4 inches, weight 1 pound.
Ordnance steel barrel, solid brass receiver.
PRICE: $ 39.95 B 10 BP / $ 39.95 B 10 RP /
$ 44.95 B 1 RP / $ 7.95 E 10 P / $ 9.95 E 1 RP /
FROM: Classic Arms International Ltd.

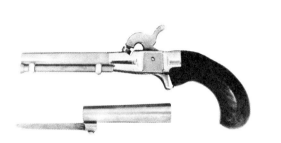

KENTUCKY PISTOL,
MODEL PP 206 / PP 205 Deluxe
Caliber .45 (.451 bore), barrel length 10 1/2 inches, overall length 15 1/4 inches, weight 40 ounces.
Rifled, octagonal, blued barrel, brass fittings, casehardened lock.
Dovetail Kentucky front and rear sights, brass-tipped hardwood ramrod.
Fully adjustable trigger pull, nipple wrench included.
PRICE: $ 54.95 PP 206 / $ 63.95 PP 205 engraved /
FROM: C. V. A.

KENTUCKY BELT PISTOL, MODEL PP 202
Caliber .45 (.451 bore), barrel length 7 inches, overall length 11 1/2 inches, weight 27 ounces.
Rifled octagonal barrel, high lustre blue, oil finished walnut stock.
Brass fittings, engraved lock, dovetail open rear sight, brass bead front sight.
Complete with steel nipple wrench.
PRICE: $ 38.95 / FROM: C. V. A.

177

PHILADELPHIA DERRINGER, MODEL PP 204

Caliber .45, barrel length 3 1/8 inches, overall length 7 1/8 inches, weight 14 ounces.
Casehardened lock, brass fittings, back action lock, stock is walnut-finished.

PRICE: $ 29.95 / FROM: C. V. A.

ENGLISH BELT PISTOL, MODEL PP 201

Caliber .45 (.451 bore), barrel length 7 inches, overall length 12 inches , weight 30 ounces.
Octagonal blued and rifled barrel, casehardened lock, dovetail rear and brass bead front sight.
Walnut stained stock, brass fittings, steel ramrod and nipple wrench.

PRICE: $ 36.95 / FROM: C. V. A.

TOWER PERCUSSION PISTOL, MODEL PP 203

Caliber .45 (.451 bore), barrel length 8 1/4 inches, overall length 14 1/4 inches, weight 39 ounces.
Original caliber reduced to more shootable .44 caliber, casehardened lock, round smoothbored and blued barrel.
Walnut stock, steel ramrod and nipple wrench.

PRICE: $ 53.95 / FROM: C. V. A.

DIXIE PHILADELPHIA DERRINGER

Caliber .41, barrel length 2 1/2 inches, overall length 5 1/2 inches, weight 1 pound.
Browned barrel with 8-groove rifling, gun is marked „DERINGER PHILADELPHIA".
Back action lock and tang are fully engraved, as is hammer.
Brass front blade sight and non-adjustable open rear sight, European walnut stock with German silver fittings.

PRICE: $ 99.50 / FROM: Dixie Gun Works

DIXIE KENTUCKY PERCUSSION PISTOL, MODEL DPP - 42

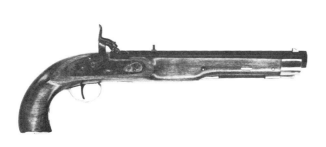

Caliber .45, barrel length 9 inches, overall length 14 inches, weight 29 ounces.
Full maple stock is stained to resemble cherry, wedge and all other fittings are brass.
Barrel is 13/16 inches across flats, Kentucky sights and rifling.

PRICE: $ 89.95 / FROM: Dixie Gun Works

PHILADELPHIA DERRINGER, MODEL DPP - 44

Caliber .41, barrel length 3 1/2 inches, overall length 5 1/2 inches, weight 8 ounces.
Barrel and lock are blued, brass furniture, walnut stock.

PRICE: $ 27.95 / FROM: Dixie Gun Works

179

DIXIE BRASS FRAME DERRINGER,
MODEL DPP - 43 / DPP - 43 E engraved

Caliber .41, barrel length 2 1/2 inches, overall length 5 1/2 inches, weight 7 ounces.
Walnut stock, brass frame, casehardened hammer and trigger.
Shoots .395" round ball.

PRICE: $ 25.50 DPP - 43 / $ 32.50 DPP - 43 E
FROM: Dixie Gun Works

DIXIE OVERCOAT PISTOL,
MODEL MX 3 plain / MX 35 engraved

Caliber .39, barrel length 4 inches, overall length 8 inches, weight 13 ounces.
Use .380 balls, barrel is smoothbored, barrel and trigger guard blued.
Breechplug and engraved lock are nicely burnished.

PRICE: $ 26.95 MX 3 / $ 34.50 MX 35 /
FROM: Dixie Gun Works

SPANISH PERCUSSION PISTOL,
MODEL DPP - 47

Caliber .40, length and weight are not specified.
Barrel is smoothbore, fires shot or a round ball.
Checkered grips, steel fittings and ramrod.
Use .395" ball, no. 11 cap, and 20 grains of FFFg black powder.

PRICE: $ 25.95 / FROM: Dixie Gun Works

DIXIE DUELLING PISTOL, MODEL DPP - 48

Caliber varies, runs from .44 to .50, barrel length 9 inches, overall length 15 1/4 inches, weight 20 ounces.
Checkered maple stock, fixed sights.
Shoots round ball or shot.

PRICE: $ 69.95 / FROM: Dixie Gun Works

THE TROPHY WINNER, MODEL D-E-001

Caliber .44, barrel length 10 inches, overall length 12 3/4 inches, weight 42 ounces.
Casehardened frame decorated with etched Western Scene on both sides.
Octagonal barrel has 7 lands and 7 grooves of equal width, fixed ramp blade sight, adjustable rear sight.
Use .435 ball, no. 11 caps on .245 x 28 nipple.
Also available is a 28 gauge smoothbore barrel with brass front sight that is easily installed.

PRICE: $ 49.50 / $ 12.95 D-E-002 shotgun barrel / FROM: Dixie Gun Works

KENTUCKY PISTOL

Caliber .44, barrel length 10 1/4 inches, overall length 15 1/2 inches, weight 43 ounces.
Rifled blued barrel, lock and side plate casehardened, lock enhanced by light engraving.
Hand finished walnut stock, brass fittings.

PRICE: $ 43.90 / FROM: EMF Co., Inc.

CUSTOM DELUXE TARGET PERCUSSION

Caliber .44, barrel length 9 inches, overall length not specified, weight 43 ounces.

Octagonal blued barrel, casehardened frame, brass back strap and trigger guard, special target sights.

PRICE: about $ 65.00 / FROM: EMF., Inc.

KENTUCKIAN PERCUSSION PISTOL, MODEL ML 7 P (not shown)

Caliber .44, barrel length 9 1/2 inches, overall length 15 1/2 inches, weight 34 ounces.

Heavy rifled octagonal barrel, polished brass fittings, ramrod.

Selected, hand finished walnut stock.

PRICE: $ 59.95 /
FROM: Firearms Import and Export Corp.

TRAPPER'S PISTOL (not shown)

Calibers .45, .50, .54, and .58.

A fine copy of the original trapper pistol from the days of the fur traders.

8 inch barrel rifled 1:20, .012" deep grooves.

Single trigger, brass fittings, maple half-stock.

Also available in kit form, for $ 95.00.

PRICE: $ 150.00 /
FROM: Green River Rifle Works

KENTUCKY PISTOL, MODEL 508 P (not shown)

Caliber .44, barrel length 9 1/2 inches, overall length 15 1/2 inches, weight 40 ounces.

Casehardened engraved lock plate, solid brass fittings, one piece walnut stock.

Rifled octagonal barrel.

PRICE: $ 82.45 / FROM: Hawes Firearms

PHILADELPHIA DERRINGER, IBM 185 394

Caliber .44, barrel length 3 1/2 inches, overall length not specified, weight about 16 ounces.
Octagonal barrel, action and barrel engraved, checkering on grip, ramrod.

PRICE: about $ 25.00 /
FROM: Liberty Arms Corp.

HUNTSMAN, MODEL SSP 701 (not shown)

Standard / SSP 702 Engraved / SBL 002 28 gauge shotgun barrel

Caliber .44, barrel length 9 inches, overall length not specified, weight 42 ounces.

Octagonal blued barrel, brass back strap and trigger guard, casehardened frame and hammer.
Walnut stock, fixed blade front sight, fully adjustable rear sight. 7 groove ordnance steel barrel, best results were obtained with a .435 round ball.
PRICE: $ 70.00 SSP 701 / $ 90.00 SSP 702 /
$ 15.00 SBL 002 / FROM: Navy Arms Co., Inc.

HOPKINS & ALLEN BOOT PISTOL

Choice of .36 or .45 caliber, barrel length 6 inches, overall length 13 inches, weight 34 ounces.
Underhammer gun has octagonal barrel, 15/16 inches across the flats. Simple firing system design that has been well proved over the years.
PRICE: $ 39.95 / FROM: Nummrich Arms Corp.

183

HARPERS FERRY DRAGOON PISTOL,
MODEL 1855

Caliber .58, barrel length 11 3/4 inches, overall length 16 inches, weight 42 ounces.
Originally made for the U.S. Mounted Rifles, shoulder stock came later. Gun was then known as Springfield Pistol Carbine, Model 1855.
Shoulder stock is now optional ($ 30.00). Gun fires the 500 grain Minie bullet, is the most powerful black powder handgun made.
PRICE: $ 95.00 /
FROM: Smokepole Musket Co., Inc.

T/C PATRIOT

Caliber .45, barrel length 9 inches, overall length 16 inches, weight 36 ounces.
Octagonal blued barrel, 13/16 inches across the flats, twist 1:48. Hooked breech system, solid brass trim, walnut stock with ebony ramrod.
Coil spring lock, decorated and color casehardened lock plate, dolphin-shaped hammer, double set triggers.
Fully adjustable target rear sight, front sight post shielded by semi-globe.
PRICE: $ 125.00 / $ 152.50 with accessory pack
FROM: Thompson/Center Arms

SINGLE-SHOT TARGET PISTOL,
MODEL 1960
Caliber .40, barrel length 8 inches – 9, 10 and 12 inch barrels on order, weoght with 8 inch barrel 33 ounces. Octagonal 6 groove barrel, blued, easy to remove.
Fixed front, windage adjustable rear sight, lacquered walnut stock.
PRICE: $ 74.95 / FROM: Tingle Mfg. Co., Inc.

PERCUSSION REVOLVERS

COLT ARMY MODEL 1860 REVOLVER

Caliber .44, barrel length 8 inches, overall length 13 5/8 inches, weight 41 ounces.

Brass trigger guard, steel backstrap, round barrel, rebated cylinder with engraved battle scene, frame cut for shoulder stock.

This is probably the best known and most popular of the cap and ball Colt sixguns. Frame, loading lever and hammer beautifully color casehardened. 6-shot cylinder.

PRICE: $ 63.00 – 115.00

FROM: Armoury, Inc., Dixie Gun Works, EMF Co., Inc., Hawes Firearms, Liberty Arms, Lyman, Navy Arms, Richland Arms

COLT NAVY MODEL 1851

Caliber .36, also .44, barrel length 7 1/2 inches, overall length 13 inches, weight depends on caliber and type frame – either steel or brass.

Famed Colt replica with brass trigger guard, blued rifled octagonal barrel, engraved cylinder, polished walnut grips.

Use no. 11 caps on most guns, .376 balls are usually best in the .36 caliber models.

PRICE: $ 35.00 – 60.00 Brass frame /
$ 82.50 – 166.50 Steel frame

FROM: Armoury Inc., Colt's Firearms, Dixie Gun Works, EMF Co., Firearms Import and Export Corp., Hawes Firearms, Jana International, Liberty Arms, Lyman, Navy Arms, Richland Arms

185

COLT NAVY SHERIFF

Caliber .36 and .44, barrel length 5 inches, overall length 11 1/2 inches, weight about 40 ounces depending on frame.

Shortened version of 1851 Navy Model.

Blued rifled octagonal barrel, brass or steel frame, brass back strap and trigger guard, casehardened hammer and loading lever, 6-shot cylinder engraved with battle scene, caliber .44 may have rebated cylinder.

PRICE: $ 50.00 – 85.00 steel frame /
$ 45.00 – 59.00 brass frame

FROM: Armoury, Inc., Dixie Gun Works, EMF Co., Inc., Liberty Arms, Richland Arms, Smokepole Musket

COLT ARMY SHERIFF (not shown)

Calibers .36 and .44, barrel length 5 inches, overall length 11 1/2 inches, weight depends on caliber.

Shortened version of the 1860 Army Model, considered as the original snub nose revolver and adopted by numerous police departments. Brass frame, blued round barrel

PRICE: $ 60.00 /

FROM: Navy Arms, Smokepole Musket

COLT POLICE MODEL

Caliber .36, barrel length 5 or 7 inches, overall length 10 1/2 or 13 inches, weight 38 or 41 ounces.

A shortened steel frame version of the Colt 1851 Navy.

Octagonal rifled and blued barrel, fluted cylinder, with lanyard ring or belt hook, brass back strap and trigger guard.

PRICE: $ 84.50

FORM: Armoury, Inc., Hawes Firearms

1862 POLICE MODEL

Caliber .36, barrel length 4 1/2, 5 1/2, 6 1/2 inches, overall length about 12 inches depending on barrel length, weight about 26 ounces.
Blued round barrel, 5-shot cylinder half-fluted and rebated, frame, loading lever and hammer casehardened, brass trigger guard and back strap.
Fixed sights and walnut stock.
PRICE: $ 95.00 / $ 199.95 cased with accessories
FROM: Dixie Gun Works, Navy Arms

COLT POCKET MODEL 1849

Caliber .31, barrel length 4 or 6 inches, weight 26 ounces. Walnut stock, fixed sights, round trigger guard.
5-shot steel cylinder with engraving showing Colt Stagecoach hold-up.
PRICE: $ 95.00 / FROM: Navy Arms
Same model only with square-back trigger guard and Indian fight scene engraved on the cylinder available at same price
FROM: Dixie Gun Works, EMF Co.

1849 WELLS FARGO

Caliber .31, barrel length choice of 3, 4, 5, 6 inches, overall length not specified, weight about 22 ounces depending on barrel length.
Walnut stock, fixed sights, V sight notch in hammer.
Blued octagonal barrel, no loading lever, 5-shot engraved cylinder, casehardened frame and hammer, brass back strap and square-back trigger guard.
PRICE: $ 55.00–95.00
FROM: EMF Co., Jana International, Liberty Arms, Navy Arms, Smokepole Musket.

187

COLT FIRST MODEL DRAGOON, M 1845

Caliber .44, barrel length 7 1/2 inches, overall length 14 inches, weight 64 ounces.
Soldier and Indian fight scene engraved on 6-shot cylinder, brass back strap and square-back trigger.
V-type mainspring, oval cylinder stops, vertical closing lever latch. Trigger, frame, hammer and loading lever are casehardened. Use .441 or .442 balls in chambers which mike .440.
PRICE: $ 115.00
FROM: Dixie Gun Works, Navy Arms, Smokepole Musket

COLT SECOND MODEL DRAGOON

Caliber .44, barrel length 7 1/2 inches, overall length 14 inches, weight 64 ounces.
6-shot cylinder fully engraved, color casehardened frame, loading lever and hammer.
Safety notches on hammer, safety pin in cylinder, on piece walnut stock, square-back trigger guard.
PRICE: $ 125.00
FROM: Dixie Gun Works, Navy Arms, EMF Co., Liberty Arms, Smokepole Musket

COLT THIRD MODEL DRAGOON

Caliber .44, barrel 7 1/2 inches, overall length 14 inches, weight 4 pounds, 2 ounces.
Engraved 6-shot cylinder uses .457 round ball.
One piece walnut grip, blade front and fixed V-notch rear sight. Hammer rest position on cylinder between nipples, provision for detachable shoulder stock.
Color casehardened frame, brass back strap and rounded trigger guard, deep blue finish.
PRICE: $ 130.00 / $ 175.00 with detachable shoulder stock
FROM: Colt, Dixie Gun Works, Navy Arms, Smokepole Musket

COLT PATERSON

Caliber .36, barrel length 6, 7 1/2, 9 and 12 inches, overall length 14 1/4 inches with 9 inch barrel weight about 2 3/4 pounds depending in barrel length. Octagonal barrel blued, as are all other metal parts. Walnut grips, fixed sights, engraved 5-shot cylinder. Uses .377 round ball.
PRICE: $ 100.00 /
FROM: Dixie Gun Works, EMF Co., Liberty Arms

COLT WALKER MODEL 1847

Caliber .44, barrel length 9 inches, overall lemgth 15 1/2 inches, weight 72 ounces.
Engraved 6-shot cylinder, brass square-back trigger guard, casehardened frame, loading lever and hammer.
PRICE: $ 110.00 – 130.00 /
$ 250.00 completely engraved with gold bands at muzzle from Navy Arms
FROM: Dixie Gun Works, Navy Arms, EMF Co., Jana International, Liberty Arms

COLT BABY DRAGOON MODEL 1848

Caliber .31, barrel length 4, 5, or 6 inches, overall length 10 1/2 inches with 6 inch barrel, weight about 24 ounces depending on barrel. Hinged loading lever, octagonal barrel, 5-shot engraved cylinder. Casehardened frame, square-back brass trigger guard, walnut grips. Safety notches on hammer, safety pin in cylinder.
PRICE: $ 50.95 – 95.00
FROM: EMF Co., Firearms Import and Export, Jana International, Navy Arms

189

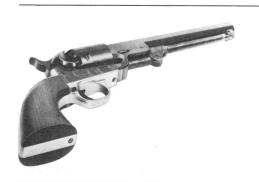

COLT NEW MODEL NAVY - YANK M 1851

Caliber .36, barrel length 7 1/2 inches, overall length 13 inches, weight 42 ounces.
6-shot cylinder roll-engraved with Navy battle scene, brass back strap and trigger guard.
Casehardened frame, hammer and loading lever, octagonal barrel.
PRICE: $ 100.00 /
FROM: Liberty Arms, Navy Arms

THIRD MODEL BUNTLINE DRAGOON

Caliber .44, barrel length 18 inches, overall length and weight not specified.
Gun comes with shoulder stock and holster that holds both gun and stock.
Engraved 6-shot cylinder, brass rounded trigger guard, casehardened loading lever, frame and hammer.
PRICE: $ 195.00 complete /
FROM: Navy Arms, Smokepole Musket

GRISWOLD AND GUNNISON

Calibers .36 and .44 barrel length 7 1/2 inches, overall length 13 inches, weight approximately 40-44 ounces depending on make and caliber. Replica of famous Confederate revolver.
Brass frame and trigger guard, round barrel and 6-shot cylinder of high lustre blue finish, walnut grips.
PRICE: $ 60.00 - 140.00 with presentation case from High Standard
FROM: Dixie Gun Works, High Standard, Navy Arms, Richland Arms, Smokepole Musket

LEECH & RIGDON, MODEL 1862

Caliber .36, barrel length 7 1/2 inches, overall length 13 3/4 inches, weight approximately 40 ounces.
Another of the famous C. S. A. revolvers.
Round Dragoon-type barrel, 6-shot cylinder, steel frame with satin nickel finish, brass trigger guard and back strap.
Walnut grips, fixed sights.
PRICE: $ 100.00 - 139.00 with presentation case from High Standard
FROM: Dixie Gun Works, High Standard, Navy Arms, Smokepole Musket

SPILLER & BURR REVOLVER

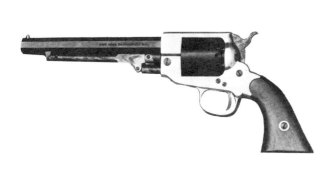

Caliber .36, barrel length 7 inches, overall length 12 1/2 inches, weight 2 1/2 pounds.
Copy of the Whitney revolvers made in the Confederacy.
6-shot cylinder, Dixie models using the .380 ball, safety cut in cylinder between nipples.
Two piece walnut grips, brass trigger guard, back strap and frame.
Casehardened hammer, trigger and loading lever.
Octagonal blued barrel with 6 lands and grooves in contrast with the original rifling of 7 and 7.
PRICE: $ 69.55 - 75.00 /
FROM: Dixie Gun Works, Navy Arms, Richland Arms, Smokepole Musket.

REMINGTON 1858 NEW MODEL ARMY

Calibers .36 and .44, barrel length 6 1/2 inches (.36) or 8 inches (.44), overall length 12 1/2 or 13 1/2 inches depending on caliber, weight about 40 ounces. Blued octagonal barrel, two piece walnut grips, brass trigger guard.

In the smaller caliber, also known as Army Model Belt Revolver.

Fixed front sight, sight groove in top strap.

Some models with brass frame, others with deep blue finish on steel frame as well as cylinder and loading lever.

Trigger and hammer casehardened.

PRICE: $ 57.00 - 109.95 / $ 114.95 engraved /
FROM: Armoury, C. V. A., Dixie, EMF, Firearms Import & Export, Hawes, Jana, Liberty Lyman, Navy Arms, Richland, Smokepole

REMINGTON 1858 NEW TARGET MODEL

Calibers .36 and .44, barrel lengths and weight same as above.

Features are the same as New Model Army above, except that rear sight is adjustable for target shooting.

PRICE: $ 125.00 /
FROM: Armoury, Dixie, Hawes, Navy Arms, Smokepole.

REMINGTON NEW MODEL NAVY

Caliber .36, barrel length 6 1/2 inches, overall length 12 1/4 inches, weight 42 ounces.

Smaller naval version of New Model Army with performance comparable to .38 Special when properly loaded.

Walnut stock, fixed sights, brass trigger guard, steel frame with top strap, heavy duty nipples.

Color casehardened trigger and hammer.

PRICE: $ 109.95 /

FROM: Armoury, Dixie, Hawes, Lyman

RUGER OLD ARMY

Caliber .44 barrel length 7 1/2 inches, overall length 13 1/2 inches, weight 46 ounces.

Blued barrel has 6 grooves, 1 : 16 twist, carries front sight.

6-shot cylinder, uses .457 round ball.

Rear sight fully adjustable.

Not a replica, but design features come from several models and were improved.

Available in stainless steel blued or with solid brass Dragoon-style frame and wide trigger.

PRICE: $ 125.00 blued / $ 140.00 brass frame /

FROM: Sturm, Ruger

OTHER MULTI-SHOT PERCUSSION HANDGUNS

CORSAIR DOUBLE BARREL PISTOL
Calibers .36 and .44, barrel length 8 1/4 inches, overal length 13 3/4 inches, weight about 34 ounces depending on caliber.
Blued, rifled barrels, brass trigger guard and butt cap, lightly engraved.
Walnut stock, ramrod.
PRICE: $ 69.50 - 91.60 /
FROM: Armoury, Hawes, Liberty

DUCKFOOT PERCUSSION PISTOL
Caliber .36, weight 2 pounds, other details not specified.
Early mutiny and riot gun, one cap fires all three barrels.
Solid brass receiver, ordnance steel barrels.
PRICE: $ 49.95 /
FROM: Classic Arms International

DUCKFOOT PERCUSSION PISTOL
(not shown)

Caliber, length and weight specifications not given.
Brass frame, four steel barrels fired with one cap, wood grip.
PRICE: $ 69.95 / FROM: Dixie Gun Works

ETHAN ALLEN PEPPERBOX
Caliber .36, barrel length 3 1/2 inches, overall length 9 inches, weight not specified.
Four barrels are fired in rotation, being indexed manually.
Solid brass receiver, ordnance steel barrels, wood grip.
PRICE: $ 49.95 /
FROM: Classic Arms International

RIFLES AND MUSKETS - SINGLE-SHOT FLINTLOCKS

KENTUCKY FLINTLOCK DELUXE,
MODEL R 122 (not shown)

Caliber .45, barrel length 36 inches, overall length 50 inches, weight 6 1/2 pounds.
Bore diameter .453 Pennsylvania Roman nose style, large brass patch box, casehardened lock.
Octagonal barrel 13/16 inches across flats, walnut stock with cheekpiece.
One piece ramrod with brass tipping at both ends, threaded at the bottom end.
PRICE: $ 146.75 / FROM: The Armoury

KENTUCKY FLINTLOCK RIFLE,
MODEL R 112 (not shown)

Caliber .45, barrel length 36 inches, overall length 50 inches, weight 7 pounds.
Bore diameter .451, casehardened lock with bolster, one piece walnut stock, brass furniture including patch box.
One piece ramrod with fitting at both ends, one end threaded.
PRICE: $ 139.00 / FROM: The Armoury

KENTUCKY CARBINE, MODEL R 113

Caliber .45, barrel length 29 inches, overall length 43 inches, weight 5 1/2 pounds.
Bore diameter .451, casehardened lock, polished brass mountings, cap box with light engraving.
One piece walnut stock, wood ramrod with brass fittings at both ends, threaded at one end.
PRICE: $ 139.00 / FROM: The Armoury

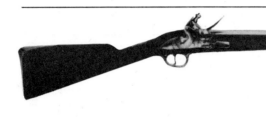

BROWN BESS MUSKET, MODEL BB 1
Caliber .75, barrel length 42 inches, overall length 59 inches, weight not specified.
Barrel and lock polished, as were the originals.
Good shooter as well as decorator for the history-minded gun buff.
PRICE: $ 200.00 / FROM: The Armoury

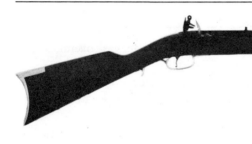

KENTUCKY RIFLE, MODEL FR 501
Caliber .45, barrel length 34 1/2 inches, overall length 50 inches, weight 7 pounds.
Bore .451, octagonal barrel 7/8 inches across flats.
Dark walnut-type stained stock, lock lightly engraved, brass tipped hardwood ramrod.
PRICE: $ 107.95 / FROM: C. V. A.

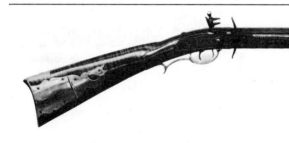

DAY SWIVEL BREECH FLINTLOCK, MODEL SBR – F 1
Caliber .45, barrel length 32 inches, overall length and weight not specified.
Semi-custom made rifle with wood panelled swivel breech, browned Douglas barrel, hand-made lock plates, front trigger unlatches barrel.
Engraving on lock and brass parts as seen on original rifles of the period of about 1840.
PRICE: $ 450.00 / FROM: Dixie Gun Works

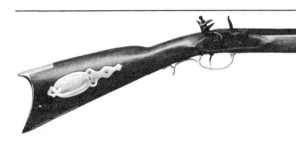

KENTUCKIAN, MODEL 1 FR - 01
Caliber .44, barrel length 33 1/2 inches, overall length 48 inches, weight 6 1/4 pounds.
Octagonal barrel 13/16 inches across flats, 6 lands and 6 grooves, takes .445 - .448 ball.
Brass furniture, casehardened and engraved lock plate, European walnut stock.
Made in Italy and proofed there.
PRICE: $ 145.00 / FROM: Dixie Gun Works

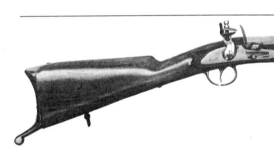

ELEPHANT GUN, MODEL DFR - 13
Six gauge smoothbore, barrel length 34 inches, overall length not specified, weight 11 pounds.
Uses round balls with 200 - 225 grains of black powder.
Hefty recoil, strictly short range gun as used to hunt elephants in Africa.
PRICE: $ 113.00 / FROM: Dixie Gun Works

FLINTLOCK MUSKET, MODEL 79 FLG
Caliber .670, barrel length 37 inches, other specifications not given.
Smoothbore, not a replica but design comes from several sources.
Very accurate, contains some old original parts. Use Dixie mold .660.
PRICE: $ 96.50 / FROM: Dixie Gun Works

197

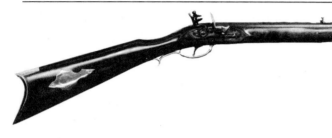

STANDARD KENTUCKY, MODEL DFR - 02

Blued barrel, 13/16 inches across flats, 6 lands and 6 grooves, twist 1:48.
Hard, plain, straight-grain maple stock, Tennessee-style cheekpiece, casehardened lock.
PRICE: $ 189.95 / FROM: Dixie Gun Works

SECOND MODEL BROWN BESS, MODEL DFR - 07

Caliber .75, barrel length 41 3/4 inches, other specifications not given.
A very good copy of the original smoothbored gun.
Lock is marked „Tower" with the mark GR over crown.
Frizzen sparks well, ignition is certain.
PRICE: $ 225.00 / FROM: Dixie Gun Works

BROWN BESS

Caliber .69, other specifications not given.
A copy of the original Tower flintlock gun.
Brass furniture, browned barrel.
PRICE: not given / FROM: EMF

HAWKEN FLINTLOCK RIFLE (not shown)

Available in .45, .50, .54 and .58 calibers and overall lengths not given, weight about 10 1/4 pounds depending on caliber.
Choice of early ornate Hawken-style trigger guard and cheekpiece.
A truly outstanding copy of the original, largely hand-made.
Maple full stock, patent breech with hook and snail.
PRICE: $ 550.00 /
FROM: Green River Rifle Works

KENTUCKY RIFLE (not shown)

Caliber .44, barrel length 35 inches, overall length 50 inches, weight 6 1/2 pounds.
Octagonal barrel, casehardened and engraved lock plate, brass furniture, hardwood ramrod, full stock.
Carbine model: same specifications, except for 27 inch barrel and overall length of 43 inches.
PRICE: $ 174.95 rifle and carbine / FROM: Hawes

TOWER FLINTLOCK RIFLE,
IBM: 189299 standard
IBM: 189399 deluxe

Caliber .69, no other specifications given.
Another copy, made abroad, of the classic Tower rifle.
PRICE: $ 78.00 standard / $ 85.00 deluxe /
FROM: Liberty Arms

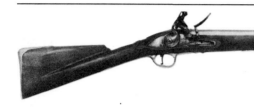

BROWN BESS MUSKET
Caliber .75, barrel length 42 inches, overall length 59 inches, weight 10 1/2 pounds.
A fine replica of the "New Land Pattern".
Barrel and lock are brightly polished, walnut-finished stock, polished brass trigger guard.
Use patched .735" round ball.
PRICE: $ 275.00 / FROM: Lyman

BROWN BESS MUSKET, MODEL JBM 809
Caliber .69, no other specifications given.
This replica musket is made in Japan, is also offered in kit form.
Aside from caliber and other minor differences, this is a fair copy of the original.
PRICE: $ 250.00 / FROM: Navy Arms

BROWN BESS, MODEL BBM 709 Musket / MODEL BBC 710 Carbine
Caliber .75, barrel length 42 inches for musket, 30 1/2 inches for carbine, other specifications not given.
A precise copy of the original "New Land Pattern" gun, including hand-engraved lock.
Made in limited quantity only.
PRICE: $ 325.00 either style / FROM: Navy Arms

BLUNDERBUSS, MODEL NMB 301

This short-range defense gun is a copy of a British original.

The blunderbuss came originally from Holland, and this replica has a 15 1/2 inch turned barrel with a cannon motif, made of highly polished brass. The trigger guard, side and butt plates are engraved.

PRICE: $ 125.00 / FROM: Navy Arms

HARPERS FERRY RIFLE, MODEL OF 1803, MODEL FRM 180

This .58 caliber copy is said to be the most authentic replica of this famous rifle.

Browned barrel, walnut stock, highly polished brass furniture.

PRICE: $ 200.00 / FROM: Navy Arms

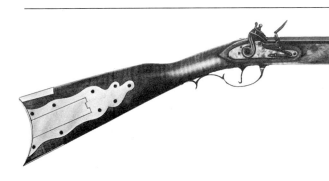

MINUTEMAN BRUSH RIFLE

Calibers .45 and .50, 24 inch barrel length, overall length not specified, weight 8 pounds.

This rifle is available either smoothbored or rifled.

Octagonal blued barrel and lock, polished brass furniture, hand rubbed maple stock.

PRICE: $ 179.50 / FROM: Numrich Arms

KENTUCKY RIFLE

Choice of .31, .36, .45 or .50 caliber, no length or weight specifications given.

This replica is available with either rifled or smooth-bore barrel, is also available in kit form.

A good quality replica of a traditionally American gun.

PRICE: $ 179.95 / FROM: Numrich Arms

BROWN BESS MUSKET, MODEL 101

Caliber .69, other specifications not given.

Hardwood stock and bright steel round barrel.

Also available in kit form.

PRICE: not given / FROM: Smokepole Musket

KENTUCKY FLINTLOCK RIFLE, MODEL 103

Caliber .44, overall length 50 inches, weight 8 pounds.

Rifled octagonal barrel, engraved lock, hardwood stock.

Also offered as a kit.

PRICE: not given / FROM: Smokepole Musket

MINUTEMAN FLINTLOCK RIFLE, MODEL 104

Caliber .69, overall length 49 inches, weight 8 pounds, 4 ounces.
Smoothbored round steel barrel, hardwood stock.
Also sold as a kit.
PRICE: not given / FROM: Smokepole Musket

T/C HAWKEN (not shown)

Caliber .45 and .50, barrel length 28 inches, overall length not specified, weight 8 1/2 pounds.
Octagonal barrel, blued, 15/16 inches across flats.
Hooked breech, color casehardened and decorated lock, double set triggers, fully adjustable rear sight, walnut stock.
PRICE: $ 215.00 / FROM: Thompson/Center

PERCUSSION SINGLE-SHOT RIFLES AND MUSKETS

BLUNDERBUSS, MODEL PB 1

Opening at belled muzzle 1 7/8 inches, overall length 30 inches, weight 4 pounds.
Half octagonal, half round barrel of heavy steel, ramrod, brass furniture, checkered straight grip.
PRICE: $ 82.10 / FROM: The Armoury

203

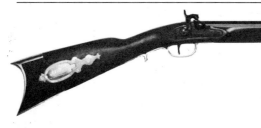

KENTUCKY CARBINE, MODEL R 111

Caliber .45, barrel length 29 inches, overall length 43 inches, weight 5 1/2 pounds.

Bore diameter is .451, octagonal barrel, one piece walnut stock.

Casehardened lock with bolster, wooden ramrod, brass tipped at both ends, one end threaded.

Carbine is 7 inches shorter than rifle, is therefore more suitable for hunting.

PRICE: $ 139.00 / FROM: The Armoury

KENTUCKY RIFLE, MODEL R 110

Caliber .45, barrel length 36 inches, overall length 50 inches, weight 7 pounds.

Bore diameter .451, octagonal barrel.

Casehardened lock with bolster, brass furniture, full length walnut stock, wooden ramrod brass tipped at both ends, one end threaded.

PRICE: $ 139.00 / FROM: The Armoury

KENTUCKY RIFLE, DELUXE MODEL R 120

Caliber .45, barrel length 36 inches, overall length 50 inches, weight 6 1/2 to 7 pounds.

Bore diameter .453, deep rifling in octagonal barrel, 13/16 inches across flats.

Casehardened lock plate with flash shield or bolster.

Roman nose walnut stock, brass furniture, light engraving on lock plate.

One piece wooden ramrod, brass tipped at both ends, one end threaded.

PRICE: $ 146.75 / FROM: The Armoury

ZOUAVE RIFLE MODEL 1863, MODEL R 130
Caliber .58, barrel length 32 1/2 inches, overall length 48 1/2 inches, weight 9 1/2 pounds.
Casehardened percussion lock, highly polished round barrel, brass furniture.
Three leaf rear sight as in the original, one piece steel ramrod.
PRICE: $ 137.00 / FROM: The Armoury

KENTUCKY RIFLE, MODEL R 150
Caliber .45, barrel length 36 inches, overall length 50 inches, weight 8 1/2 pounds.
Casehardened lock with bridle, polished blue octagonal barrel.
Brass mountings, two piece walnut stock, patch box, wood ramrod, brass tipped at both ends.
An economy model without frills.
PRICE: $ 82.10 / FROM: The Armoury

CVA KENTUCKY RIFLE, MODEL PR 401
Caliber .45, barrel length 34 1/4 inches, overall length 50 inches, weight 7 pounds.
Bore diameter .451, octagonal barrel with deep blue finish, 7/8 inches across flats.
Walnut stained stock, brass hardware, hardwood ramrod is brass tipped, nipple wrench furnished.
PRICE: $ 104.95 / FROM: C. V. A.

205

CVA ZOUAVE RIFLE, MODEL PR 404

Caliber .58, barrel length 32 1/2 inches, overall length 48 1/2 inches, weight 9 1/2 pounds.
Cold forged barrel, color casehardened lock, polished brass hardware.
Authentic three leaf rear sight, blade front sight, hardwood stock, steel ramrod.
PRICE: $ 149.95 / FROM: C. V. A.

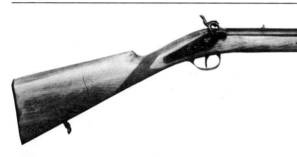

HALF-STOCK TARGET RIFLE,
MODEL DPR - 09

Caliber .45, barrel length 32 inches, overall length not given, weight 7 1/2 pounds.
Designed for off-hand target shooting and for snap shots at game.
Uses .455" ball.
Steel buttplate and trigger guard have mottled casehardened color.
PRICE: $ 92.00 / FROM: Dixie Gun Works

DIXIE DELUXE PENNSYLVANIA RIFLE,
MODEL DPR - 03

Caliber .45, barrel length 40 inches, overall length 55 inches, weight 10 pounds.
Six lands and grooves, barrel 13/16 inches across flats, twist 1:48.
Color casehardened lock, brass furniture including expensive brass patch box and extra wide buttplate.
Buttstock style differs vastly from standard Pennsylvania rifle on this model, for example, the Roman nose comb.
Straight grain maple stock stained chestnut.
PRICE: $ 209.95 / FROM: Dixie Gun Works

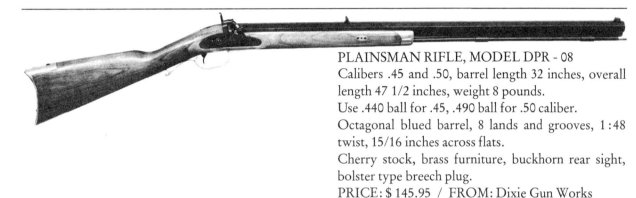

PLAINSMAN RIFLE, MODEL DPR - 08
Calibers .45 and .50, barrel length 32 inches, overall length 47 1/2 inches, weight 8 pounds.
Use .440 ball for .45, .490 ball for .50 caliber.
Octagonal blued barrel, 8 lands and grooves, 1:48 twist, 15/16 inches across flats.
Cherry stock, brass furniture, buckhorn rear sight, bolster type breech plug.
PRICE: $ 145.95 / FROM: Dixie Gun Works

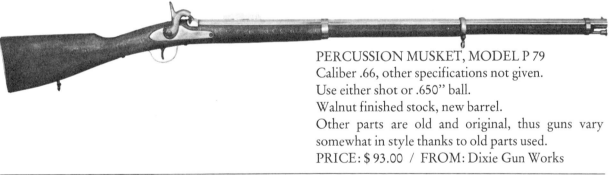

PERCUSSION MUSKET, MODEL P 79
Caliber .66, other specifications not given.
Use either shot or .650" ball.
Walnut finished stock, new barrel.
Other parts are old and original, thus guns vary somewhat in style thanks to old parts used.
PRICE: $ 93.00 / FROM: Dixie Gun Works

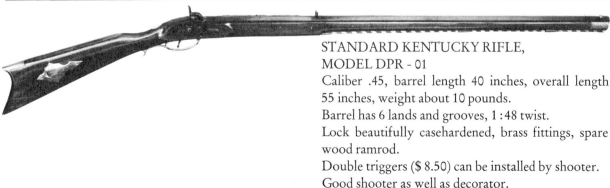

STANDARD KENTUCKY RIFLE, MODEL DPR - 01
Caliber .45, barrel length 40 inches, overall length 55 inches, weight about 10 pounds.
Barrel has 6 lands and grooves, 1:48 twist.
Lock beautifully casehardened, brass fittings, spare wood ramrod.
Double triggers ($ 8.50) can be installed by shooter.
Good shooter as well as decorator.
PRICE: $ 179.95 / FROM: Dixie Gun Works

KENTUCKIAN PERCUSSION RIFLE, MODEL 1 PR - 02

Caliber .44, barrel length 33 1/2 inches, overall length 48 inches, weight 6 1/4 pounds.
Suggested ball size .445 - .448".
Barrel with 6 lands and grooves, 13/16 inches across flats.
Walnut stock, casehardened and engraved lock plate, brass fittings.
Made in Italy.
PRICE: $ 145.00 / FROM: Dixie Gun Works

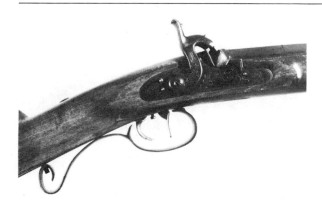

HAWKEN FULL STOCK RIFLE

Calibers .45, .50, .54 and .58, barrel length 36 inches, overall length not given, weight about 10 1/4 pounds
A fine copy of the guns produced by Sam and Jake Hawken between 1820–1840.
Full maple stock, completely hand finished, fancy open rear and blade front sight.
Full patent breech with hook and snail, all steel accoutrements, including ferrules and nose cap.
Specify early or late Hawken style trigger guard and cheekpiece.
Also offered in kit form.
PRICE: $ 500.00 /
FROM: Green River Rifle Works

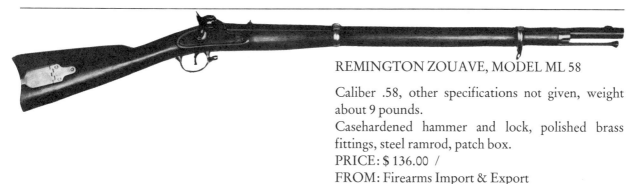

REMINGTON ZOUAVE, MODEL ML 58

Caliber .58, other specifications not given, weight about 9 pounds.
Casehardened hammer and lock, polished brass fittings, steel ramrod, patch box.
PRICE: $ 136.00 /
FROM: Firearms Import & Export

HALF-STOCK LEMAN
INDIAN TRADE RIFLE

Calibers .45, .50, .54 and .58, barrel length 33 inches, overall length not given, weight about 9 pounds.
A precise copy of a famed rifle, offered in three authentic styles.
Most of the finishing touches are done by hand.
Maple half-stock finished with stain and oil, open rear and blade front sight.
Traditional percussion lock with bolster and Ampco nipple, single trigger.
Brass buttplate, trigger guard and fittings, other metals finished in traditional brown.
14 inch pull.
The three styles of Leman rifles are also offered in kit form.
These guns are for the dedicated muzzleloader who wants authenticity in his guns.
PRICE: from $ 250.00 /
FROM: Green River Rifle Works

209

KENTUCKY RIFLE

Caliber .45, barrel length 36 inches, other specifications not given.
Walnut-type stock, polished brass fittings, octagonal barrel.
Casehardened lock, hammer and trigger.
Engraved model also available.
PRICE: $ 104.00 / $ 112.00 engraved
FROM: EMF, Firearms Import & Export

ZOUAVE RIFLE, MODEL 905   (not shown)

Caliber .58, barrel length 33 inches, overall length 49 inches, weight about 9 1/2 pounds.
A copy of the most accurate military rifle of the period.
Rich walnut stock, casehardened lock, ornate brass fittings and brass patch box.
PRICE: $ 139.95 / FROM: Hawes

KENTUCKY RIFLE AND CARBINE,
MODEL 907P rifle / 908P carbine (not shown)

Caliber .44, rifle barrel length 35 inches, overall length 50 inches, carbine barrel length 27 inches, overall length 43 inches, weight about 6 1/2 pounds depending on model.
Casehardened and engraved lock plate, brass patch box, solid brass trigger guard and fittings.
Open sights, hardwood ramrod, octagonal barrel, full stock.
PRICE: $ 174.95 both models / FROM: Hawes

SPRINGFIELD STALKER

Calibers .45 and .58 barrel length 28 inches, overall length 43 inches, weight 7 1/2 – 8 pounds.

A traditional caplock rifle with American walnut stock, blue-black metal finish, stainless steel nipple for //11 caps.

Wooden ramrod with metal handle, nipple wrench furnished.

Also available in deluxe version with selected wood and hand checkering on pistol grip and forend.

PRICE: $ 190.00 standard / $ 275.00 deluxe /

FROM: Harrington & Richardson

HUNTSMAN

Calibers .45 and .58, barrel length 28 inches, overall length 43 inches, weight 7 1/2 – 8 pounds.

Blue-black finish, color casehardened frame, knock-out breech plug in patented breech system.

Walnut finished hardwood stock, stainless steel nipple for // 11 caps. Solid brass ramrod with wooden handle, nipple wrench furnished.

PRICE: about $ 90.00 /

FROM: Harrington & Richardson

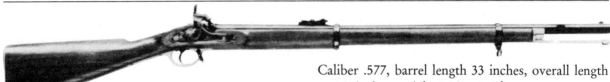

1858 ENFIELD RIFLE, NAVAL PATTERN

Caliber .577, barrel length 33 inches, overall length 48 1/2 inches, weight 8 1/2 pounds.

A superb copy of a famed rifle, also known as the two band model. Blued barrel, British proof, 5 grooves of progressive depth, 1 :48 twist.

Folding leaf sight with slide for 1100 yard shooting.

Made by Parker-Hale on old Enfield patterns and with original gauges. Walnut stock, color casehardened lock parts, issue tool furnished.

PRICE: $ 225.oo / FROM: Jana International

1861 ENFIELD MUSKETOON

Caliber .577, barrel length 24 inches, overall length 40 1/4 inches, weight 7 1/2 pounds.

Original pattern tapered rifling, 5 grooves.

Seasoned walnut stock with brass furniture, issue tool furnished.

Rear sight graduated for 600 yards.

A limited edition of this carbine will be made.

PRICE: $ 225.00 / FROM: Jana International

GALLAGER CARBINE (not shown)

Caliber .54, barrel length 22 1/3 inches, overall length 39 inches, weight 7 1/4 pounds.

A faithful replica of a relatively little-known breechloading percussion carbine. See Chapter VIII for discussion of this loading system.

Walnut stock, deep blue metal finish.

Made in Germany by Erma Werke.

PRICE: Not given / FROM: Jana International

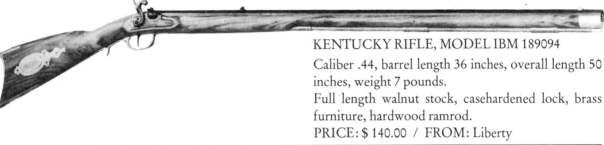

KENTUCKY RIFLE, MODEL IBM 189094

Caliber .44, barrel length 36 inches, overall length 50 inches, weight 7 pounds.

Full length walnut stock, casehardened lock, brass furniture, hardwood ramrod.

PRICE: $ 140.00 / FROM: Liberty

LYMAN 1863 ZOUAVE

Caliber .58, barrel length 32 1/2 inches, overall length 48 1/2 inches, weight 9 1/2 pounds.

Color casehardened lock, brass furniture, patch box an butt plate, walnut stock.

Lyman also offers a shooting kit, containing mold with handles, lube, spare nipple and instruction booklet.

PRICE: $ 160.00 / $ 175.00 with kit
FROM: Lyman

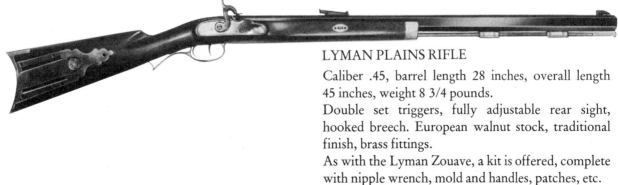

LYMAN PLAINS RIFLE

Caliber .45, barrel length 28 inches, overall length 45 inches, weight 8 3/4 pounds.

Double set triggers, fully adjustable rear sight, hooked breech. European walnut stock, traditional finish, brass fittings.

As with the Lyman Zouave, a kit is offered, complete with nipple wrench, mold and handles, patches, etc.

PRICE: $ 190.00 / $ 205.00 with kit
FROM: Lyman

213

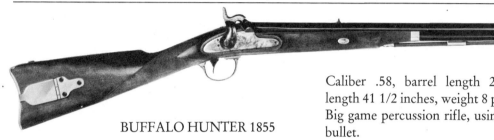

BUFFALO HUNTER 1855

Caliber .58, barrel length 25 1/2 inches, overall length 41 1/2 inches, weight 8 pounds.
Big game percussion rifle, using the 500 grain Minie bullet.
Walnut finished stock, handcheckered with brass furniture, ramrod. Lock and hammer color case-hardened, deep finish on barrel.
PRICE: $ 160.00 / FROM: Navy Arms

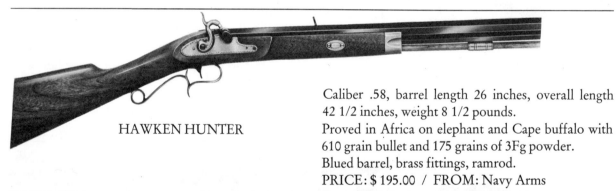

HAWKEN HUNTER

Caliber .58, barrel length 26 inches, overall length 42 1/2 inches, weight 8 1/2 pounds.
Proved in Africa on elephant and Cape buffalo with 610 grain bullet and 175 grains of 3Fg powder.
Blued barrel, brass fittings, ramrod.
PRICE: $ 195.00 / FROM: Navy Arms

MORSE/NAVY MAGNUM

Caliber .58, barrel length 26 inches, overall length 41 1/2 inches, eight 7 1/2 pounds.
Highly polished action, oil finish American walnut stock, pistol grip.
Also offered in .45 and .50 calibers and in 12 gauge.
PRICE: $ 85.00 in all calibers and 12 gauge
FROM: Navy

MISSISSIPPI RIFLE 1841

Caliber .58, barrel length 32 1/2 inches, overall length 48 1/2 inches, weight 9 1/2 pounds.
An authentic copy of the original United States model. Browned barrel, polished brass fittings including patch box.
PRICE: $ 160.00 / FROM: Navy

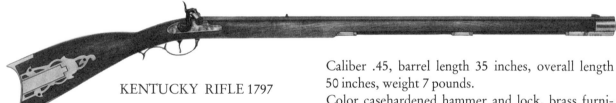

KENTUCKY RIFLE 1797

Caliber .45, barrel length 35 inches, overall length 50 inches, weight 7 pounds.
Color casehardened hammer and lock, brass furniture including patch box, ramrod of hardwood.
Also in flint system.
PRICE: $ 175.00 / FROM: Navy

KENTUCKY CARBINE (not shown)

Same specifications as for 1797 rifle but with 28 inch barrel and overall length of 40 inches.
Also in flint system.
PRICE: $ 175.00 / FROM: Navy

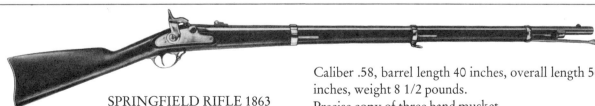

SPRINGFIELD RIFLE 1863

Caliber .58, barrel length 40 inches, overall length 56 inches, weight 8 1/2 pounds.
Precise copy of three band musket.
Open, step adjustable rear sight, walnut stock, all metal parts finished bright, steel ramrod.
PRICE: $ 200.00 / FROM: Navy

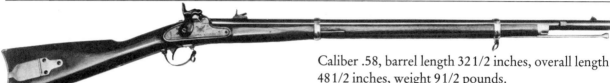

ZOUAVE RIFLE

Caliber .58, barrel length 32 1/2 inches, overall length 48 1/2 inches, weight 9 1/2 pounds.
Excellent copy of the most accurate military rifle.
Walnut-toned stock, deep blue barrel, casehardened lock, brass fittings and patch box.
A 20 gauge shotgun barrel can readily replace the rifled barrel.
PRICE: $ 150.00 / $ 50.00 shotgun barrel
FROM: Navy

ENFIELD CAVALRY CARBINE

Caliber .58, barrel length 22 inches, overall length 44 inches, weight 7 1/2 pounds.
Swivel ramrod, smoothbored barrel, oil finished walnut stock. Brass fittings, brightly polished metal work.
PRICE: $ 100.00 / FROM: Navy

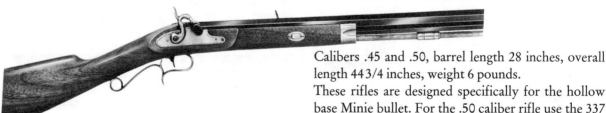

HAWKEN HURRICANE

Calibers .45 and .50, barrel length 28 inches, overall length 44 3/4 inches, weight 6 pounds.
These rifles are designed specifically for the hollow base Minie bullet. For the .50 caliber rifle use the 337 grain Minie bullet ahead of 140 grains of 3Fg powder. For the .45 use the 225 grain Minie and 125 grains of 3Fg powder, which equals the ballistic performance of the .30–06.
PRICE: $ 195.00 / FROM: Navy Arms

ZOUAVE MODEL 1864 CARBINE (not shown)

Same specifications as for above rifle, but with 22 inch barrel.
PRICE: $ 150.00 / FROM: Navy

HERITAGE MODEL

Calibers .36 and .45, barrel length 32 inches, overall length 49 inches, weight 8 1/2 pounds.
Hopkins & Allen best underhammer gun.
Brass butt plate, patch box and trigger guard extension.
Walnut stock, octagonal barrel 15/16 inches across flats.
Two standard open sights plus H & A aperture long range rear target tang sight.
PRICE: $ 99.50 / FROM: Numrich Arms

OFFHAND DELUXE

Calibers .36 and .45, barrel length 32 inches, overall length 49 inches, weight 8 1/2 pounds.
Similar to Heritage Model, but lacks patch box and tang sight.
PRICE: $ 94.50 / FROM: Numrich

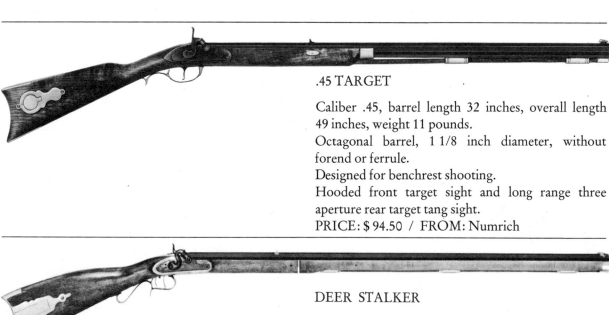

.45 TARGET

Caliber .45, barrel length 32 inches, overall length 49 inches, weight 11 pounds.

Octagonal barrel, 1 1/8 inch diameter, without forend or ferrule.

Designed for benchrest shooting.

Hooded front target sight and long range three aperture rear target tang sight.

PRICE: $ 94.50 / FROM: Numrich

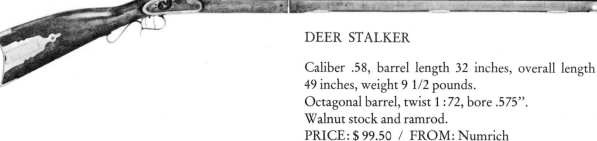

DEER STALKER

Caliber .58, barrel length 32 inches, overall length 49 inches, weight 9 1/2 pounds.

Octagonal barrel, twist 1:72, bore .575".

Walnut stock and ramrod.

PRICE: $ 99.50 / FROM: Numrich

BUGGY DELUXE

Calibers .36 and .45, barrel length 20 inches, overall length 37 inches, weight 6 1/2 pounds.

Octagonal barrel, walnut stock, hooded front sight and open notched rear sight.

Carbine designed for NMRA's "Seneca Match," ideal for deer hunter.

PRICE: $ 94.50 / FROM: Numrich

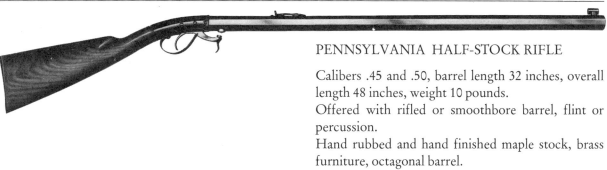

PENNSYLVANIA HALF-STOCK RIFLE

Calibers .45 and .50, barrel length 32 inches, overall length 48 inches, weight 10 pounds.

Offered with rifled or smoothbore barrel, flint or percussion.

Hand rubbed and hand finished maple stock, brass furniture, octagonal barrel.

PRICE: $ 179.50 / FROM: Numrich

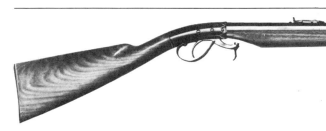

YORKSHIRE RIFLE

Caliber .45, barrel length 36 inches, overall length 51 3/4 inches, weight 7 1/2 pounds.

Octagonal barrel 7/8 inch diameter, adjustable double set triggers. Front and rear sight, trigger guard, patch box, butt plate and all other fittings are polished brass.

Casehardened lock, select maple stock.

Also in flint system.

PRICE: $ 144.00 percussion / $ 153.00 flintlock
FROM: Richland Arms

MICHIGAN CARBINE (not shown)

Caliber .45, barrel length 26 inches, overall length 41 3/8 inches, weight 5 pounds 15 ounces.

Ordnance steel barrel 7/8 inch diameter, octagonal.

Hand finished select maple stock, adjustable double triggers.

Patch box, butt plate and all other fittings polished brass.

Also in flintlock version.

PRICE: $ 144.00 percussion / $ 153.00 flintlock
FROM: Richland

219

T/C SENECA

Calibers .36 and .45, barrel length 27 inches, overall length not given, weight 6 pounds.

Hooked breech, coil springs, blued octagonal barrel 13/16 inches across flats.

Walnut half stock with cheekpiece, polished brass furniture, color casehardened lock, dolphin-shaped hammer.

Accessory pack available.

PRICE: $ 205.00 / $ 232.50 with accessories / FROM: Thompson/Center

T/C RENEGADE

Caliber .54, barrel length 26 inches, overall length not given, weight 8 pounds.

Blued octagonal barrel 1 inch across flats, hooked breech, coil springs. Lightly decorated and color casehardened lock plate, fully adjustable rear sight.

This no-frills gun was especially designed for the hunter.

Accessory pack with Maxi-lube, starter, powder measure and 20 cast Maxi-Balls; mold 6 and mold handle not included.

PRICE: $ 165.00 / $ 177.35 with accessories / FROM: Thompson/Center

T/C HAWKEN

Calibers .45 and .50, barrel length 28 inches, overall length not given, weight 8 1/2 pounds.

Hooked breech system, octagonal barrel 15/16 inches across flats, deep blue finish.

Lightly engraved, color casehardened lock, coil springs in action, adjusting double set triggers, fully adjustable rear sight.

Brass trim and furniture, walnut stock with cheekpiece.

Accessory pack with mold and handles, ball starter, etc, is available with the gun.

Also offered in flintlock system.

PRICE: $ 205.00 / $ 232.50 with accessories

FROM: Thompson/Center

TARGET RIFLE, MODEL OF 1962

Calibers .36, .45 and .50, barrel length 32 inches, overall length 48 inches, weight 10 pounds.

Patent breech for easy take-down, octagonal barrel 1 inch across flats, twist 1:52, 8 wide grooves and narrow lands.

Brass fittings, blued barrel, lock and trigger plates, adjustable double set triggers.

Lacquered walnut half stock, fully adjustable rear sight.

PRICE: $ 159.95 / FROM: Tingle Mfg. Co.

221

KENTUCKY RIFLE, MODEL 102

Caliber .44, barrel length not given, overall length
50 inches, weight 8 pounds.
Octagonal barrel, engraved lock, hardwood stock.
PRICE: not given / FROM: Smokepole Musket

TEXAS CARBINE

Caliber .58, barrel length 24 inches, overall length
39 inches, weight 8 pounds.
Octagonal barrel, 1 inch across flats, 4 groves, twist
1:60, uses .575 Minie bullet.
Walnut stock, adjustable front and rear sights, solid
bronze box, lock and action.
PRICE: $ 189.50 / FROM: Trail Guns Armoury

MULTI-SHOT RIFLES

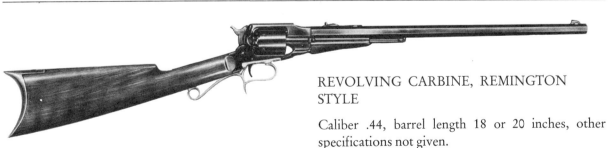

LEONARD DAY SWIVEL BREECH,
MODEL SBR - F1 flintlock
      SBR - P2 percussion

Caliber .450, barrel length 32 inches, other specifications not given.

Rotation breech with O/U barrels which are browned, and wood panelled.

Curly maple stock and engraving on metal parts typical of the flintlock period on the flinter, while the percussion model is equally authentic with straight grain maple stock and no metal engraving.

Hand-made lock plates, single trigger, front trigger unlatches barrels, wide butt plate, brass furniture.
PRICE: $ 450.00 flinter / $ 325.00 percussion /
FROM: Dixie Gun Works

REVOLVING CARBINE, REMINGTON
STYLE

Caliber .44, barrel length 18 or 20 inches, other specifications not given.

Six shot carbine, deep blue metal finish, adjustable front sight, buckhorn rear sight.
PRICE: $ 165.00 / FROM: Navy Arms

223

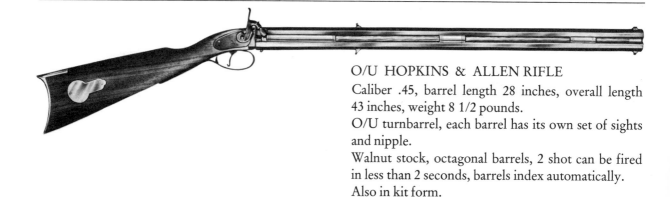

O/U HOPKINS & ALLEN RIFLE
Caliber .45, barrel length 28 inches, overall length
43 inches, weight 8 1/2 pounds.
O/U turnbarrel, each barrel has its own set of sights
and nipple.
Walnut stock, octagonal barrels, 2 shot can be fired
in less than 2 seconds, barrels index automatically.
Also in kit form.
PRICE: $ 139.95 / FROM: Numrich Arms

SINGLE-SHOT FLINTLOCK SHOTGUNS AND FOWLING PIECES

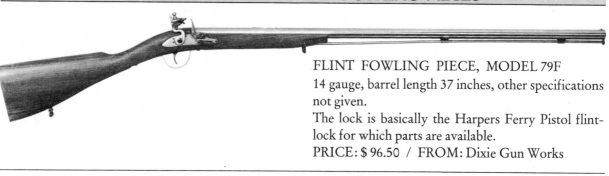

FLINT FOWLING PIECE, MODEL 79F
14 gauge, barrel length 37 inches, other specifications
not given.
The lock is basically the Harpers Ferry Pistol flintlock for which parts are available.
PRICE: $ 96.50 / FROM: Dixie Gun Works

FOWLING PIECE (not shown)

12 gauge, weight about 8 pounds, other specifica-
tions not given.
Cylinder bore, a true copy of a Colonial fowler.
Maple half-stock, 1/3 octagonal and 2/3 round bar-
rel, front bead sight.
Largely hand-crafted and semi-custom made.
Also in kit form.
PRICE: $ 360.00
FROM: Green River Rifle Works

SINGLE-SHOT PERCUSSION SHOTGUNS

SINGLE BARREL SHOTGUN, MODEL DPS-22

28 gauge, barrel length 32 inches, other specifications not given.

Blued barrel, steel furniture with cap box on these Spanish guns.

PRICE: $ 35.95 / FROM: Dixie Gun Works

FOWLING PIECE (not shown)

12 gauge, weight about 8 pounds, no other specifications given.

This gun is offered in flintlock as well as percussion.

Semi-custom made and a true copy of a Colonial original.

Also in kit form.

PRICE: $ 360.00

FROM: Green River Rifle Works

THE HUNTSMAN

12 gauge, barrel length 28 inches, overall length 43 inches, weight 6 1/4 pounds.

Patent knock-out breech plug, stainless steel nipple for No. 11 caps, cap is protected in breech.

PRICE: about $ 80.00

FROM: Harrington & Richardson

225

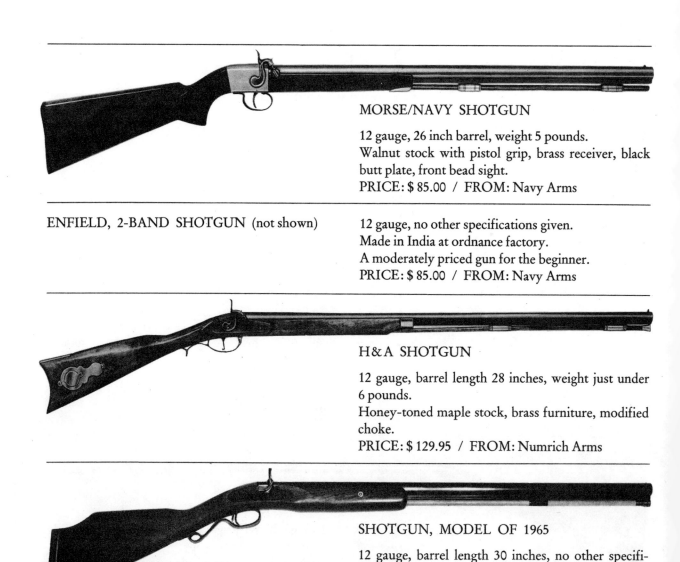

MORSE/NAVY SHOTGUN

12 gauge, 26 inch barrel, weight 5 pounds.
Walnut stock with pistol grip, brass receiver, black
butt plate, front bead sight.
PRICE: $ 85.00 / FROM: Navy Arms

ENFIELD, 2-BAND SHOTGUN (not shown)

12 gauge, no other specifications given.
Made in India at ordnance factory.
A moderately priced gun for the beginner.
PRICE: $ 85.00 / FROM: Navy Arms

H & A SHOTGUN

12 gauge, barrel length 28 inches, weight just under
6 pounds.
Honey-toned maple stock, brass furniture, modified
choke.
PRICE: $ 129.95 / FROM: Numrich Arms

SHOTGUN, MODEL OF 1965

12 gauge, barrel length 30 inches, no other specifications given.
Cylinder bore, walnut stock, rubber butt plate, blued
barrel, lock and triggers guard.
PRICE: $ 114.95 / FROM: Tingle Mfg. Co.

DOUBLE BARREL PERCUSSION SHOTGUNS

DOUBLE BARREL SHOTGUN, MODEL S 101

12 gauge, no specifications given for barrel or over-all length, weight about 6 pounds.
Modified and full choke.
Engraved sidelocks, browned barrels, brass tipped wooden ramrod and worm.
PRICE: $ 136.65 / FROM: The Armoury

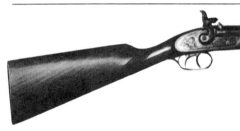

DELUXE SHOTGUN, MODEL PR 403

12 gauge, barrel length 30 inches, overall length not given, weight 6 1/8 pounds.
Modified and Improved.
Hand rubbed oil finished walnut stock, bead front sight, patent breech, threaded breech plug.
PRICE: $ 139.95 / FROM: C.V.A.

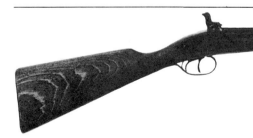

20 GAUGE SHOTGUN, MODEL PR 402

28 inch barrels, weight 5 3/4 pounds.
Light-colored walnut stock, blued barrels and lock, front bead sight.
Brass tipped hardwood ramrod, nipples take No. 11 caps.
PRICE: $ 89.95 / FROM: C.V.A.

227

MUZZLELOADING DOUBLE BARREL
SHOTGUN, MODEL PER 206 (not shown)

12 gauge, 32 inch barrels, weight 8 pounds 3 ounces.
Cylinder bored so that shot or solid balls can be used.
Bar locks, tapered tubular steel ramrod, all metal is blued except front bead and small patch box.
Scroll engraving on trigger guard and barrel tang, checkered steel butt plate.
Exotic hardwood stock.
Made in India.
PRICE: not given / FROM: EMF Co.

DELUXE MAGNUM SHOTGUN

Weight about 6 pounds, neither gauge nor length of barrels are specified.
Choked IC and MOD, rabbit ears sidelock with a forward locking pin holding the barrels.
Browned barrels, color casehardened locks and fittings, hand checkered walnut stock.
PRICE: $ 150.00 / FROM: Navy Arms

KITS

As the interest in kits has grown, more and more importers began to offer new kits, some of them duplicating kits already on the market. And now, the demand for more sophisticated kits and guns has also grown. One importer plans to introduce at least six new shortly, but was unable to furnish any details at press time.

As pointed out in Chapter IX, there is a very definite difference in the amount of skill required to complete these kits. The advanced kits – such as those offered by Dixie Gun Works, which come without instructions – are becoming more and more popular, and more kits of this type will become available.

The following list of kits is by no means complete, as more kits are being added to the various lines all the time. Hand in hand with the growing interest in building your own muzzleloader comes the demand for custom barrels, standard and custom locks, stock blanks and semifinished accessories as well as rough castings which require a considerable amount of skill and work before they can be affixed to a gun.

The Armoury, Inc.

Kentucky full stock pistol kit, caliber .44
    percussion, # KP 20 . . . . $ 42.75
Kentucky full stock pistol kit, same as above,
    but flintlock, # KP 21 . . . . $ 49.45
Corsair pistol kit, available in .36 and .44 caliber,
    percussion lock, double barrel, # KP 30 (.36)
    # KP 31 (.44) . . . . $ 49.45

Kentucky percussion pistol kit, caliber .45,
    plain barrel and lock, # KP 10 . . . . . . $ 26.80
– Deluxe kit of above with fully engraved barrel
    and lock, # KP 2 . . . . $ 36.85
Philadelphia derringer kit, caliber .41,
    # KP 3 . . . . $ 21.75
Kentucky flintlock pistol kit, caliber .45,
    plain barrel and lock, # KP 4 . . . . . . $ 36.85
– Deluxe kit of above with fuuly engraved
    barrel and lock, #KP 5 . . . . $ 41.85
New Model Army Remington kit, caliber .44,
    parts all finished, requires minor fitting,
    instruction manual, # RK 1 . . . . $ 58.65
Kentucky rifle kit – Standard, caliber .45, requires
    some sanding, inletting, brass furniture require
    polishing, # KR 102 . . . . $ 57.45
– Deluxe kit of above, inletting and sanding com-
    pleted, all metal parts polished, # KR 101
                        $ 76.00

Classic Arms International Ltd.

New Orleans Ace, .44 caliber single-shot pistol
    offered in three different combinations, with
    extra barrels, smoothbored or rifled, percussion
                        $ 25.95
Ethan Allen pepperbox, .36 caliber percussion pistol
                        $ 39.95
Duckfoot three barrel percussion pistol . . $ 39.95
This company is also planning to introduce rifle kits in the near future.

Connecticut Valley Arms

Philadelphia derringer kit, .45 caliber percussion,
  # KA 712 . . . . $ 21.95
Colonial pistol kit, .45 caliber,
  percussion # KA 702 . . . . $ 24.95
  flintlock # KA 701 . . . . $ 30.95
– Deluxe of above, engraved,
  percussion # KA 704 . . . . $ 26.95
  flintlock # KA 703 . . . . $ 32.95
Kentucky pistol kit, caliber .45,
  percussion # KA 709 . . . . $ 38.95
  flintlock # KA 710 . . . . $ 43.95
Kentucky rifle kit, caliber .45,
  percussion # KA 707 . . . . $ 68.95
  flintlock # KA 708 . . . . $ 74.95
Zouave rifle kit, caliber .58,
  percussion # KA 711 . . . . $ 109.95

Dixie Gun Works

At latest count, this company is offering over 30 kits, and several new ones will be available shortly. Complexity of assembling these kits ranges from very simple to very complex, requiring expert workmanship. The catalog of this company sells for two dollars and is a worthwhile investment. This is a lot more than a catalog – it might well be called the black powder vademecum.

Green River Rifle Works

This company produces a number of kits, all based on their semi-custom muzzleloader, see rifle section of this catalog.

Hawken, basic half-stock kit . . . . $ 205.00
    basic full stock kit . . . . . . $ 230.00
    basic flintlock kit . . . . $ 260.00
Leman Indian trade rifle, semi-finished kit
                                        $ 230.00
    basic kit . . . . $ 185.00
Leman squirrel rifle, semi-finished kit . . $ 230.00
    basic kit . . . . $ 185.00
Leman 1858 Indian rifle, basic kit . . . . $ 200.00
Fowling piece, basic kit . . . . $ 200.00
Trapper's pistol, basic kit . . . . $ 95.00

Lyman Products for Shooters

Caplock belt pistol, caliber .45 . . . . $ 29.95
Caplock Pennsylvania pistol, caliber .45 . . $ 42.95

Navy Arms Co., Inc.

Brown Bess musket kit . . . . $ 195.00
    carbine kit . . . . $ 195.00

Numrich Arms Corp.

Kentucky Rifle kit, calibers .31, .36, .45, .50,
  percussion or flint . . . . $ 109.95
Minuteman brush rifle kit, caliber .45 or .50,
  flint or percussion . . . . $ 109.95
Turnbarrel rifle kit, caliber .45 percussion $ 101.75

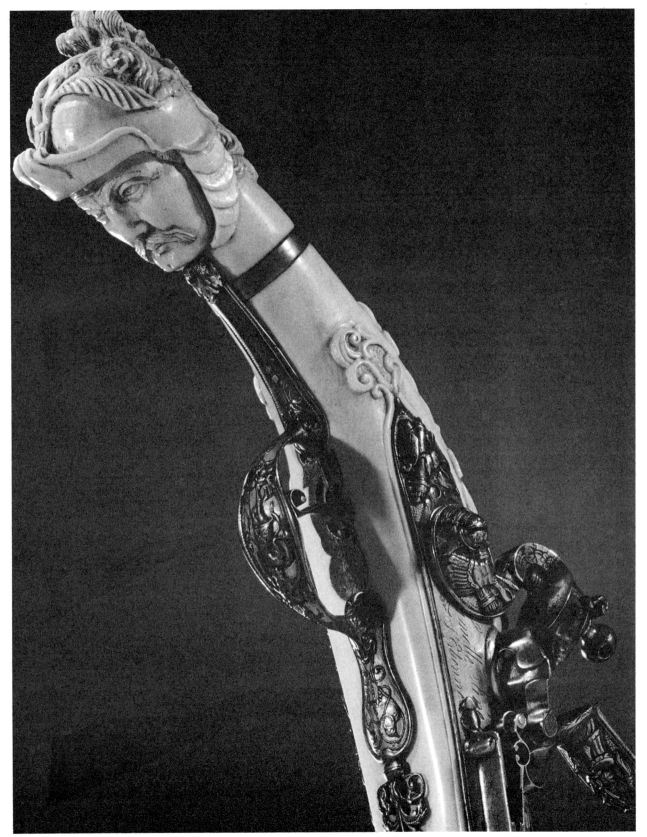

Flintlock pistol of Lamotte at St. Etienne, carved ivory stock, Maestricht work, end of the 17th century.

231

Chapter 12 GLOSSARY

As already mentioned in Chapter I, a number of words and terms, originally derived from black powder shooting, have become an integral part of our language. Many of the gun terms used by black powder shooters of today date back to the early days of firearms, but equally as many phrases currently in use by shooters, hunters and gunsmiths are more of a modern derivation. For the sake of brevity, the latter group has not been included here. The reader who seeks definitions for such words and phrases is referred to the reprint edition of the author's THE FIRE-ARMS DICTIONARY which is available from Paladin Press, Box 1307, Boulder, Colo. 80302.

***

ACID ETCHING: This method of marking gun barrels was widespread during the early 19th century. The metal to be marked was first coated with wax, and the desired markings were then scratched into the wax until the metal below was exposed. Nitric acid was most frequently used for this etching process. Such etching did not last long under use, hence the method was abandoned. The etching appeared as a discoloration of the metal wherever the metal was not protected by the wax coat.

AMPCO NIPPLE: A modern percussion nipple made from a Beryllium alloy that looks like brass but is much harder and also resists corrosion better than any other metal tried for nipples. To provide a hotter flame, AMPCO nipples have a much smaller flash hole at the bottom than other nipples. The hotter flame produces better ignition, hence somewhat better ballistics.

APERTURE SIGHT: Frequently also called a peep sight, the aperture sight, often fully adjustable for elevation and infrequently for windage, is mounted on the tang or at the rear of the barrel. In conjunction with a post sight at the muzzle, the aperture sight is widely used for hunting as well as match shooting. A few match rifles carry a variation of a peep sight at the muzzle, allowing very precise aiming.

ARQUEBUS: One of the early matchlock shoulder guns. Hakenbüchse, the German hook rifle, was probably the first of this type of rifle. The French translated the first part of the word – Haken became arque – and büchse was bastardized, hence arquebus. The arquebus was usually of better quality than its military counterpart, including some of the wheel-locks of the period.

BACK ACTION LOCK: A percussion side lock that appeared late in the evolution of the percussion gun. In this type of action, the mainspring is located toward the rear of the hammer and tumbler.

BALL: The round projectile used in most muzzle-loading rifles and pistols. Balls must be cast from pure soft lead to prevent damage to the relatively shallow lands and grooves customary in black powder barrels. Sometimes the word is used incorrectly with such names as Minie, as in Minie balls instead of Minie bullets.

BALL AND SWAN DROPS: In this type of load, the ball was at the bottom, and large shot pellets – swan drops of about .27 caliber – were placed on top of the ball and held in place by a wad. These loads were used for hunting swans, as well as in coach pistols and a few duelling guns.

BALL SCREW: A special device that is screwed onto the threaded end of the ramrod to remove a ball from a loaded gun without having to fire the gun.

BALL STARTER: A handy wooden tool which can either be purchased or easily made. It consists of a wooden ball about 2 1/2" in diameter, and fastened to it at right angles to each other are two short pieces of doweling, one about 1/4" long, the other about 5 1/2" long. The short piece of dowel is used to start the ball and patch down the barrel, the longer one drives ball and patch farther down the rifle barrel until a ramrod can be used.

BALTIC LOCK: A rather primitive flintlock design used in the early part of the 17th century.

BAND SPRING: A small spring which, when depressed, allows removal of the barrel band from a musket.

BAR ACTION LOCK: The most popular type of side lock where the mainspring is located forward of the action. If the mainspring is located to the rear of the action, the design is known as back action lock, the latter being the stronger of the two designs.

BARLEYCORN: A blade-type front sight which usually is quite low, somewhat resembling an upside-down V.

BARREL BAND: Found primarily on military muskets, the barrel band serves to hold the barrel in the forend. One or more of these narrow, often blued, metal bands are usually used, and they are held in place by band springs.

BARREL KEY: A relatively short and somewhat tapered metal bar that holds barrel and forend together on most of the half-stock rifles and many shotguns.

BARREL PIN: Seen mostly on early, full-stock muzzleloading rifles where the barrel pin served to hold forend and barrel together.

BELTED BALL: The belt on a lead ball gives a somewhat better gas seal, and thanks to the use of a mechanical starter, the ball also engages rifling somewhat more reliably, hence belted balls are usually more accurate. The belted ball is used primarily in English guns which have the deep two-groove rifling.

BLACK POWDER, also BLACKPOWDER: The only propellant that should be used in muzzleloading guns, comes in various granulations. Black powder is produced by mixing potassium nitrate, sulfur and charcoal. Although the early pioneers often made their own black powder, home manufacture of black powder is dangerous and should not be encouraged.

BLUNDERBUSS: Characterized by its belled or flared muzzle, this type of gun was widely used aboard ships to repel boarders. Whether the flared muzzle really spread the charge at the close range at which these guns were used seems doubtful, and modern tests have proved inconclusive, with some testers reporting a spreading of the charge and others reporting that the belled muzzle does not spread the charge. Slim Ackermann points out that many pictures show the early pilgrim fathers carrying blunderbusses and further points out that this was not the usual firearm carried by them.

BOLSTER: That raised portion at the rear of the barrel where the nipple is screwed in. A bolster may be screwed into the barrel, welded on, or may be an integral part of the barrel.

BOOT: A leather cover, treated to make it water repellent, that covers the flash pan of some flintlock rifles, thus keeping the priming charge dry in inclement weather.

BOX LOCK: A type of lock in which the hammer is located inside the lock plate and protrudes above the plate.

BREECH: The rear part of the barrel.

BREECH PLUG: A threaded and gas-tight metal plug that fits into the open rear end of the barrel. In some muzzleloading guns, the tang is fastened to the breech plug.

BREECH PROTECTOR: A small piece of leather, most often tanned deer hide, that is fastened around the nipple of a percussion gun to protect the wood finish of the stock. A small hole is punched into the leather so that the nipple of the gun protrudes and can be capped, and so that the hammer makes the needed hard contact with the cap.

BREECH SEAL: A metal seal that provides obturation, often encountered in U.S. military breech-loading guns, so that the arm could be used as a muzzleloader.

BREECH WRENCH: A special tool designed to facilitate removal of the breech plug.

BRIDLE: A plate inside of some conventional locks that holds tumblers and pins or sear in proper relation with each other.

BROWN BESS: The smoothbore flintlock long gun issued to British troops during the time they were stationed in the Colonies. This was a .75 caliber gun, was distinguished by the brown residue left by treating the metal parts of the gun, hence the reference to the color in the name.

BROWNING: A chemically induced rusting process used for barrels and actions. Browning was the forerunner of our bluing, which essentially is also a rusting or oxidation process.

BUCK AND BALL: A devastating short-range load that originated during the Civil War. Such a musket load usually consisted of three buckshot ahead of a conical bullet, all projectiles being cast from soft or pure lead.

BUCKSHOT: Relatively large round lead projectiles, ranging in diameter from .240 to about .360. Several of these were loaded for hunting and for some close-range fighting, Buckshot loads are still in use today, both in black powder and in smokeless powder loads.

BUGGY RIFLE: Most often a small-caliber light rifle, sometimes a single-shot pistol with rifle-like sights and detachable shoulder stock, and with a barrel that was somewhat longer than usual. Buggy rifles were usually about .36 caliber, were used for protection and small game hunting, even though the caliber is a bit too small to afford much protection. These guns were popular into the latter part of the 1800s.

BULLET: A non-spherical projectile designed to be fired through the rifled barrel of a gun. Minie and other conicals bullets were, and still are, used in muzzleloading guns.

BULLET MOLD or MOULD: Traditionally, molds for black powder bullets and balls were made of brass, and though still being offered, the steel and aluminum molds have largely replaced the brass molds. A mold may contain one or more precisely cut cavities which, when filled with molten lead, produce bullets or balls, each, design requiring a separate mold.

BULLET PATCH: A piece of material that is seated with the ball into the muzzle of a black powder rifle, to serve as gas seal. The material can be cotton, bed ticking, linen, buckskin or special patching material which is being sold by numerous dealers specializing in black powder guns and gear.

BUTT MASK: Sometimes seen on early pistols, often brass or even silver, and fastened to butt of the grip. Some of the butt masks represented grotesque faces or masks.

BUTT PLATE: A metal plate, usually brass, fastened to the butt or rear of the stock where the stock makes contact with the shooter's shoulder.

CALIBER: The bore diameter of a rifled barrel, usually measured from land to land. In the United States and England, the caliber is given in decimals of an inch, elsewhere the measurement is given in the metric system's smallest unit, the millimeter.

CANNELURE: A groove around the circumference of a bullet. In metallic cartridges, this groove is often used to crimp the case mouth into the cannelure of the bullet, hence it is often called a crimping groove. For lead projectiles to be fired in centerfire cases, the groove or grooves are filled with a lubricant, hence are known as grease grooves. Conical bullets for muzzleloaders which have a cannelure are also lubricated.

CAP BOX: A small metal container or box, with either a hinged or sliding cover, in the butt of percussion shotguns and sometimes handguns. The issue belt pouch for musket caps was also called a cap box during the Civil War.

CAPLOCK: Another term to describe the percussion system.

CAPPER: A spring-activated device which allows the user to store percussion caps in either a circular or straight-line metal container. The use of a capper is not essential, but on cold days, a capper will be appreciated when a percussion cap must be installed on a nipple. Only one cap at a time is released from the capper.

CASEHARDENING: Metal, when heated with bone and leather scraps, and these days by means of special chemicals, takes on a mottled appearance with varying colors. Casehardened metal has a great deal of eye appeal, and the surface of the metal also becomes quite hard.

CHAMBER: The non-rifled portion of the barrel that contains the powder charge, projectile, patch or wadding.

CHARGER: Either a fixed or an adjustable device that delivers a predetermined charge of powder. A charger can be found on powder flasks, shot pouches, powder horns or any other containers suitable for the job on which a charger can be installed.

CHERRY: The precisely made steel burr that is used to cut the desired cavities into the faces of two perfectly mated mold block blanks.

COACH PISTOL: Most often a smoothbore pistol used as protection against highwaymen. Accuracy of most of these guns was poor since they were intended as close-range defense guns.

COCK: The hammer of a flintlock was sometimes called that. Also means the drawing rearward of the hammer.

COMBUSTIBLE CARTRIDGE: A paper, sometimes linen or other material, tube or "cartridge" that contains charge and ball. Inserted via the muzzle, the covering material burns by the ignition flame. This

235

type of "cartridge" was most often used in percussion revolvers.

CONE: Another term for percussion nipple which appeared before the term nipple became popular.

CORNED POWDER: Describes early attempts to produce black powder in specific granulated sizes. Corned powder was found to be somewhat more stable and less hygroscopic than earlier mixes.

CORROSION: Is due either to rust or to chemical reaction of powder residues in the barrel or on all other metal parts that are exposed to such chemical actions, such as the area around the bolster.

CULOT: This iron wedge was originally a part of the Minie bullet, designed by French Capt. Minie. Designed to aid in the expansion of the Minie bullet, the culot was abandoned by the U.S. Ordnance.

DAMASCUS BARREL: Made by twisting together strips of unlike metals, then welding them together over a mandrel. Because of the differences in the metals, heating produced various colors and configurations in the finished product. Damascus barrels are not very strong, must never be fired with smokeless powder loads, and care should be exercised even when using black powder.

DERRINGER: Small pocket pistols based on, or somewhat resembling in design, those invented by Henry Deringer. Copies and variations of the original are named derringer with two "r's" to differentiate them from the original Deringer pistols.

DETENT: A catch, pawl or fly. A detent is added to the tumbler so that the sear nose is moved downward during firing whenever a set trigger is installed. The half-cock notch is missed during firing, but otherwise the gun can still be put on half-cock.

DETONATING POWDERS: A number of high explosives which detonate when struck a blow. Introduction of these powders led to the first percussion caps, and indirectly also to modern primers. Alexander Forsyth pioneered the detonator lock in the early 1800s, but the concept did not catch on for many years. The highly explosive fulminate of mercury was considered too dangerous by Forsyth, and he developed a mixture of potassium chlorate, sulfur and charcoal.

DISC PRIMER: A type of primer often seen on transitional Sharps rifles. As the hammer is cocked, a disc primer is moved from a small primer magazine onto the nipple. The disc primer is also known as the Lawrence patent.

DOG HEAD: On wheellocks, the spring-loaded arm that holds the pyrite against the wheel.

DOG LOCK: A small latch, activated manually, located at the rear of the hammer on some early flintlocks. Also, those locks having a dog catch which hooks into the rear section of a cock and acts as safety device. A great many of the early locks had such safety devices, each varying somewhat according to maker and designer.

DOUBLE-NECK HAMMER: Essentially a somewhat beefed up or reinforced hammer, found primarily on late military flintlocks. More rugged than the standard goose-neck hammer. As steel was improved and better hammers were made, the double-neck was replaced again by the goose-neck type hammer.

DRIVELL: Said to be another and early term for ramrod.

DUELLING PISTOL: Usually a better-than-average flintlock or percussion single-shot handgun. Only a few of the duelling guns now seen were really

made for that purpose, and fancy gold and silver inlays are never found on genuine duelling pistols since such decorations tended to reflect too much unwanted light into the eyes of the duelling participants.

DUPLEX LOAD: To improve burning rate and ignition, plus less barrel residue, some shooters favor the use of a small charge of smokeless powder as primimg charge and a somewhat reduced load of black powder behind it. Although such duplex loads are quite feasible, their use cannot be recommended, and they should be left to the experts and ballisticians.

EPROUVETTE: Also known as powder tester, this device somewhat resembles a pistol which is fired by a flintlock mechanism. It was used to test the strength of black powder, and once the quality of this had been improved, the use of the eprouvette declined.

EROSION: The wearing away of metal thanks to the high heat of ignition, plus the wear created by projectile friction in the barrel.

ESCUTCHEON: A decorative metal covering or inlay, usually brass and sometimes silver, that covers and strengthens the opening in the forend through which the barrel key is inserted.

FALSE MUZZLE: Found only in match and target rifles, this device is placed on the actual muzzle of the rifle while starting the bullet. It is used to prevent deformation of the bullet during insertion of the bullet into the muzzle and also forestalls possible damage to the rifling at the muzzle.

FENCE: Also known as Flash Guard. A raised section of the flintlock pan that deflects the flash from the face of the shooter.

FINIAL: The ornamental ends of brass furniture, such as patch boxes, trigger guard, lock plate. Furniture may also be silver or other metals, although brass was, and still is, the most widely used metal for this purpose.

FLASH: The ignition, caused by the sparking of the flint on the frizzen, of the priming charge of black powder in the flash pan, when the charge in the barrel fails to detonate or burn.

FLASH PAN: The small pan on flintlock rifles and pistols where the priming charge, usually 4Fg or FFFFg powder, is placed.

FOWLING PIECE: An early shotgun, usually a single-barrel gun.

FRENCH LOCK: An early French flintlock design, said to be one of the first successful flintlocks which appeared around the early 1600s.

FRESHENING: By recutting and deepening the grooves and polishing the tops of the lands, the useful life of a barrel can be extended considerably. Freshening, however, requires a new mold since the operation enlarges somewhat the actual caliber of the barrel. Freshening should only be done if the barrel has not been shot out too much. It is less costly than re-rifling or replacing the barrel.

FRIZZEN: The most common and frequently used term to describe the hardened steel part which the flint strikes, thus igniting the powder in the flash pan of a flintlock gun.

FRIZZEN BOOT: Usually home-made from tanned deerskin, the boot is used as cover for the frizzen in wet weather. The frizzen boot is removed before firing, of course, and makes ignition more certain thanks to a dry frizzen. Undoubtedly, this is very similar to the boot already discussed.

237

FRIZZEN SPRING: This external spring controls the position of the frizzen.

FULMINATING POWDERS: The explosive properties of the fulminates had been known, but it was not until the actions of fulminate of mercury became known in March 1800, that use was made of the characteristics of the compound. It took about 20 years before fluminate of mercury lead to the invention of the percussion cap.

FURNITURE: The decorative metal parts which are not essential to the gun's function. Furniture is usually brass, but may also be made in silver, german silver and other metals. Today, the term includes trigger guard, patch box, butt plate and grip caps.

FUSIL, also FUSEE: A French flintlock musket which was lighter, hence more convenient than contemporary matchlock muskets.

GAIN TWIST: A method of rifling a barrel where the degree of twist increases from breech to muzzle.

GERMAN SILVER: An alloy of copper, nickel and zinc, also known as nickel silver. It is relatively easy to work and when polished, is very decorative.

GLOBE SIGHT: A thin front sight with a small bead at the top which is frequently equipped with a tube-like metal cover to shade and protect the sight.

GOOSE-NECK HAMMER: Delicately shaped hammer found on many early flint and percussion sporting guns.

GUN FLINT: More frequently referred to just as "flint." A special, selected flint or stone, shaped to form a chisel-edge on the forward part, required for firing a flintlock gun.

HALF-STOCK: Found on rifles of U.S. origin mostly, where the stock does not extend to the full length of the barrel. It has been claimed that the half-stock was created for frontiersmen who found that full-stocks were often damaged during hard use, hence required repairs or replacement of stock all too frequently.

HAMMER: The external part of the action that strikes the percussion cap on a caplock gun or holds the flint in a flintlock gun.

HAMMER SPUR: The rearward extension of the hammer used as an aid in moving the hammer to the rear.

HAND CANNON: Probably the first gun design to appear in the middle of the 15th century. Widely used by the military, the designs varied greatly, and its effects in battle seem to have been more psychological than physiological.

HANGFIRE: The delayed firing of a charge. A dangerous situation calling for care in handling the gun that produced the hangfire. Remember, a hangfire can still go off!

HARQUEBUS: see Arquebus.

HORSE PISTOL: Usually a large pistol of military persuasion carried in a special holster fastened to the saddle.

HUNTING POUCH: A leather pouch, frequently carried over the shoulder, which contains the essentials for reloading, spare flints and the like. The originals were often highly decorated.

HYDRAULIC BULLET: A special bullet for muzzleloading rifles with a hole which is plugged after being filled with water. The bullet, when used for hunting, is said to expand more completely thanks to the hydraulic effect of the water in it.

IRON PYRITES: A yellow mineral, often called "fool's gold", which sparks when it strikes steel. It is used for this purpose in wheellocks and pyrite lock guns.

JAEGER RIFLE: A German form of hunting rifle which was probably the basis for our Kentucky rifles.

KENTUCKY RIFLE: The traditionally long flintlock rifle of our forefathers. Although derived, at least in part, from the German Jaeger rifle, the Kentucky rifle is truly an American development, reaching its peak of perfection between 1775 and 1830.

KNAPPER: A skilled artisan who prepares flints with hand tools exclusively. Despite the upswing in black powder shooting, knappers are decreasing, and knapping is truly a dying art.

LINEN: A preferred material for ball patches.

LOADING BLOCK: Usually a home-made hardwood board with suitable holes that hold one patched ball per hole. A loading block makes reloading easier and faster, can be carried either in the leather pouch or on a belt with a rawhide lanyard.

LOADING LEVER: In percussion revolvers, the rod, similar to the ejection rod in single action revolvers, which allows the proper seating of the ball on the powder charge in each chamber of the cylinder.

LOCK PLATE: The external plate of a lock, which on the inside holds the firing mechanism, spring, etc.

LOCK SCREW: A long screw that extends from one side to the other of a lock, not only holding the lock together, but also keeping it in the stock.

LONG RIFLE: Some historians have tried to pin this term to any of the American-made guns which appeared between 1700–1750. This was to replace the somewhat ambiguous description of Kentucky rifle, especially since many of these rifles were not made in Kentucky. More frequently the term is used to differentiate between a rifle (long gun) and a handgun.

MAGAZINE CAPPER: see Capper.

MAINSPRING: Usually a heavy, flat spring that is linked to the hammer.

MATCH CORD: A hemp cord or match which, when ignited, glowed and was used to fire the matchlock gun.

MATCHLOCK: The earliest form of firing system known. On early matchlocks, the match was moved into the touch hole by hand, later a mechanical device was used.

MINIE BULLET, also known incorrectly as MINIE BALL: Designed by French Capt. Minie, these projectiles are really bullets, not balls. The conical bullet expanded well, notably the base. Can be seated even in a dirty bore, usually is surprisingly accurate with suitable charges.

MIQUELET: A very early flintlock with outside spring and one-piece frizzen and pan cover.

MUSKET: A full-stock rifle of military persuasion, but smoothbored. Rifled muskets were just that, muskets identical in appearance to the smoothbored ones, but with rifled barrels.

MUZZLELOADER: Any firearm that is loaded from the muzzle, and this includes, by definition, cap and ball revolver, although here the chambers of the cylinder are loaded rather than the barrel.

239

NIPPLE: The threaded tube on percussion arms on which the percussion cap is seated. The nipple, being hollow, guides the fire from the cap to the charge in the gun. Nipples, when damaged, should be replaced.

NIPPLE PICK: A short length of wire, sometimes with a small handle, that is used to ascertain that the passageway in the nipple is clear of obstructions.

NIPPLE WRENCH: A special key-like tool for the removal of nipples. Since nipples come in various sizes, so do nipple wrenches.

PAN: A container or receptacle that contains priming powder in some early ignition systems, such as the flintlock.

PATCH BOX: A container, complete with spring-activated lid, inletted into the buttstock of some muzzleloaders, used to carry greased patches, tallow for greasing, worm and the like. Most often made from brass, the patch box is included in the furniture.

PATCH CUTTER: A sharp-edged tool which punches out patches with the aid of a mallet or hammer.

PATCH KNIFE: A specially shaped, very sharp knife used for cutting the patch after the ball has been partially started.

PATCHING: Any material from which a patch is made.

PATENT BREECH, also known as FRENCH BREECH: On this breech, the breech plug and nipple seat are cast from one piece.

PEPPERBOX: A percussion pistol with multiple barrels which turn with each pull of the trigger. Guns were usually of small caliber, were fired double action, and barrels were rifled.

PERCUSSION: Any gun fired by means of the percussion system, this using a cap with an explosive charge, and a nipple on which the cap is seated. In revolvers, the term "cap and ball" is frequently used. The last of the ignition systems to be used before the introduction of self-contained cartridges.

PERCUSSION CAP: A small copper or brass cup, a forerunner of the modern primer, that contains a small detonating charge of fulminate. Caps are sometimes waterproofed or foil-wrapped to give them greater resistance to the elements.

PICK: see Nipple Pick. Sometimes also called pricker.

PICKET BULLET: An early conical bullet in which only the base was bore-size. Had to be loaded with great care to prevent its tipping, thereby losing its inherent accuracy.

PILL LOCK: One of the earlier percussion systems. A small pill of fulminate of mercury was delivered through a special tube. When hit by the floating firing pin, the fulminate detonated and fired the charge in the barrel. This design is usually credited to Joseph Manton, an outstanding British gunmaker.

PIPES: The short pieces of metal tube, fastened onto the barrel and into the stock's forend, which hold the ramrod. Sometimes also called ferrules.

PLAINS RIFLE: A development of the westward movement when plainsmen found that the longer guns were more difficult to handle (see Half-Stock, Kentucky). Moreover, plains rifles usually were of larger caliber and the best examples are the Hawken rifles.

POWDER FLASK: A metal container for black powder, usually shaped to fit a pocket, with a powder delivery tube with spring-activated closure. Often made from brass, copper or zinc, the current replicas are usually browned (see Browning) or treated chemically to resemble the original browning used on powder flasks. Typical of the percussion era.

POWDER HORN: Made either from buffalo or other bovine horn, the powder horn is typically American and is linked to the flintlock era. Most of the powder horns do not have an adjustable measure, hence the charge must be measured in some other way.

POWDER MEASURE: Most often a brass tube with an adjustable rod moving up and down that can be locked in place. This allows the user to measure the amount of powder volumetrically, and if the setting of the rod is not changed during use, this is a reliable method of delivering constant amounts of powder.

POWDER TESTER: see Eprouvette.

PRICKER: see Nipple Pick.

PRIMER HORN: A small powder horn for 4Fg (FFFFg) priming powder.

PYRITES: see Iron Pyrites.

PYRITE LOCK: A successor to the matchlock system, where iron pyrites made hard contact with a steel frizzen, thus creating sparks which set off the priming charge.

QUEEN ANNE PISTOL: A flintlock handgun with a removable barrel. On this flintlock, the barrel unscrews and the charge is placed into the breech of the barrel. Most of these guns do not have a forend.

RAMROD: Usually a hickory rod which is used to push the ball down the barrel until a proper seating of the ball on the powder charge is felt. Some ramrods have a provision at one end so that cleaning jags or a worm can be screwed on. Also see: Pipes.

REVOLVING RIFLE: A rifle with a rotating cylinder which has chambers in which individual charges (powder and projectile) are loaded. Pulling the trigger fires the chamber in line with the barrel, releasing the trigger brings the next chamber in line with the barrel. Although Colt and Remington are the best known examples of revolving rifles, a number of fine flintlock revolving rifles of German origin are known.

RIFLED MUSKET: Muskets were smoothbored military long guns. When rifling became popular, some thin-walled muskets were rifled, but cannot be considered true rifles since they retained the thin barrel walls.

SALTPETER: The popular name for potassium nitrate.

SCREW BARREL PISTOL: Many flintlock and percussion guns had a barrel which could be removed and the charge inserted into the breech end of the barrel.

SEE: Queen Anne Pistol.

SEAR: That part of the lock that mechanically engages the tumbler and the hammer. It is released by trigger pressure.

SEAR SPRING: The spring that acts on the sear.

SERPENTINE POWDER: An early crude black powder of non-uniform granulation.

SHORT STARTER: see Ball Starter.

241

SHOT DIPPER or MEASURE: A scoop, usually with a handle, that delivers a predetermined amount of shot. Some of these are adjustable, others are not.

SHOT POUCH or FLASK: Most often made from leather with a spout that delivers a fixed, or sometimes adjustable amount of lead shot for reloading afield.

SIDE PLATES: The decorative metal plates on the sides of the patch box.

SIZING: Most of the modern materials suitable for patching contain some sort of chemical sizing. This must be removed by thorough washing before the material is suitable for use as patching material.

SKIN CARTRIDGE: An early form of combustible cartridge designed for use in some percussion six-guns. The skin used was hog intestine treated chemically before use.

SNAIL: A type of percussion nipple base that is seen on some of the best of the percussion guns.

SNAPHAUNCE: An early type of flintlock, but where the frizzen and pan cover were two separate pieces.

SPANNER: The special wrench required for cocking a wheellock.

SPERM OIL: Sperm Whale oil was once the main ingredient in gun oils, has largely been replaced by more modern products, partly because it is no joy to use, and partly because sperm oil is getting very scarce and soon will no longer be produced.

SPRUE: The small flat surface produced on a cast ball by the sprue cutter plate of the mold. Balls are always seated sprue up when loading.

STARTER: see Ball Starter.

STEADY PIN: The small projection at the edge of the mainspring – a flat spring is used in most black powder guns – that fits into a mating hole in the lock plate.

STIRRUP: In some locks, a moving piece of metal that connects the mainspring with the tumbler.

STRAIGHT CUT RIFLING: Found only in very early guns. This type of rifling does not rotate in the barrel.

STRIKING A BARREL: A sort of draw-filing, with a special file, used when making octagonal barrels.

SUPERIMPOSED ROUNDS: Some very early guns had two locks for the same barrel. For such guns, two charges were inserted, each charge being located next to the lock that was to fire it. An advanced design that, however, did not find great favor.

TANG SIGHT: Any sight, usually an aperture or peep sight and adjustable for elevation, mounted on the tang, an extension of the breech plug.

TAPE PRIMER: Maynard's tape primer was probably the best known of this type of self-contained primers. The same idea is used in today's cap pistol tapes. A specially treated paper containing fulminate of mercury pellets was fed automatically into position and each pellet was in turn detonated by the striking hammer.

TENON: The piece of metal welded to the underside of the barrel. A slot was cut into the tenon so that the barrel key would fit through it, thus fastening the barrel to the forend.

THIMBLE: see Pipe.

TINDER: Usually charred linen or flax tow which caught the sparks from a flintlock. Often also used to start camp fires.

TINDER BOX: A special small box in which tinder was carried.

TOMPION: Most often a wooden plug used in the muzzle of a gun during prolonged storage periods. Wood, however, attracts and holds moisture, hence should not be used. Nevertheless, wood tompions are still sold.

TOP JAW: The upper part of the flintlock hammer that holds the flint against the lower jaw by means of a threaded rod – the top jaw screw.

TOUCH HOLE, also TOUCHHOLE: The hole or vent in the pan of a flintlock gun that permits passage of the flash to the main charge.

TOW: Unspun flax, now almost impossible to find, was used for cleaning patches, and sometimes as patching material in shotguns. The fibers of tow are too coarse for patching rifle or handgun balls.

TOWER LOCK: A particular type of flintlock, as found on the Brown Bess. Locks marked with the Tower mark are in the collector's class, and replica Tower locks are now being offered.

TRIGGER PLATE: A narrow metal bar with milled-out slot, inletted into the stock, that limits lateral trigger motion. The trigger group may or may not be assembled to it.

TUBE LOCK: Developed during the early part of the 19th century, this type of percussion lock was invented by John Manton, British gunmaker. In this system a copper tube, with both ends open, contained fulminate which was crushed by the hammer. The both-end-open system was soon changed to one-end-open since the flash of the fulminate from both ends proved to be dangerous. The tubes were known as Tube Primer.

TUBE SIGHT: A forerunner of our telescopic sight. The slender metallic tube was often as long as the barrel, did not contain either lenses or other sighting devices, but served to concentrate the sight picture without external light affecting it. In some tube sights, especially the later ones, the front sight was located in the forward end of the tube sight.

TUMBLER: That part of the lock that permits hammer movement. The edge of the tumbler carries the half and full-cock notches and the detent, if the lock has one.

UNDERHAMMER LOCK, also

UNDER-STRIKER LOCK: A percussion lock where the hammer is located below the line of the barrel. The mainspring of such locks also serves as trigger guard.

UNDER-RIB: The metal bar that carries the pipes on half-stock rifles.

V-SPRING: A flat spring in the shape of a V, and better than the single-leaf spring.

VENT: The small hole or passage in muzzleloading locks that allows the flame of ignition to reach the main charge in the rear of the barrel.

VERNIER SIGHT: see Aperture Sight.

WAD CUTTER: A tool with sharpened edge used to cut wads or small patches for balls.

WHEELLOCK: The successor to the matchlock ignition system. Complex to make, difficult to maintain, the ignition depended on iron pyrites being pressed against the serrated edges of a wheel, the resulting sparks igniting the powder charge.

WIPING ROD: A special cleaning rod used to remove fouling and to clean the barrel between shots.

243

Chapter 13
DIRECTORY BLACK POWDER

ARMS MANUFACTURES AND IMPORTERS

The Armoury, Inc.
Route 202
New Preston, CT 06777

Arms International
P. O. Box 95
Malverne, NY 11565

Centennial Arms Corp.
3318 W. Devon
Chicago, IL 60645

Century Arms, Inc.
3–5 Federal Street
St. Albans, VT 05478

Cherry Corners Mfg. Co.
11136 Congress Road
Lodi, OH 44254 (kits only)

Classic Arms International Ltd.
14 Fifth Street
Valley Stream, NY 11581

Colt Industries
Colt's Firearms Division
150 Huyshope Avenue
Hartford, CT 06102

Connecticut Valley Arms
Candlewood Hill Road
Higganum, CT 06441

William Damewood
27 Gordon Road
Springfield, OH 45504
(custom guns)

Dixie Gun Works
Union City, TN 38261

EMF Co, Inc.
Box 1248
Studio City, CA 91604

English Longrifles
RFD 2, Troy Road
Washington, IN 47501
(custom rifles, supplies)

Clark K. Frazier
RFD 1
Rawson, OH 45881
(custom match rifles)

Golden Age Arms Co.
Box 825
Worthington, OH 43085

Green River Rifle Works
Roosevelt, Utah 84066

Harrington & Richardson, Inc.
Industrial Rowe
Gardner, MA 01440

Hawes Firearms
8224 Sunset Blvd.
Los Angeles, CA 90046

High Standard Sporting Firearms
1817 Dixwell Avenue
Hamden, CT 06514

House of Hawken
Rt. 5, 11009 122nd Street
Kenosha, WI 53140

Hurricane Creek Muzzle
Loading Supplies
Route 4, Box 51
Hyden, KY 41749

Jana International Co.
Box 1107
Denver, CO 80201

Lewis & Clark Trading Co.
Box 777
Salt Lake City, Utah 84110

Liberty Arms Corp.
Box 306
Montrose, CA 91020

Lyman Products for Shooters
Middlefield, CT 06455

Navy Arms Co., Inc.
689 Bergen Blvd.
Ridgefield, NJ 07657

Numrich Arms Corp.
West Hurley, NY 12491

Richland Arms Co.
325 W. Adrian Street
Blissfield, MI 49228

Smokepole Musket Co., Inc.
Powersbridge Road
Peterborough, NH 03458

South Bend Replicas, Inc.
61650 Oak Road
South Bend, IN 46614

Sturm, Ruger & Co.
Lacey Place
Southport, CT 06490

10-Ring Precision, Inc.
1449 Blue Crest Lane
San Antonio, TX 78216

Thompson/Center Arms
Farmington Road
Rochester, NH 03867

Tingle Mfg. Co., Inc.
1125 Smithland Pike
Shelbyville, IN 46176

Trail Guns Armory
2115 Lexington
Houston, TX 77006

LOCKS

W. L. Cochran
6432 N. Xanthus
Tulsa, OK 74130 (Flint)

R. T. Golebiewski
27286 Jean Street
Warren, MI 48093 (Flint)

C. Doc Haddaway
5728 New Cut Road
Louisville, KY 40214 (Flint)

Russ Hamm
2617 Oleander Blvd.
Fort Pierce, FL 33450

Long's Lock
6360 W. Colfax
Denver, CO 80214 (Hawken)

Morgan's Buffalo Works
Box 838
Alief, TX 77411 (Flint)

Harold W. Robbins
653 S. Hewitt Road
Ypsilanti, MI 48197

C. E. Silver
181 Sand Hill School Road
Asheville, NC 28806 (Flint)

STOCKS

Ernie Paulsen
Rt. 71, Box 11
Chinook, MT 59523

Al Winn
190 Upland Drive
Petaluma, CA 94952

BARRELS

William Large
JJJJ Ranch
Gun & Machine Shop
Route 1
Ironton, OH 45638

Joseph W. Mellott
334 Rockhill Road
Pittsburgh, PA 15243

Sharon Rifle Barrel Co.
Box 106
Kalispell, MT 59901

Dave Taylor
Box 1
Little Hocking, OH 45742

CASTING EQUIPMENT

Connecticut Valley Arms
Candlewood Hill Road
Higganum, CT 06441

Dixie Gun Works
Union City, TN 38261

Firearms Import and Export
Corp.
2470 N. W. 21st Street
Miami, FL 33142

Lee Custom Engineering
Route 2
Hartford, WI 53027

Lyman Products for Shooters
Middlefield, CT 06455

Navy Arms Co.
689 Bergen Blvd.
Ridgefield, NJ 07657

RCBS, Inc.
Box 1919
Oroville, CA 95965

245

SAECO Reloading Inc.
Courtyard Bldgs.
726 Hopmeadow Street
Simsbury, CT 06070

Shiloh Products Inc.
37 Potter Street
Farmingdale, NY 11735

ACCESSORIES & MISCELLANEOUS

Belding & Mull
100 North 4th St.
Philipsburg, Penna. 16866

Luther Adkins
Box 281
Shelbyville, IN 46176
(breech plugs)

Antique Gun Parts, Inc.
1118 S. Braddock Avenue
Pittsburgh, PA 15218 (parts)

Birchwood Casey
7900 Fuller Road
Eden Prairie, MN 55343
(barrel and stock finishing kits)

C & M Gun Works
2603 41st Street
Moline, IL 61265
(powder magazines)

Gearhart-Owen Industries, Inc.
Belin Plant
Moosic, PA 18507 (gunpowder)

GTR
N33W22-101 Memory Lane
Pewaukee, WI 53072
(adjustable pistol charger)

Hodgdon Powder Co.
7710 W. Highway 50
Shawnee Mission, KS 66202
(powder and shooting supplies)

Hoppe's Division of
Penguin Industries
P.O. Box 97
Parkersburg, PA 19365
(shooting supplies)

Log Cabin Sport Shop
P.O. Box 275
Lodi, OH 44254 (shooting
and historical accessories)

The Minute Men
3465 Edgewood Drive
Wooster, OH 44691
(breech plugs)

Ox-Yoke Originals
West Suffield, CT 06093
(pre-cut patches)

Wayne Robidoux
4230 Normal Blvd.
Lincoln, NB 68506 (plans &
drawings for making Hawken
rifle)

Rush's Old Colonial Forge, Inc.
106 Wiltshire Blvd.
Baltimore, MD 21221 (parts,
kits)

SNS Enterprises
Box 759
Coronado, CA 92118 (clothing)

Tecumseh's Indian Trading Post
Strausstown, PA 19559
(clothing)

Mike Tocci
Box 4561
Columbus, OH 43212
(browning fluid)

Uncle Mike's
P.O. Box 13010
Portland, OR 97213
(gun parts and accessories)

Mrs. C.H. Weisz
Box 311
Arlington, VA 22210 (parts)

Western Industries
(gunpowder – temporarily out
of business)

Chapter 14
MUZZLELOADER'S LIBRARY

To gain a full understanding of, and enjoyment from, your black powder guns, and from shooting them, you should be familiar with some of the standard works and a few of the classics concerned with black powder and muzzleloaders. While this list is by no means complete, it will form the basis for a good black powder library.

MONTHLY PUBLICATIONS...

Muzzle Blasts, the official publication of the National Muzzle Loading Rifle Association, Box 67, Friendship, IN 47021. Dedicated to early American muzzleloading firearms, matches and greater safety with all guns, especially black powder guns. A great deal of material for the novice as well as the advanced black powder shooter in each issue, also in-depth evaluations of replicas. Carries advertisements on black powder guns, paraphernalia and gear.

The Buckskin Report, official monthly publication of the National Association of Primitive Riflemen, Big Timber, MT 59011. Dedicated to the perpetuation of primitive muzzleloaders and shooting them. Included many short how-to articles for the advanced black powder shooter, plus historical sidelights.

Of the monthly gun magazines, only *Guns* carries a monthly column for black powder shooters. Most of the other publications carry articles about new replica guns as they appear. *The Gun Digest,* although an annual, is included here since this publication also carries black powder articles, with most of them being evaluations of new guns.

BOOKS...

HAWKEN RIFLES, Baird, J. D., Big Timber, MT 59011. 1968.
A well done book on one of the most important historical muzzleloading rifles.

MUZZLE FLASHES, Lenz, E. C., Standard Publications, Inc., Huntington, WV. 1944. Now out of print.
Though not exclusively concerned with black powder shooting, this book contains a great many interesting and historical features about black powder shooting and early pioneers.

INSTRUCTION OF MUSKETRY, abridged edition, Parker Hale Ltd., Birmingham, England. 1972.
A fascinating booklet, available in the U.S. through Jana International of Denver.

LONGRIFLES OF NOTE, PENNSYLVANIA, Shumway, G., published by author, R.D.7, York, PA 17402. 1968.
One of a series of excellent small books which are well done and essential for those who are interested in the development of historically important gun makers of the early U.S.

RECREATING THE AMERICAN LONG-RIFLE, Buchele, W., and Shumway, G., George Shumway, R.D.7, York, PA 17402. 1970.
Detailed instructions on how to build your own authentic replica. For the skilled hobbyist only, but worth reading and studying by every black powder shooter.

MAKE MUZZLE LOADER ACCESSORIES, McCrory, R. H., Box 13, Bellmore, NY 11711. Second edition, 1971.

The basic and probably the best of the how-to books on the subject. Full descriptions in words and drawings that can be followed by anyone who can handle basic tools.

LOCK, STOCK AND BARREL, McCrory, R. H., Box 13, Bellmore, NY 11711. 1966.

When and how to restore old muzzleloaders, complete with detailed instructions by a man who knows whereof he speaks. From simple repairs, such as replacing a lock, to the most complex job.

HANDFEUERWAFFEN, Lugs, J., Deutscher Militarverlag, translated into German from the original Czech. 1956.

One of the best and most concise surveys of the development of firearms, from the early hand cannon to modern multi-shot rifles and handguns.

COLT FIREARMS, Serven, J. E., Foundation Press, Santa Ana, CA 92701. Several editions.

The standard reference work on Colt guns and Colt history. This book traces the evolution of the cap and ball guns, as well as production dates of all Colt guns.

THE STORY OF COLT'S REVOLVER, Edwards, W.B., Castle Books, New York, NY. 1957. An in-depth study of Col. Colt's guns, his methods of promoting his wares, and much historical background.

THE EARLIEST HAND FIREARMS, Clephan, R.C., reprinted by Standard Publications. N.d., out of print.

An interesting volume that describes and traces the evolution of the gun in general and in England specifically.

CIVIL WAR GUNS, Edwards, W.B., Stackpole, Harrisburg, PA 17105. 1962.

This is probably the most definitive work on this complex subject. Thoroughly researched and documented.

THE STORY OF POPE'S BARRELS, Smith, R.M., Stackpole, Harrisburg, PA 17105. 1960.

Pope's work and his rifles occupy a special place in the history of black powder shooting, and his muzzleloaders are still setting records today.

THE PLAINS RIFLE, Hanson, O.E., Jr., Stackpole Books, Harrisburg, PA 17105. 1960.

The Plains rifle is something typically American and this volume is the best of the books covering this sometimes elusive subject.

SYSTEMS OF PROJECTILES AND RIFLING, Butler, J. G., D. van Nostrand, New York, NY. 1875.

Though primarily concerned with projectiles fired through rifled cannon barrels, this scarce volume contains a wealth of ballistic information, and some misinformation, based originally on black powder performance.

THE MUZZLE-LOADING CAP LOCK RIFLE, Roberts, N. H., Stackpole Co., Harrisburg, PA 17105. Fourth printing, 1952.

This book, now a collector's item, is the most definitive book on the subject. Roberts, who fathered the .25 caliber rifle catridge bearing his

name, was one of the most outstanding caplock experts of his day.

MEHRLÄUFIGE FEUERWAFFEN (Multi-Barrel Firearms), Mueller, H. G., Journal-Verlag Schwend, Schwaebisch Hall, West Germany. 1973. A short, but thorough study of all multi-barrel firearms, complete with sketches, patent drawings, and detailed descriptions. Of special interest are the early muzzleloaders and the multi-barrel wheellock and flintlock guns, as well as the percussion duckfoot pistol.

DER PERKUSSIONS-REVOLVER (The Percussion Revolver), Schmitt, G., Journal-Verlag Schwend, Schwaebisch Hall, West Germany. 1973. An excellent history with exceptional photographs of the percussion system revolver and handguns in German. Covers all of the better known guns as well as many which are almost unknown.

BEWAFFNUNG UND AUSRÜSTUNG DER SCHWEIZER ARMEE SEIT 1817, Volume I, Hand Firearms, Muzzleloaders & Revolvers, Reinhart, C., and am Rhyn, M., Verlag Stocker-Schmid, Dietikon, Zurich, Switzerland. 1974. A beautifully done volume with well documented data, including some of the ultra-scarce Swiss guns and an experimental cavalry percussion gun caliber 10.5 mm (.41). Several other almost unknown guns, both single and double barrel, are shown in detail, complete with history, name of manufacturer and other pertinent data.

PERCUSSION REVOLVERS OF THE UNITED STATES, Thalheimer, R., P. O. Box 22163,

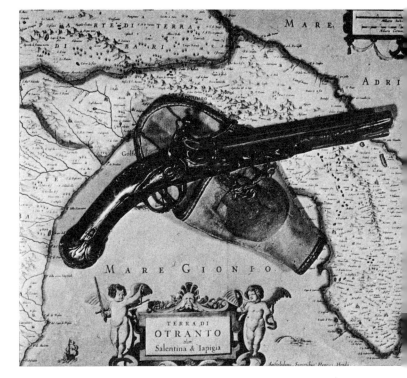

St. Louis, MO 63116. 1970.
Each of the guns mentioned in this volume is described in some detail and a picture, somewhat dark in most cases, serves to help in identifying the various revolvers.

AMERICAN PERCUSSION REVOLVERS, Sellers, F. M., and Smith, S. E., Museum Restoration Service, Ottawa, Ontario, Canada. 1971. This book, without a doubt, is the most valuable overall book on the subject of percussion revolvers. Inventors, makers and companies are alphabetized, and much of the information presented

249

here is the result of painstaking and long-lasting research. Of particular interest is the section on unidentified revolvers, and the photo index which permits quick identification of a gun by means of a photograph.

NOTES ON CAVALRY WEAPONS OF THE AMERICAN CIVIL WAR, 1861–1865, Lewis, B. R., American Ordnance Assoc., Mills Building, Washington, DC. 1961.
A concise and well-illustrated brochure which outlines the salient points well.

EARLY ENFIELDS ARMS, THE MUZZLE LOADERS, Reynolds, E. G. B., Profile Publications Ltd., Windsor, Berkshire, SL 4 1EB, England. 1972.
An extremely well done and well illustrated small volume covering the most important historic landmarks in the evolution of the Enfield rifle.

RULES FOR THE MANAGEMENT AND CLEANING OF THE RIFLE MUSKET, MODEL 1863, anon., War Department U.S. Government, Government Printing Office, 1863. Reprinted by Normount Technical Publications, P. O. Drawer N-2, Wickenburg, AZ 85358, rerinted in 1969.
Even if your interests are not along the military lines, this reprint should be of interest to all black powder shooters. A good source of material for the nomenclature of percussion rifles and muskets.

TECHNICAL BOOKS...

BALLISTICS IN THE SEVENTEENTH CENTURY, Hall, A. R., Harper & Row, New York, NY. Reprint edition of 1969.
The origin of most of the early ballistics study was founded in the study of the behavior of projectiles fired from a cannon barrel. This slender volume, considered now a classic in ballistics, covers all cannon studies and behavior, especially the work done in England.

INTERNAL BALLISTICS, JAMES WATT LECTURE, delivered before the Greenock Philosophical Society by Capt. Noble on the 12th February, 1892. W. P. Griffith & Sons, Ltd., Old Bailey, London, England. 1892.
This study was concerned primarily with the burning of black powder and the brand-new Cordite in cannons, and the effect burning rate has on velocity and chamber pressure.

TREATISE ON AMMUNITION, anon., 10th edition, War Office, Harrison and Sons, London. 1915.
The British standard work on ammunition, propellants, and explosives. Interesting are the data on black powder and notes on the manufacture of this propellant.

MANUFACTURING GUNPOWDER AT THE ISHAPORE MILLS IN BENGAL, Anderson, W., John Weale, London. 1862.
Considerable experimental work was conducted at this British powder plant both for cannon, primarily mortars, and for muskets. The chapters

on the history and manufacturing methods are interesting, and the experimental work is worthwhile studying.

BLACK POWDER HANDBOOK, Ramage, C. K., et al., Lyman Products for Shooters, Middlefield, CT 06455. 1975.
A valuable book for the beginner since it gives a great deal of ballistics information as well as load data for revolver, rifle and musket, and shotgun.

SHOOTING BLACK POWDER GUNS, anon., Thompson/Center Arms, Rochester, NH 03867. No date.
This promotional booklet offers product information about the company's black powder guns, load data for same and some how-to-load information, plus cleaning instructions for black powder guns.

BLACK POWDER DATA MANUAL NO. 1, anon., Hodgdon Powder Co., Inc., Shawnee Mission, KS 66202. 1971.
This small booklet offers black powder load data for muzzleloading rifles, shotguns and handguns, as well as black powder loads for centerfire handgun, rifle and shotgun ammo.

BALLISTICS AND THE MUZZLE LOADING RIFLE, Herring, W. C., N.M.L.R.A., Friendship, IN 47021. 1974.
This paperback is well worth studying. Although there are some poorly conducted tests and experiments described, and in some cases vital information, such as bullet weight, is lacking, the author has done a creditable job. Since this is the first time that an attempt was made to conduct ballistics

experiments with a valid base – and the author has succeeded in most cases – shortcomings and failures must be forgiven.

There is one more publication that is highly recommended, although it is actually a catalog. Every year, Turner Kirkland and his crew at Dixie Gun Works, Inc., Union City, TN 38261, produce a big, fat catalog. The 1974 issue was over 400 pages, and within the covers of this "book" you will find a wild and wooly assortment of gun lore, commercials for the Dixie Gun Works products, plus information and tips that are not found anywhere else. The catalog sells for $2.00, and is worth that much in how-to information alone.

251

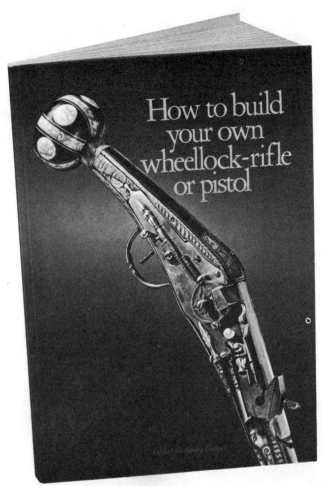

A Jolex publication for
1975 release!

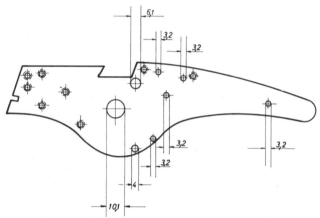

HOW TO BUILD YOUR OWN WHEELLOCK RIFLE OR PISTOL
By Georg Lauber

This sophisticated text will teach the reader how to build his own wheellock rifle or pistol. From the muzzle to the butt, every component has been meticulously drawn, actual size, and these drawings cover everything from the barrel and stock down to the smallest pin and screw. Many of the larger drawings are printed on fold out leafs...none are partitioned for layout convenience; consequently, it is possible for the craftsman to make tracings or templates quickly and easily.

All dimensions are given in both metrics and inches!

The text carefully describes the process of selecting materials, shaping parts, heat-treating, hardening, annealing as well as polishing and finishing. Assembly, fitting, tuning and testing processes are likewise adequately covered.

The wheellock was invented during the early sixteenth century (circa 1517) and the design selected for this book is representative of the classic style most generally employed by the better gun-makers of that era.

Mr. Lauber, a prominent German master gunsmith has done an exceptional job of creating this highly educational volume with the amateur craftsman in mind. Even those who would never get around to the actual task of building a wheellock will revel in this wealth of gunsmithing knowledge.

PAPERBACK, 8 1/4 x 11 5/8" . . . . $ 5.05

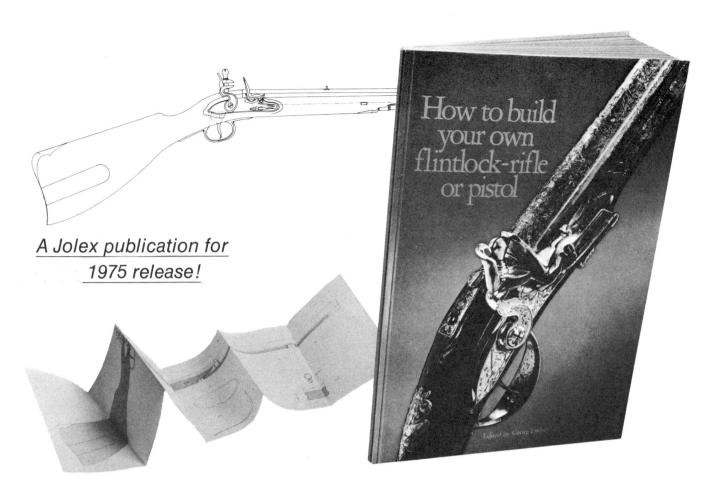

A Jolex publication for 1975 release!

How to build your own flintlock-rifle or pistol

Edited by Georg Lauber

The second in Mr. Lauber's three-volume series on the art and science of building muzzle-loading black powder firearms.

The flintlock, invented by Marin le Bourgeays of France about 1615, was used by Napoleon's troops, American colonists and countless others in its two-hundred some-odd-year reign as the ultimate weapon, before the percussion lock replaced it. It is the romance and color of the flintlock that is largely responsible for the development and interest in modern black-powder sport shooting.

Again, with the rifle and pistol designed for this book, Mr. Lauber was careful to select designs and sizes that were most typical of the period. Every component is drawn to scale (the larger pieces actual size) and shown with both metric and inch dimensions. Many drawings are on foldout leafs for easy tracing.

Instructions include details on selecting materials, shaping, fitting, hardening and finishing. Stock shaping and finishing is also carefully explained.

The talented, though inexperienced, craftsman will delight in working with this book and should have no difficulty fabricating a shootable flintlock.

PAPERBACK, 8 1/4" x 11 5/8" . . . . $ 5.95

**HOW TO BUILD
YOUR OWN
FLINTLOCK RIFLE
OR PISTOL**
By Georg Lauber

253

*A Jolex publication for
1975 release!*

**HOW TO BUILD
YOUR OWN
PERCUSSION RIFLE
OR PISTOL**
By Georg Lauber

This is the third and final volume of Georg Lauber's set of books on the building of muzzle-loaders, and probably the most popular. Today's black powder sportsmen favor the percussion lock because of its faster and surer ignition.

It was the development of the percussion lock in 1848, by the American-Sharps, that provided the bridge between the flintlock and self-primed cartridges that made the modern breechloader possible. Those designs selected by Mr. Lauber for this edition are representative of the guns that achieved the greatest popularity in the percussion era.

Every part, from the smallest screws and pins to the barrels and stocks are carefully drawn to scale and shown with both inch and metric dimensions. The stocks and barrels are drawn actual size for easy tracing or template-making.

The text covers information on selecting materials, shaping, hardening, polishing and finishing together with step-by-step instruction for fitting and assembling.

PAPERBACK, 8 1/4 " x 11 5/8" . . . . $ 5.95

3rd World Championship International Muzzle-loading Rifle & Pistol Matches

(Schwaebisch Hall, Germany, Oct. 5th & 6th 1974)

I. COMPETITIONS

No.	Code Name	Description	Type	Range	Position
1	MIQUELET	Smooth bore flintlock musket	Military	50 m	standing
2	MAXIMILIAN	Flintlock Rifle	Free	100 m	prone
3	MINIE	Percussion Rifle	Military	100 m	prone
4	WHITWORTH	Percussion Rifle	Free	100 m	prone
5	COMMINAZZO	Single shot Flintlock Pistol	Free	25 m	standing
6	KUCHENREUTER	Single shot Percussion Rifled Pistol	Free	25 m	standing
7	COLT	Percussion-Revolver	Free	25 m	standing
8	WALKYRIE	Percussion Rifle (Ladies only)	Free	50 m	prone
9	GUSTAV ADOLPH	Team: as No. 1	Military	50 m	standing
10	PAULY	Team: as No. 3	Military	100 m	prone
11	AGGREGATE	Team: aggeregate of Nos. 9 & 10			
12	REPRO REVOLVER	Reproduction Percussion-Revolver (see note)	Free	25 m	standing
13	REPRO REVOLVER	Team: as No. 12	Free	25 m	standing

II. RULES

(A) COMPETITION

(a) Competitors are to be selected by their National Association.

(b) Targets: Competitions 1 and 9 use the French 200 m Rifle Target; all other Competitions use the 50 m I.S.U. Target.

(c) Ties will be decided according to I.S.U. Rules, i. e. the winner has the highest number of shots in each scoring ring in descending order.

(d) Where a shot hole cuts a line it must be a minimum of 50% across the line to count in the higher scoring ring.

(e) Scores will be witnessed by one officer of the host country and countersigned by one officer of an invited country.

(f) Where possible practice targets will be available at each range.

(g) All competitions will be:
1. 13 shots in 30 minutes; the best ten shots to count for score.
2. Prone and standing positions according to I.S.U. Rules.
3. Telescopes allowed for spotting, but no coaching permitted.
4. No weapon to be loaded until the signal for "Open Fire". All weapons to be unprimed during a "Temporary Cease Fire" and to be unloaded on "Cease Fire".
5. It is permitted to fire one warming shot into the bank after the signal for "Open Fire".
6. Signals. The orders during the competitions will be made by the Range Officer on a whistle:

"OPEN FIRE"	– TWO WHISTLE BLASTS
"TEMPORARY CEASE FIRE"	– SERIES OF SHORT WHISTLE BLASTS
"CEASE FIRE"	– ONE LONG WHISTLE BLAST

(B) WEAPONS AND LOADS

(a) **Military Weapons (Service Rifles and Muskets).** Arms manufactured in accordance with military pattern, unaltered and with original pattern sights. Slings may be modern but of a military type. Bore diameter in excess of 13.5 mm (0.5315")! Set triggers, butt pads or check pads not permitted. Wiping out barrels between shots and the use of a long loading tube not permitted. (Competitions 1, 3, 9, 10, 11.)

(b) **Free Weapons.** Any original muzzle loading weapon of any calibre with contemporary sights (**NOT** telescopic or optical.) Any alteration made to the original which would spoil its historical value will disqualify its use.

(c) **Replicas.** Reproduction weapons of any type are not permitted (see note.)

(d) **SMOKING** IS NOT PERMITTED ON THE FIRING LINE.

(e) **Powder.** Factory made black powder only is permitted. Loading must be from a measuring powder flask or from pre-packed single charge containers.

(f) **Bullets.** Round ball for all flintlocks and smooth bored pistols. Any type for percussion rifles and rifled pistols.

(g) Any weapon may be used only once in the same event with the sole exception of by one lady and one man, where time permits.

(h) **Artificial sighting aids.** Aperture and iris diaphragms at the shooting spectacles as well as corrective lenses are allowed.

(i) The use of safety spectacles, tinted or otherwise, is encouraged but not obligatory.

III. ORGANIZATION OF THE ANNUAL CHAMPIONSHIP

1. The organizing country will send out official invitations at least two months before the event. The Annual Championship will be held between June 15th and July 15th or September 20th and 30th.

2. Visiting teams will submit, at least two weeks in advance, names of all members of their party, clearly stating the person in charge, and also their proposed Ports of Entry. They must also send a full list of all weapons they may bring, showing make, type, calibre and, where possible, serial number or identifying marks.

3. Entry Forms will be sent out by the organizing country at least one month before the event, to be returned at least two weeks in advance of the event.

4. Teams for competitions No. 10, 11 and 13 will consist of four members, and whenever possible, two substitutes The maximum number of competitors and substitutes will be determined by the organizing country, according to local conditions. All competitors must belong to a National Muzzle Loading Association of their own country and be in possession of a valid shooting license.

5. Range Officers will be provided by the organizing contry and the M. L. A. I. C.

6. Any dispute will be settled by those members of the M. L. A. I. C. present on the range at the time.

Competitions:

1. Flintlock guns	Individual	20 birds	Sporting
2. Percussion guns	Individual	20 birds	Sporting
3. Percussion guns	Team No. 2		Sporting

Guns:	Any shotgun (including army weapons) under 11 bore may be used; double barrel guns may be used in single barrel events using one barrel per bird; reproduction guns may only be used if they are true to original.
Loads:	Maximum 6,2 gr. of black powder; shotload 35 gr.
Misfires:	Flintlock guns allowed: 4 Percussion guns allowed: 1
Ranges:	5 ranges, Automatic Trap range

Gun Position:

The gun butt must be under the elbow when the shooter is calling for his target.

Repeat targets:

A repeat target is only allowed if the shooter has to discontinue the competition in case of malfunction of the gun and sufficient time is left for a repeat target. This shall be decided by the Range Officer.

Entrance fees:

The entrance fee for the individual events will be $ 5.00 per competition. No fees will be charged for the team events.

Prizes:

The medals for the World Championship will be awarded as follows:

Individual events:	The Winner:	A "Gold"
	2nd Place:	A "Silver"
	3rd Place:	A "Bronze"
	further prizes will be awarded to 4th, 5th and 6th places.	
Team events:	Winning Team:	4 "Golds"
	2nd Team:	4 "Silvers"
	3rd Team:	4 "Bronzes"

ENTRANCE FEES: The entrance fee for individual events will be $ 3.50 competition. No fees will be charged for team events.

PRIZES: The medal for the World Championship will be awarded as follows:

Individual Events:	The Winner:	A "Gold"
	2nd Place:	A "Silver"
	3rd Place:	A "Bronze"
Team Events:	Winning Team:	4 "Golds"
	2nd Team:	4 "Silvers"
	3rd Team:	4 "Bronzes"
Clay Pigeon Event:	M.L.A.I.C. 3rd World Championship, Schwäbisch Hall 5th/6th October, 1974	

Shooting the Muzzleloaders